FOUR T

4th ed.

ALL MORTGAGES

Insider Tips to Finance or Refinance Your Home in Today's Economy

Julie Garton-Good

KAPLAN)

PUBLISHING

New York

This publication is designed to provide accurate and authoritative information in regard to the subject matter covered. It is sold with the understanding that the publisher is not engaged in rendering legal, accounting, or other professional service. If legal advice or other expert assistance is required, the services of a competent professional person should be sought.

© 1994, 1999, 2004, and 2008 by Julie Garton-Good

Published by Kaplan Publishing, a division of Kaplan, Inc.
1 Liberty Plaza, 24th Floor
New York, NY 10006

Printed in the United States of America

July 2008
10 9 8 7 6 5 4 3 2 1

ISBN: 978-1-4277-5473-8

Kaplan Publishing books are available at special quantity discounts to use for sales promotions, employee premiums, or educational purposes. Please email our Special Sales Department to order or for more information at kaplanpublishing@kaplan.com, or write to Kaplan Publishing, 1 Liberty Plaza, 24th Floor, New York, NY 10006

DEDICATION

To the memory of my incredible daughter, Crystal Ann Branch, (1973-2006) who was my heart and will forever be "the wind beneath my wings."

There's been a world of change since I wrote the first edition of *All About Mortgages* in 1994, the second edition in 1999, and the third edition in 2004. Consumers now access their credit scores prior to meeting a lender, empowering them with the same information the lender will see. And because more than 80 percent of buyers use the Web to begin their home search, many also embrace it to locate the lender and obtain the mortgage loan. These market changes provide consumers with a more streamlined process that includes quicker closings, often in three weeks or less.

That's why it's imperative that consumers are well prepared to take on the mortgage process and troubleshoot their purchase. This means being armed with little-known, insider facts that make the difference between not only getting a mortgage, but obtaining the right one to meet the borrower's financial needs for the long run.

You'll get a behind-the-scenes look at:

- What or who caused the mortgage meltdown and the impact it has on today's borrower
- How to check your credit report, clean up errors, and put your best financial foot forward to garner a "yes" from the lender
- Tips for evaluating loan programs to make sure you don't overpay including what to negotiate with the lender

Marginally qualified buyers will discover:

- Low/no-down payment financing using home affordability programs, gifted down payments, and lease purchases
- What to do if the lender says no
- Little-known compensating factors that help you qualify for the mortgage you need

And to successfully manage your equity after the closing, you'll learn:

- How to evaluate whether refinancing makes financial sense
- When to and when not to prepay your loan plus an affordable prepayment system to cut years off your mortgage
- How to work with the lender when your payments fall behind

Let *All About Mortgages* be your financial companion and guide to obtaining a cost-effective mortgage, growing your home's equity, and helping secure your financial future!

Enthusiastically,
Julie Garton-Good, DREI, C-CREC

1

MORTGAGE MARKET
OVERVIEW
Players and Process

The mortgage market of a decade ago in no way resembles today's world. With just a few key strokes, the lender can enter the borrower's information into an automated underwriting system (AUS), taking light years off the application process. Savvy borrowers know their credit score as well as the importance it plays in obtaining a cost-effective mortgage loan. And more than 80 percent of borrowers first begin their home search via the Internet.

Yet the more things change, the more they remain the same. Many homebuyers are still confused about the requirements, the process, and the role of the myriad players involved. This chapter provides insight into how the borrowing process works and how technology has expanded the industry and, therefore, the consumer's options. It serves as a template to help the borrower understand and more successfully navigate the mortgage process.

THE MORTGAGE LENDING PROCESS

Q. The mortgage loan process seems so complicated. Is there any way the consumer can make it easier?

The mortgage lending process can seem daunting. I fondly remember a first-time homebuying couple who received word that their loan closing would be delayed because of "a Fannie Mae underwriting glitch." The wife responded, "I don't care who that Fannie Mae woman is, we just want to buy a house!" Had someone taken the time to explain to her that Fannie Mae (FNMA—Federal National Mortgage Association) and other players in the secondary market are vital for recycling lent funds (and in turn pass on greater loan affordability to buyers), she might have been a bit more patient! Thus, it's important that buyers and sellers alike understand the delicate inner workings of the primary market, the secondary market, and the private mortgage insurer. I refer to this as the *triple challenge*. Understanding it can help clarify the mortgage process.

Q. Who are the three main players in the mortgage market and how do they work together?

The players in the triple challenge are (1) the primary lenders, (2) the secondary market, and (3) the private mortgage insurance market. The early years of mortgage lending found local lenders working alone, holding loans originated *in portfolio*. This meant that when ABC Bank made a mortgage loan to the Brown family, the bank held that loan in its loan portfolio of investments, collecting the monthly payments until the loan was paid in full. This was actually beneficial for the Browns because they developed an ongoing business relationship with the lender. If hard times came and their loan payments fell behind, the Browns had a much better chance of negotiating with someone who was aware of their personal situation and perhaps more empathetic.

Q. Why did lenders change from the portfolio practice?

Keeping the loan in portfolio for 30 years was not necessarily in the lender's best interests. As interest rates fluctuated (typically moving upward), it became increasingly evident to many lenders that they should recycle these mortgages to receive not only higher interest rates but also increased loan origination fees. Thus, in the late 1930s the secondary market was born.

The first player in the secondary market was the Federal National Mortgage Association (FNMA), lovingly called Fannie Mae. She was soon followed by a sister, Ginnie Mae, the Government National Mortgage Association (GNMA), and later by a brother, Freddie Mac, the Federal Home Loan Mortgage Corporation (FHLMC). Although each of the siblings serves a particular market segment, the scope of their duties is very similar. They recycle lent funds from primary markets (e.g., banks) to return funds to circulation at the local level while creating additional collateral and investment vehicles for the secondary market. For example, ABC Bank's $5 million in mortgage loans written to Ginnie Mae's specifications can be sold to Ginnie with the lender taking a slight reduction on the face value received for the privilege of converting the loans to immediate cash. Ginnie uses these loans, and their monthly payments received, as collateral for issuing GNMA pass-through securities to purchasers. In other words, if the Browns' loan was sold into GNMA in the secondary market, and the Browns subsequently purchased some GNMA pass-through securities, they would actually be purchasing their own flow of cash! (See figure 1.1.) This is the mortgage-backed securitization process we hear so much about today.

Q. Was the addition of private mortgage insurance necessary to the secondary market?

Yes, over time. With more and more loans being sold into the secondary market, the players needed to hedge against potential losses on the loans purchased. So private mortgage insurance (PMI) became the third integral part of the triple challenge.

PMI typically insures the top 20 percent of the new conventional loan against the borrower's default. This was exactly the payment assurance needed by the secondary market. General guidelines of private mortgage insurance companies were added to the secondary market's existing list of loan requirements. Local lenders then added these criteria to their buyers' qualifying guidelines.

Q. If linking the three groups was so positive, why is it called a challenge?

Although the melding of primary lenders, secondary markets, and private mortgage insurance companies has greatly increased the options and scope of lending in the United States, it has its shortcomings. The lender, the secondary market, and the private mortgage insurance companies each have their own set of underwriting guidelines and costs,

FIGURE 1.1 *How the GNMA Mortgage-Backed Securities Program Works*

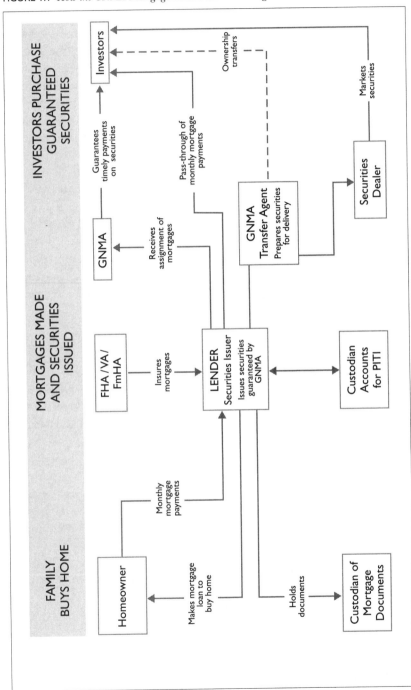

some of which can prove too restrictive for borrowers. In an effort to qualify, a borrower might leverage into an ill-fitting program that's not financially feasible for the long run. This "challenge" was most recently played out in the mortgage market meltdown.

THE MORTGAGE MELTDOWN

Q. What and whom do you believe is at the root of the mortgage meltdown?

I'm reminded of the adage that when you point a finger of blame at someone, the balance of your fingers point back at you! The mortgage morass and foreclosure fiasco were created by many parties using a dangerous combination of greed and ignorance. And while subprime loans have been seen as the primary whipping boys, the problems go much deeper and wider.

The number one roadblock for first-time buyers has always been accumulating the down payment. Earlier in this decade, mortgage lenders and investors began to focus on inventing a slew of new loan products designed to put home affordability within easier reach of first-time buyers. Not only were they incredibly successful (and continue to be), they skyrocketed U.S. home ownership rates to record highs of nearly 70 percent.

Meanwhile, another market segment of the industry was being underserved—the credit-blemished borrower. Enter subprime, also known as nonprime mortgages. Although at higher-than-prime (market rate) interest and typically more points, they were touted as a stop-gap loan while borrowers repaired their credit and could then qualify for a cheaper, more cost-effective mortgage. And because the yield spread premiums (read "profit") to lenders was more attractive on subprime than other mortgage products, lenders wanted every opportunity to make them and did so—sometimes even to people who turned out not to have bad credit after all. Those lenders, many now defunct, are the poster children for predatory lending.

But subprime/nonprime mortgages weren't the only culprits in the mortgage mess. Another loan product that has helped borrowers use leverage to purchase homes that they really couldn't afford was the hybrid mortgage, also known as the fixed-period adjustable rate mortgage (ARM). Set at a fixed rate for a predetermined initial period of time (usually three, five, seven, or ten years), the loan then converts to an ARM for the balance of the term, adjusting annually. And since many of these loans were made at unrealistically low short-term "teaser rates" to entice consumers, a borrower could qualify to purchase more house, and did just that! To top it all off, these mortgages were often made using little or no documentation from the borrower (low-doc/no-doc loans) requiring more than their fair share of points and lender fees to boot.

What was designed as a short-term fix and leverage tool for borrowers is now a living nightmare in homes across America. With these hybrid loans now transitioning to ARMs, monthly payments are slipping out of reach for many buyers, often more than doubling the monthly payment.

Then came the exotics—mortgages for anyone who could fog up a mirror. They included no down payment mortgages, interest-only mortgages, and an interesting new twist, the payment option mortgage. With the latter, a borrower had the option each month to make one of four types of payments. One that (1) amortized the loan during the loan term, i.e. 30 years; (2) amortized the loan for a shorter loan term, i.e. 15 years; (3) required a payment of interest only on the loan; or (4) required a "minimal" payment of less than interest only whereby the unpaid interest would be added back onto the principal each month (termed "negative amortization"). While there's no such thing as a bad mortgage program, originating a leveraged loan without regard for the applicant's financial situation and/or ability to repay coupled with a borrower who knows he can't make payments for the long run is a recipe for disaster.

It's interesting to note that the majority of these highly leveraged mortgages were built around the faulty premise that perpetual double-digit home appreciation would save the day and financially bail the consumer out, no matter how rotten and misbegotten the loan program. In 2007, more than $1 trillion worth of adjustable rate mortgage products had upward rate adjustments causing payment shock and potential foreclosure for American homeowners. Meanwhile, dozens (and still counting) of sizable national mortgage lenders have closed operations, primarily since they are required to repurchase loans from investors in the secondary market if the loan becomes delinquent within a few months after it's sold. These "collateral calls" or "buybacks" are expensive and the major cause of lender failures.

Everyone wants to get their piece of the action in a booming market. Enter the speculators. Some bought property, quickly flipped it, paid off their exotic loan product, and made money. But as the market shifted from a seller's to a buyer's, some were left holding the property and a mortgage they couldn't pay with an inability to charge enough rent to cover the debt service. In order to cut their losses and run, these properties became some of the first to foreclose.

Additionally, there were two equally strong components that impacted the housing market and contributed to the problem of home affordability—a marked increased in the cost of property taxes and homeowner's insurance. The previously buoyant housing market raised values, resulting in a substantial increase in assessed value resulting in higher property taxes. Today, some homeowners must work two or more months of the year just to pay their property taxes. Then there's Mother Nature. The hurricane triplets, wild fires in the West, and other natural disasters have impacted home insurance across the board nationwide. If your policy isn't canceled because your underwriter is out of business, you can at least rely on your premiums increasing. The grim reaper is that the financial complexion of the mortgage market is vastly different from what it was just several years ago and will most likely continue to morph into something different all together before the dust settles.

To sum up the answer to your question about what or who is to blame for the mortgage mess, we all are—overzealous lenders wanting to make a larger profit, investors wanting to cash in on the big returns of the subprime market, "flippers" wanting to double their investment, and consumers who didn't use their heads and got saddled with mortgage products they couldn't understand and/or afford long term.

But there's good that's come from the mortgage firestorm. The mortgage industry is getting "back to basics," focusing once again on full documentation, transparent lending, stronger equity positions for borrowers, and, in general, making sensible, cost-effective mortgages that consumers can afford for the long run. While some programs will disappear, many will remain unchanged, while yet others will require tighter underwriting guidelines, larger down payments, and/or premiums based on the borrower's amount of risk to the lender/investor.

There's never been a better nor more important time for consumers to take an active role in understanding mortgage borrowing and equity management. When the consumer wins, everyone wins.

CONSUMER EMPOWERMENT VIA THE WORLD WIDE WEB

Q. To what degree has online access empowered consumers in the mortgage loan process?

To an incredible degree. In fact, latest statistics from the National Association of Realtors® (NAR) estimate that more than 80 percent of all buyers begin their mortgage (and homebuying) hunt online! Not only can consumers peruse the vast choices in loan types, lenders, and available properties, but they can do so in anonymity in the comfort of their own homes. (Check out the wide array of Uniform Resource Locators [URLs] found in the Resource Guide section of this book.)

Q. What's the most time-efficient plan for a homebuyer who wants to check out the Web?

Here's an approach I've found simple and helpful. If you're a first-time homebuyer (or it's been a while since your last purchase), check out information-gathering sites such as www.interest.com, www.realtor.com, and, of course, yours truly at www.juliegartongood.com. On your initial trip, don't get bogged down filling in time-consuming forms and micromanaging your visit. Your initial mission is to gather enough information to feel comfortable about homebuying and get a flavor for the online marketplace.

Next, visit several of the interest rate and mortgage sites— www.lendingtree.com, www.hsh.com, and www.eloan.com. If you're feeling comfortable enough with the process, go ahead and try one of the "how much home can you afford?" calculators you'll see and check out your credit report online by accessing www.annualcreditreport.com.

Q. Once I've gone that far in the online process, is it wise to go ahead and make a formal application for a mortgage at that time?

It's your call and it should be based to a large extent on what you feel comfortable with. Some buyers feel more comfortable providing the site with their e-mail address, name, and telephone number so that a real person can contact them or can fax or e-mail back possible loan options. Others don't mind filling in screens full of information. Much of that information, however, is rarely at your fingertips when you're sitting in front of a computer screen.

Many mortgage sites allow you to send them a streamlined, skeletal application that includes your name, telephone number, e-mail address, best time to call, approximate income and debts, and the state in which you wish to buy property. By using the online qualifying calculators and this approach, you can get an idea of what you can afford, but the detail gathering is still in the hands of the lender.

Q. What about Internet safety when transmitting personal and financial information about yourself?

While most mortgage companies use encrypted transmission to send personal information (turning it from text to a secure code), some people are still leery of online security. But think about this: Information about your credit, medical history, and far more personal buying habits is freely circulating around the planet. So Web security could perhaps be one of your least personal worries!

Seriously, if you have any doubt about the security of the site or the ultimate destination of any information you might submit, either (1) do nothing or (2) use only your e-mail address initially until you can gather further information.

Q. What are the cautions when mortgage shopping online?

Consumers should remember that there's no Web God of Mortgaging who patrols the information, guarantees the source, or even checks to see if the information is current (though most mortgage companies do keep rates current on their sites because it's their stock-in-trade). Each borrower should double-check the accuracy, timeliness, and availability of the information as it applies to his or her specific needs.

Q. What about obtaining a mortgage from an online interstate lender?

Loans originated online and closed in another state can require an even higher level of troubleshooting. Forms and disclosures must be state-specific, based on the location of the property not on the state where the loan originates. It's not uncommon for interstate lenders to overlook a state-specific form or a nuance of title, for instance requiring a second set of signatures on documents. Some interstate lenders will send you documents to sign, have notarized, and return. Others will select a title company in your area to close the transaction. There are even some lenders who merely hire a notary public in your area to show up at your door with the documents for you to sign! For your own protection, you should close with a knowledgeable closing officer (i.e., title company) or attorney or at least have a local professional review the documents prior to closing. You must protect yourself against signing mortgage documents that don't meet the legal requirements in your state and/or create a title error.

Q. What kind of property information can you find online?

A lot. Millions of properties are listed at sites such as www.realtor.com, www.hud.gov, and in the for-sale-by-owner category of www.forsalebyowner.com and www.byowner.com. You can obtain information about pricing at sites such as www.zillow.com and www.domania.com.

THINK LIKE AN APPRAISER TO SELECT A PROPERTY

Q. Because pricing and appraisals are important in obtaining a mortgage, what's the best way to select a home the lender will approve?

Most mortgage appraisal guidelines specify that the property is located in a stable neighborhood where values are strong. Even after multiple decades, the top three criteria of the homebuying process are still location, location, and location. Four reasons why this is true are:

1. Stable property generates a stronger appraisal for the transaction. Because most loans are contingent on securing a certain loan size based on appraised value, a favorable appraisal can make or break the sale.
2. Private mortgage insurance (and homeowners insurance, too) is more readily available if the home is in a good neighborhood.
3. The borrower can consider a wider variety of loans if the home and the neighborhood are of good quality.
4. A home in a good neighborhood has a strong potential for appreciation, giving it a better resale value. This factor can also be important to the lender should the loan default.

Q. If the stability of the neighborhood and the quality of the home are so important, what kinds of things should a prospective homebuyer consider before purchasing?

An in-depth review of the property and the surrounding area would help the borrower evaluate the strength of the purchase. Here are some things to consider:

Looking Around

- *Check the traffic flow.* Make several trips to the property during different days of the week and various times of the day to make sure accessibility is good. If commuting is a concern, make sure traffic flows well to and from the property.
- *Take different routes to access the property.* Make sure there are no unsightly concerns near the property such as wrecking yards, dumpsites, or overgrown vacant lots.
- *Check for noise pollution.* Properties easily accessible to main highway arteries and commercial zoning risk higher levels of noise bleeding into the neighborhood. Is the home under an airport flight pattern? Test the noise level from inside and outside the home. Take a stroll up the street to uncover any dog kennels, handyman garages, or day care centers.
- *Is outside lighting good?* Incidents of crime and traffic accidents increase if the neighborhood lighting is poor. Check the home's exterior lighting as well, especially near entrances and garage doors.
- *Analyze the condition of the streets, sidewalks, and services available.* Is there ample street and sidewalk drainage? How many fire hydrants are there and how close is the nearest fire station? These factors also will affect your homeowners insurance.

Asking Around

If the opportunity is available, personally contact the neighbors before making an offer. They are often a great source of unbiased information about the neighborhood. Here are some possible questions to ask:

- *Is the area generally quiet?*
- *Where do you shop near the area and why?*
- *What is the quality of the schools? You can access online resources like www.homefair.com to check this out for yourself*
- *Do you think you would have any trouble selling your property? Why or why not?*
- *Would you buy here again? Why or why not?*
- *Have you seen much crime or vandalism in the neighborhood? If so, were police and ambulance responses satisfactory?*

Checking with several residents can provide a well-rounded view of the area, as well as help sidestep any prejudiced remarks.

Checking Around

It's wise to verify material facts before you select a property. If you're working with a real estate agent, he or she can provide much of the following information:

- *Check the public records.* Although the title report you receive at closing will reveal items of public record, it's wise to double-check for any current or pending assessment to the area, such as for sidewalk repair, or water or sewer line addition.
- *Check the level of crime for the area.* The city police department can provide an overview of the type and volume of crime in the area. By calling the nonemergency number for the police department and stating the location of the property and the cross streets, the public service officer can provide you with an analysis for the area. Some police departments even do safety checks, coming to the property to offer suggestions for exterior lighting and burglary protection. Online sources such as www.homefair.com (city profile) also can assist your information gathering.
- *Confirm general property values.* Ask real estate agents or appraisers to confirm that property values in the area are stable and have not recently softened. A copy of comparable sales from the Multiple Listing Service (MLS), which can be obtained from an agent, should help confirm this. A neighborhood with eroding property values might make the house difficult to sell and could be especially tough if you purchased using a small down payment and needed to sell in a short time. Online resources, like www.zillow.com, can help determine market value.
- *Analyze the property itself.* A good way to begin is by asking the seller to provide a property disclosure sheet (required by law in more than 30 states) itemizing the contents and condition of the property, including the working order of all heating and cooling units and appliances. Be sure to test the air conditioner in the winter and the heating system in the summer to make sure they'll work when you need them. Turn on all appliances to guarantee their working order, and move throw rugs and other obstructions so you get a complete view of the property.

The buyer may be tempted to jump at purchasing a home based on the gleam of the imported ceramic tile countertops, the quality of the parquet floor, or the lush garden-like backyard. By looking around, asking around, and checking around, the borrower helps ensure the financial investment is a sound one. For a property checklist, see figure 1.2 on next page.

FIGURE 1.2 *Home Inspection Checklist*

MECHANICAL SYSTEMS

HEATING

Age, condition, and operation of main system _____

_____

Thermostat(s) _____

_____

Room-by-room heating _____

_____

COOLING

Age, condition, and operation of main system _____

_____

Thermostat(s) _____

_____

Room-by-room cooling _____

_____

ELECTRICAL

Adequacy of service _____

_____

Light switches _____

Doorbells _____

Exterior lighting _____

PLUMBING

Overall _____

Water heater _____

WASTE (SEWERS OR SEPTIC)

Flush toilets _____

Consult owners on condition _____

_____

Obtain service record _____

_____

APPLIANCES

Range _____

Oven (all controls) _____

_____

Dishwasher (run full cycle) _____

_____

Refrigerator/Freezer _____

_____

Compactor _____

Disposal _____

Washing machine _____

Dryer _____

Other _____

_____

INTERIOR SPACES

WALLS, CEILINGS, AND FLOORS

Overall condition _____

_____

Water stains _____

Cracks _____

Settlement _____

Decay _____

BASEMENT AND CRAWL SPACES

Walls _____

_____

Floor _____

_____

Water penetration _____

_____

KITCHEN

Cabinets _____

Countertop _____

Floor _____

_____

FIGURE 1.2 *Home Inspection Checklist*

BATHROOMS

Toilets (tank and operation) _____

_____

_____

Floor (around tub, shower, and toilet)

_____

_____

Shower (check controls)_____

_____

Tub (check controls) _____

_____

Tile _____

GARAGE

Doors _____

Floor _____

Walls _____

EXTERIOR CONDITIONS

Roof _____

Floor _____

Windows/Doors _____

_____

Steps and stairs _____

_____

Decks/Porches _____

_____

Pools and accessories _____

_____

Sprinkler _____

Landscaping _____

_____

Drainage _____

_____

PROTECTING YOURSELF IN THE PURCHASE AGREEMENT

Q. When a buyer finds a home he or she likes, what kinds of financing contingency clauses should be included in the purchase agreement?

If the purchaser must obtain adequate financing (as most do), it's imperative to make the purchase contingent on receiving suitable financing. If financing cannot be obtained within the parameters spelled out on the purchase agreement or in the time frame specified, the buyer would not have to complete the sale and, barring other conditions, the earnest money deposit would be returned.

The buyer should be specific, stating exactly what maximum size loan (usually a percentage of the sales price) is needed, the type of loan with a maximum rate of interest, the term of the loan, and the maximum amount of discount points the buyer will pay.

With this information, a financing contingency might read as follows: "Purchase contingent upon the borrower applying for and receiving a 90 percent thirty (30)-year fixed-rate loan, with interest not to exceed 7 percent. The buyer will pay up to two (2) discount points to obtain the loan." A real estate agent or real estate attorney can help buyers structure the language to use in the agreement.

Q. If you've talked to a lender about how much mortgage you can afford, is there any kind of purchase agreement language that would give you an added edge in a competitive market?

Following is a little-known clause/technique to provide additional leverage to a buyer's financial negotiating position. Not only does it provide a built-in counteroffer, it helps you stay afloat in negotiations when the seller is bombarded with multiple offers from various potential buyers. As with any type of leverage tool, it should be used sparingly and only in the proper circumstances.

Here's how it works. You make an offer to the seller that states something like "Should the seller receive multiple offers, the buyer agrees to pay X dollars over the highest offered price, up to a ceiling of Y. This allows you to automatically meet and beat another offer in a competitive multiple-offer situation. Note, however, that this does require you to predetermine how high you're willing to go. You or your agent would want to add clarifying language to require the seller to show you copies of other potential buyers' viable written offers before your counteroffer clause would be enforceable. The seller can do this by providing you with copies of the other buyers' offers with the buyers' names and addresses blocked out to protect the privacy of the parties.

There are downsides to using a built-in counteroffer clause. First, the seller knows that you're eager to obtain the property. This could mean a counteroffer that asks for a higher price or more flexible terms even if there aren't offers from multiple buyers—yet another reason to demand that the seller provide you with proof that another bona fide offer does exist.

A second negative is that you transfer a portion of your negotiating power to the seller. He or she now can dictate the price ceiling and could create a bidding war that could push offered prices in excess of the market value. Correspondingly, this could impact the amount of down payment you need and increase your closing costs, and even affect the appraisal required to obtain a loan. The bottom line is that too much competitiveness could cause you to overpay for the house. That's why prior to using this language, you should predetermine the maximum price, terms, and conditions that are prudent for you as preapproved with the lender. Should negotiations exceed these parameters, consider it a deal breaker and be prepared to walk away.

THE BASICS OF LOAN DISCLOSURE

Q. What does a lender have to tell a borrower about the lending process and the loan?

A mortgage lender is required to make certain disclosures to a borrower on application or within three days after application. The disclosures describe costs incurred with the loan (closing costs, origination fees, etc.), the effective interest rate being charged, and the possibility that the lender will transfer the servicing rights (payment collection) on the loan (also called selling the loan).

Good Faith Estimate

The Real Estate Settlement Procedures Act (RESPA) requires disclosure of estimated settlement costs to homebuyers based on the parameters of the loan. The Department of Housing and Urban Development (HUD) has a settlement statement that itemizes these costs, including fees to be paid at closing. Fees can vary based on changes in the loan that occur between the time of application and the closing. In addition, the lender is required to provide the borrower with HUD's *Settlement Cost Guide* booklet, which describes the homebuying process. You can obtain a copy of it at www.hud.gov.

Q. Is it true that RESPA is finally revamping their disclosure guidelines?

At long last, yes. After five years of debating and many fits and starts, the federal government is unveiling a new, more "consumer friendly" 30-year old Real Estate Settlement Procedures Act.

Primary among the reforms:

- A standard, revamped good faith estimate (GFE) that will disclose all of the important aspects of the loan, including: the interest rate and monthly payment; whether the interest rate and principal balance can increase and by how much; and whether the loan has a prepayment penalty or balloon payment.
- The GFE consolidates closing costs into major categories to prevent "junk fees" and displays total estimated settlement

charges prominently on the first page so that consumers can easily compare loan offers.

- The new HUD rule would specify the charges that can and cannot change at settlement. If a fee does change, HUD proposes to limit the amount it can change.
- The good faith estimate would require that lender payments to mortgage brokers, often called yield spread premiums (YSP), be disclosed. HUD believes that these payments are directly dependent on the interest rates that consumers agree to and therefore ought to be disclosed.
- The revamped RESPA would require that settlement agents read a "closing script" to borrowers at the settlement table and that a copy be provided to the borrower. A different script for each loan type, the document restates in a clear and specific manner every loan term and also provides a graphic showing borrowers which numbers can change from that provided in the GFE and by how much. This script will provide a ready post-closing reference to the loan.

It's sad to reflect that if this legislation had been adopted years ago in a timely fashion, perhaps some of the toxic mortgage mania could have been prevented.

Truth in Lending

The purpose of the federal Truth-in-Lending Law and regulations is to ensure that borrowers are aware of the terms and costs of credit so that they can knowledgeably compare loan programs and lenders. For example, the lender must disclose the annual percentage rate (APR) of the loan, defined as the cost of credit to the borrower expressed as a yearly rate. This finance charge includes any charge paid directly or indirectly by the borrower and imposed by the lender as a condition of extending credit (including appraisals, credit reports, etc.).

Transfer for Servicing

This document shows the lender's intent regarding servicing the loan after the closing, and tells what percentage of loans it has transferred servicing on in the past. Lenders also must give adjustable-rate mortgage (ARM) applicants a worst-case scenario of how the monthly payment could adjust over the life of the loan. This requirement will be discussed later in this book.

Ask Up Front about Other Nuances of the Mortgage

Q. Nothing in the disclosure list refers to mortgage particulars such as whether or not the loan I'm considering has a prepayment penalty. Don't lenders disclose those types of things up front?

While most good lenders attempt to, some of the nuances of mortgages (like prepayment penalties) often don't arise during the initial application appointment.

First, it may be tough for the lender to initially tell which loan program might best benefit the borrower. Until all the information is gathered and processed, the borrower's strengths and weaknesses may not be completely known.

Second, a lender may start processing a borrower under one program then switch to another that's more beneficial to him or her. The reason could be that a loan with a prepayment penalty, for example, might carry a lesser interest rate. In fact, unless you specifically tell the lender that you don't want a prepayment penalty, the lender may err on the side of getting you the best interest rate including a loan with a prepayment penalty. (I know this from experience!)

The borrower should ask the lender up front to enumerate the pros and cons of the loans being considered. If the lender switches you to another loan program, ask again for the pros and cons as well as completely new disclosure documents. This is yet another reason why, at the very least, you should thoroughly review and understand the mortgage documents prior to signing them.

PREDATORY LENDING AND MORTGAGE FRAUD

Q. You hear so much about predatory lending today. Is there a working definition for it?

The Mortgage Bankers Association (www.mortgagebankers.org) defines predatory lending as "intentionally placing consumers in loan products with significantly worse terms and/or higher costs than loans offered to similarly qualified consumers in the region for the primary purpose of enriching the originator and with little or no regard for the costs to the consumer."

Q. What are some examples of predatory lending?

Lending practices that are readily identifiable as "predatory" include:

- Selling a high-cost, high-interest loan to a borrower who would qualify for a lower-cost, lower-interest loan that the same lender offers
- Adding products or services, like credit life insurance, to a loan without adequately informing the borrower about the need or cost of the items
- Refinancing a mortgage repeatedly within a short period of time and charging higher than normal loan origination fees and points each time

Q. Is it possible for a consumer to innocently get involved in mortgage fraud?

Yes, and, unfortunately, it's occurring with greater frequency. Let's say you find a house you love, but the seller has it priced a little high in order to pay off his mortgages, cover his closing costs, and pocket a bit of equity. If you buy the house, he promises to give you back $4,000 after closing to help offset the higher purchase price. Sounds innocent enough, right?

Wrong. This cash-back-at-closing scheme constitutes mortgage fraud and is punishable under federal law including federal prison time and/ or tens of thousands of dollars in fines. The reason is that you're keeping a side contract a secret from the lender while trying to trick her into approving a mortgage loan for more money than the property is worth.

But, as the borrower, you're hurt as well. You've overpaid for the property and are saddled with a loan that you may not be able to afford. Housing values drop and you're stuck owing more on the property than you can sell it for. The lender is forced to foreclose and you lose the house.

Then there's the matter of the $4,000 cash to you at closing. What makes you think you'll ever see the money? Since you'd be participating in something illegal, the cash-back agreement won't be part of your purchase agreement or your closing statement, and you legally won't have a leg to stand on to enforce him to compensate you. You will have overpaid for a property, be stuck with higher payments and property taxes, and have nothing to show for it but a painful life lesson.

Mortgage fraud is nothing to mess with, no matter how rosy the situation appears.

THE LOAN APPLICATION PROCESS

Q. What does the applicant need to provide to the lender to have a mortgage application considered?

The lender's requirements from the borrower depend to a great degree not only on the type of loan you're seeking—conventional compared to Federal Housing Administration (FHA)—but also on the approach the lender uses in processing and underwriting the loan. For example, a lender using technological tools such as an automated underwriting system (AUS) employing computer software may require fewer pieces of information than a lender who relies solely on human resources to process the paperwork.

This is because the AUS asks the lender/loan officer to input the basic information from your application, the 1003 (pronounced ten-oh-three, the form number that Fannie Mae has assigned to the five-page application). Once entered into the computer, AUS then determines which information it needs for the type of loan you're seeking. For example, you might need three months of bank statements. No problem. And two most-recent check stubs. Depending on your credit score, your down payment, and the property you're purchasing, you may be amazed at how very little paperwork you'll be required to provide. It's a radical improvement over the good old days when you had to document everything but your birthmark! The key is to provide complete, truthful information to the lender when it's requested, but only when it's requested. With automated underwriting, less can be more. Otherwise, the underwriter might spend wasted days documenting information that had no bearing on whether or not you qualified for the loan.

Although it's unlikely that you'll have to produce a majority of the following, here's a thorough list.

Property Information

- *A copy of the purchase agreement; if a construction loan, a copy of plans and specifications.* The lender also may need information about the purchase and the property to complete the loan application. This could include the number of units (e.g., single family or duplex), the year built, and how title will be held.
- *Legal description of the property*
- *A Multiple Listing Service (MLS) information sheet,* if available

Borrower Information

- Social Security numbers for all borrowers and coborrowers
- A list of the borrowers' home addresses for the past two years
- *The names and addresses of landlords for the past two years,* if the borrowers are renters
- *The names and addresses of all employers for the past two years.* Borrowers should give the addresses of the human resources offices, because they might be different from the office locations. Any employment gaps should be explained.

Asset Verification

- *Internal Revenue Service (IRS) W-2 forms; personal tax returns from the past two years with schedules.* A buyer needs to demonstrate two years of full-time or part-time employment in the same line of work; however, time spent in technical career training (such as a physician's medical internship or union apprenticeship) could count toward the two-year requirement.
- *Two most recent paycheck stubs*
- *Bank statements for the past three months*
- *Checking account numbers and locations*
- *Savings account numbers and locations*
- *Credit union account numbers and locations*
- *Mutual fund account numbers and locations*
- *Individual retirement accounts (IRAs) and/or 401(k) information*
- *Explanation of any other income the borrower wishes to be considered toward qualifying,* including the following:
    - *Child support.* The buyer needs to show proof of receipt, through a printout from the courts or 12 months of canceled checks. (Payments must have been received for at least 12 months on time and must be scheduled to continue at a minimum of another 36 months to count as qualifying income, depending on the loan program.)
    - *A bonus.* This can be counted if the buyer has received it for the past two years (the lender will average it).
    - *Overtime.* Lenders look for a two-year history, and consider the average amount of overtime likely to continue (unless the employer volunteers something to the contrary). If the overtime can't be counted toward qualifying income, it still might be considered as a compensating factor.

- *Social Security and/or disability payments.* The buyer must provide a copy of the award letter and a recent check stub, or a copy of a bank statement if payment is electronically deposited.
- *Pension income.* The buyer should provide a check stub and any forms showing the duration of payments.
- *Rental property income.* This information can be provided in income tax returns from the past two years. The buyer should bring leases, if possible. Only 75 percent of rental income is counted, but 100 percent of the expenses are deductions. For example, if rental income is $500 per month and the mortgage is also $500, the lender considers this a net loss each month of $125, because only 75 percent of the income is counted for qualifying.
- *Copies of documents and explanations of any other money owed to the borrower,* e.g., receivable contracts

Debt Verification

- *Payment book or monthly billing statement for all debts.* If neither is supplied, the lender needs the name and address of the creditor, account number, monthly payment amount, and the approximate amount owed in order to verify.
- *Documentation of current mortgages and home equity loans,* including any recently paid-off mortgages. If the buyer is in the process of selling a home, the new lender should receive a copy of the HUD-1 closing statement on that home before closing on the new home.
- *If renting old home* (rather than selling upon moving), a copy of a lease (at least one year), signed by the new tenant, prior to the closing of the new home
- *Documentation of car payments*
- *Information about outstanding student loans*
- *Divorce decree or separation agreement* to document alimony or child support due or payable
- *Clarification of divorced person's debts.* For formerly joint debts that the other spouse is now supposed to pay, the buyer may need to prove that he or she isn't paying those bills, unless the debt was refinanced and the buyer's name was taken off the obligation. This may be required even though according to the divorce decree, it's not the buyer's obligation. Proof can include canceled checks from the former spouse to show that he or she is paying that obligation,

and on time. Otherwise, the debt may go against the borrower's long-term debt ratios for qualifying. This varies based on the loan program.

- *Information about any payments made as direct withdrawals from a checking account or credit union*
- *A copy of any bankruptcy proceedings,* if applicable, with status and explanation
- *A gift letter or explanation of a fund's source for closing costs*
- *If obtaining a Department of Veterans Affairs (VA) loan, original Certificate of Eligibility and DD214*
- *Explanation letter for any late payments, judgments, liens, bankruptcy, or foreclosure*
- *A copy of a Certificate of Resident Alien Status (green card),* if applicable
- *A check for the application fee, credit report, and appraisal,* if applicable

Q. What other mortgage loan application questions should the borrower be prepared to answer?

A section of the uniform residential loan application called "Information for Government Monitoring Purposes" requests that you state your race, nation of origin, and sex. While it's not mandatory that the applicant answer these questions, if the borrower declines to answer them, the lender is required to complete the questions based on meeting the applicant or by his or her surname. This information monitors the lender's compliance with the equal credit opportunity, fair housing, and home mortgage disclosure laws. It also monitors the number and types of minorities being afforded the opportunity to apply for a home loan. Because this information becomes part of a national database to help monitor fair housing laws and reduce discrimination, it's advisable that the applicant answer the questions in this section rather than having the lender guess the answers.

All information given the lender on the application should be truthful and complete. Penalties for falsifying information are stiff. Intentional and negligent misrepresentations can result in criminal penalties and monetary damages under Title 18 of the United States Code.

Q. If the lender wants information, can't he or she just search for it?

First of all, the borrower is expected by law to give all pertinent information to the lender. Moreover, this "find it out yourself" attitude usually catches up with the borrower. By checking credit, verifying assets and employment, and noting facts of public record, usually very little escapes the lender's underwriting process. Up front and honest is definitely the best policy if the borrower wants to get the mortgage.

THE LOAN UNDERWRITING PROCESS

Q. What happens after the application is taken?

Several things. The borrower's employment, income, and funds on deposit for the down payment and closing costs are all verified. An appraisal also may be ordered at this time. Depending on the loan type, other documentation may be requested. Figure 1.3 summarizes the process and shows some common causes of delays.

This phase is called *underwriting the loan.* It's perhaps the most difficult part of the loan process because information must be collected and thoroughly analyzed in order to decide whether the loan will be made. As mentioned previously, much of this can be sidestepped or streamlined by the lender's use of automated underwriting; but sometimes the process bogs down if the borrower is requested to produce proof that a debt was paid, a credit error repaired, and so on. No matter how the loan is processed, this type of request is likely to slow down or stall the process.

The underwriter, or loan endorser, carefully reviews the borrower's documentation and decides whether he or she would be a sound lending risk. If segments of the borrower's employment, credit, or overall financial picture are vague or appear to be contradictory, the underwriter requests more information. This decision process can take hours or weeks to complete. But as mentioned earlier, much of the process is streamlined today using technology and electronic underwriting and electronic credit scoring to help interpret the borrower's loan qualifications.

The underwriting phase also may include the approval of the borrower and the property for private mortgage insurance, if required on the loan. This insurance protects the lender from the borrower's default, usually on the top 20 percent of the loan, and requires a separate approval based on the private mortgage insurance company's underwriting guidelines.

Underwriting guidelines for major types of loans are discussed later in this book.

FIGURE 1.3 *The Loan Underwriting Process*

Common Time Delays in New Financing

1. Borrower is slow to apply.

2. No check to start process.

3. Creditors will not respond.

4. Creditors respond incorrectly.

5. Employers will not respond.

6. Employers do not complete verification form properly.

7. Explanation needed on late payments.

8. Bad credit complicates the file.

9. Income is less than reported on application.

10. More bills than reported on application

11. Appraisal is lower than sale price.

12. Property is unacceptable to lender.

13. Inspections and/or repairs

14. File must be restructured due to change.

15. Closing documents incorrectly signed.

16. Closing requirements not satisfied.

17. Lender and underwriter workloads

Financing Sequence

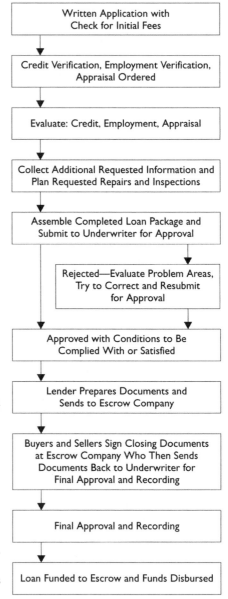

Written Application with Check for Initial Fees

Credit Verification, Employment Verification, Appraisal Ordered

Evaluate: Credit, Employment, Appraisal

Collect Additional Requested Information and Plan Requested Repairs and Inspections

Assemble Completed Loan Package and Submit to Underwriter for Approval

Rejected—Evaluate Problem Areas, Try to Correct and Resubmit for Approval

Approved with Conditions to Be Complied With or Satisfied

Lender Prepares Documents and Sends to Escrow Company

Buyers and Sellers Sign Closing Documents at Escrow Company Who Then Sends Documents Back to Underwriter for Final Approval and Recording

Final Approval and Recording

Loan Funded to Escrow and Funds Disbursed

Source: Adapted with permission of Gary Everett, Steve Scott & Co. REALTORS®, 910 NW Harriman, Bend, OR 97701.

Underwriting Roadblocks

Q. Can a borrower get a loan even if he or she doesn't meet the underwriting guidelines?

This depends on many factors: the size of the down payment, the borrower's creditworthiness, and whether the lender is selling the loan to the secondary market. Later chapters that cover the major loan types include information on these and other compensating factors. If a borrower has one or more of these pluses, the loan may be made even though all the underwriting guidelines aren't met.

Q. What major roadblocks can come up during the underwriting process?

Many problems occur with verifying employment, down payments, and income from such sources as child support and alimony. Borrowers sometimes change their financial pictures while the loan is being processed. Whether pro or con, these changes can invalidate the paperwork produced up to that point.

It may seem bizarre to mention, but after the borrower applies for the loan, he or she should not change jobs or give notice to quit. If loan processing takes more than a month or so, the lender may reverify everything, including employment.

The same is true with taking on new debt. Just because the application has been taken doesn't mean that the lender won't know if the borrower purchased a new washer and dryer using time payments. A credit inquiry from the appliance dealer will show up on the credit report, and even adding a new small monthly debt may be enough to tip the scales against the loan.

In short, the rule of thumb for borrowers to follow after application and before closing is simply, "Don't change a thing!"

Problems also can occur when verifying the borrower's funds, called *verification of deposit.* The lender wants to make sure that the down payment has not been borrowed or gained by illegal means. That means that the lender is likely to verify that the money has been accumulating in an account, usually undisturbed for a minimum of 60 days.

Funds that mysteriously disappear and reappear may send up a red flag, putting the validity of the funds into question and perhaps causing the lender to deny the loan. So if funds have increased or decreased radically (through transfers of accounts to other banks and so on), the borrower should make sure the lender understands why.

Any documentation required to verify child support, alimony, and debts incurred in a previous marriage may seem deep and cumbersome, but complying with paperwork requests may make the difference between getting and not getting the loan.

If anything changes, and that includes changes for the better, the buyer should make sure to notify the lender. Salary increases to become effective within 60 days of the loan closing may be considered for qualifying, and a larger down payment can make the buyer stronger in the eyes of the lender.

Automatic Underwriting System (AUS): Technology Streamlines the Process

Q. What is an automatic underwriting system (AUS), how does it work, and is it reliable and fair?

When automatic underwriting was first explained to me, it sounded like the mortgage industry's rendition of the "great and powerful Oz" behind the curtain—mysterious and possibly omniscient. But after more than a decade of application in a variety of formats, obviously automatic underwriting has considerably streamlined, improved, and helped objectify the mortgage process for lenders and consumers alike.

Fannie Mae lead the industry with her Desktop Underwriter® (DU) followed by Freddie Mac's Loan Prospector®(LP). These computerized underwriting systems and others employed by smaller investors use statistical models based on traditional underwriting criteria involving factors such as collateral (the property) and the borrower's credit experience plus the borrower's likelihood to repay the loan. The most important individual factors as predictors of repayment are the borrower's total equity in the property, the loan type, and his or her credit scores.

One of the greatest benefits from AUS is that it eliminates the dreaded waiting period inherent in the paper-trailing/paper-chasing processing method of the past and lets the borrower hear "You're approved" within a matter of minutes. While paper is still part of the process, with this technology, the process is more seamless with less duplicated efforts.

As for fairness, AUS allows the mortgage industry to process and approve mortgages in a color-blind approach without improprieties of race, color, creed, sex, and national origin that were more likely to occur under the old process. While not every lender currently uses an AUS, approximately 90 percent of all loans are processed using some form of technology.

Q. What are the outcomes in automatic underwriting? If a borrower is rejected as an unsuitable risk, is there any way he or she can appeal?

First, the AUS does not automatically reject anyone. Once the borrower's information is entered into the computer and processed, depending on the AUS program used, a message of "accept" (approve) or "caution" or "refer" will appear. The latter two mean that there is either insufficient data to make a decision and/or a real person in the underwriting department needs to perform a manual, nontechnological review before making a final decision. AU is only a computerized system that evaluates the information. It doesn't know the details of the application, for instance, why a borrower was late on a car loan last year or that the two mortgages the borrower is carrying are temporary until the houses sell. All it sees are the facts not the rationale behind the facts. That's why even though technology has improved the mortgage process, it won't be completely replacing human beings anytime soon! You can see a comparison of automatic underwriting systems in figure 1.4.

FIGURE 1.4 *Automated Underwriting Systems:*

	Approved	Suspended	Declined
Desktop Underwriter® "DU"– FNMA Conventional Loans, some Jumbo Loans.	**Approve – Eligible:** The loan is approved and a live underwriter must simply review required conditions or exhibits	**Approve – Ineligible:** The loan meets guidelines and receives an approval recommendation, but due to one or more characteristics, a human underwriter must approve it.	**Ineligible:** The loan does not meet A.U. parameters and must be underwritten and approved by a human underwriter.
Loan Prospector® "LP" – FHLMC Conventional Loans, some Jumbo Loans, FHA and VA Loans	**Accept:** The loan is approved and a live underwriter must simply review required conditions or exhibits.	**Refer:** The loan meets guidelines and receives an approval recommendation, but due to one or more characteristics, a human underwriter must approve it.	**Decline:** The loan is ineligible for sale to FHLMC: must be underwritten to other guidelines by a human.

Your lender can "tweak" the automated underwriting system. Tweaking is not lying, it's just adjusting/modifying certain elements of information to obtain loan approval. For example, could you borrow less and qualify? What about adding a co-borrower to the loan? Or perhaps, a 40-year term would help lower your payments into the qualifying zone? What used to take days of resubmitting the application in the old world of loan processing takes just key strokes today.

THE LOAN CLOSING

Q. So, after all the documentation is collected and the underwriter approves the loan, then the closing occurs?

That's correct. The lender or an appointed closing officer—such as a title company or an attorney—prepares the closing statement, checks the title report, prepares the mortgages and deeds to be recorded, and closes the transaction. Figure 1.5 shows a sample closing statement. It is good to familiarize yourself with these costs, because many could be negotiating points with the seller.

In addition, balances for any outstanding loans are checked and the seller gives his or her permission to pay off that loan.

Legal Right to Review Documents prior to Closing

Q. Is it possible for the buyer to review the mortgage papers and closing documents prior to closing?

Yes. Under the federal Real Estate Settlement Procedures Act (RESPA) the borrower has the right to read and inspect all closing documents one business day prior to closing upon request. Unfortunately, most consumers don't know this law exists and few closing companies/lenders extend this option to buyers as a matter of general practice. In other words, if you don't know to ask for this right to inspect, it may not be made available to you.

FIGURE 1.5 *Sample Closing Statement*

SELLER'S STATEMENT			BUYER'S STATEMENT	
DEBIT	CREDIT	ITEM	DEBIT	CREDIT
		Total Purchase Price		
		Binder Deposit		
		First Mortgage		
		Second Mortgage		
		Prorations and Prepayments		
		Rent		
		Interest (first mortgage)		
		Interest (second mortage)		
		Prepayment Penalty		
		Insurance		
		Mortgage Insurance		
		Insurance Reserves		
		Taxes (city)		
		Taxes (county)		
		Tax Reserves		
		Expenses		
		Attorney's Fees		
		Escrow Closing Fees		
		Escrow Holding Fees (Long Term)		
		State Tax on Deed		
		Recording Mortgage		
		Recording Deed		
		Title Insurance		
		Brokerage		
		Miscellaneous		
		Total Debits and Credits		
		Balance Due		
		Seller and from Buyer		
		Grand Totals		

FIGURE 1.5 *Sample Closing Statement (Continued)*

RECONCILIATION STATEMENT	RECEIPTS	DISBURSEMENT
Bank Loan (less points/origination fees)	——————	——————
Deposit	——————	——————
Check from Buyer at Closing	——————	——————
Brokerage Fee	——————	——————
Check to Seller at Closing	——————	——————
Seller's Expense	——————	——————
Buyer's Expense	——————	——————
Grand Totals	——————	——————

The major problem lies with the fast pace of the mortgage industry. Lenders want to push loans quickly to closing to appease consumers and create cash flow. And, similarly, buyers want to close their purchase. So when loan payoff amounts, title reports, and other pertinent closing information are delayed, timetables get pinched even tighter. Couple that with the fact that the majority of closings occur at month's end and you've got a house of cards. That's why in most closings, the closing agent has finalized the documents only minutes before the buyer signs them.

Some buyers will skim over the cost breakdowns on the HUD-1 form, but proportionately fewer read the fine print, especially the legalese relating to the mortgage. This is particularly dangerous if, unknown to the buyer, the loan contains a prepayment penalty the buyer wasn't expecting.

If you make it known to the closing agent well in advance of closing that you'll exercise your right to inspect the documents one business day before closing, you'll be better able to catch errors and troubleshoot problems.

Q. Does this RESPA document inspection law extend to the seller?

No, it does not. If the seller makes a request to the closing agent well in advance of the closing date, however, most agents will extend the seller the same review option.

WHAT TO DO IF THE LENDER SAYS NO

Q. What can the buyer do if the lender says no?

As discussed earlier in this chapter, a lender can reject a loan application for myriad reasons. Following are some ways in which a buyer can attempt to piece the sale back together if previous efforts to get the loan approved have failed.

Identify the Source of the Problem

If the problem is borrower-related. The borrower may ask the lender to reanalyze the borrower's financial situation, based on answers to the following questions:

- *Have any debts been paid off since the application was taken?*
- *Could any assets be converted to cash?*
- *Does any of the buyer's income now fall within the two-year track-record time frame?* Could this income be used to help the buyer qualify for the loan?
- *Would the borrower be willing to forgo this year's vacation to increase the down payment?*
- *Is a raise from the employer scheduled for the near future?* Raises in income that are scheduled to occur within 60 days of closing may be counted as income by the lender.

The borrower may ask to have the loan held in portfolio (not sold to an outside investor) so that underwriting exceptions can be made. The success of this approach depends on the lender and its programs.

Another approach is to identify the borrower's strengths and ways to showcase them. Be realistic: If a problem is so overwhelming that only time will correct it (such as a recent mortgage foreclosure), getting any loan right now might be impossible.

If all else fails, the borrower may wish to seek a less restrictive loan program or a more lenient lender. (This is usually a last resort. Because precious time and money already have been expended in obtaining the loan, moving the loan may cause duplication of costs.)

If the problem is property-related. Determine strategies for repairing the property. Identify the person who has the most to gain by the sale going through. That person might be willing to pay for repairs and could be someone besides the buyer and the seller; for example, the seller's sellers (the people whose house your seller is buying) may need to have the primary sale closed before theirs will close.

Another approach is to determine a creative time frame for completing needed repairs. One option might be to close now and hold funds in escrow. You may be able to escrow two times the amount of the highest bid in order to complete repairs later, for instance, in better weather.

You also might consider options other than cash. Perhaps the buyer could use sweat equity such as contributing personal work time, construction materials, or other items of value in lieu of cash for repairs.

The lender might be more likely to make the loan if the loan-to-value ratio (the amount of the loan compared to the property's appraised value) were different, or if you paid a higher rate of interest.

The bottom line is, "It ain't over till it's over!"

CONSUMER BOOKLETS TO THE RESCUE

Q. It seems as though there's a lot to learn about the homebuying process. Are there any consumer booklets you'd recommend?

The following are some useful homebuying fact booklets that can be obtained free of charge:

Unraveling the Mortgage Loan Mystery
  Federal National Mortgage Association
  Drawer MM
  3900 Wisconsin Avenue, NW
  Washington, DC 20006
  www.fanniemae.com

You may wish to request a list of other homebuyer pamphlets available through FNMA.

A Consumer's Glossary of Mortgage Terms, Self Test (for buyers wishing to determine how well they would do in qualifying for a mortgage) and *What Happens after You Apply for a Mortgage?*
  Mortgage Bankers' Association
  1125 15th Street, NW
  Washington, DC 20005
  www.mortgagebankers.com

The Mortgage Money Guide (comparisons of homebuying options)
  Federal Trade Commission
  Bureau of Consumer Protection
  Pennsylvania Avenue and 6th Street, NW
  Washington, DC 20580
  www.ftc.gov

Other publications can be obtained for free or at a nominal cost (to $1.50) through the federal government's Consumer Information Center. To obtain a free catalog, write to the Consumer Information Center, P.O. Box 100, Pueblo, CO 81002. www.pueblo.gsa.gov. You can find other booklets (as well as Web site URLs) in the Resource Guide section in this book.

TRENDS: LEARN FROM THE VALUABLE LESSONS OF THE PAST

While speaking at Queen's College in Cambridge, England, in 2007, I witnessed a phenomenon few people under 80 years of age have experienced—a "run on a bank." If you remember the movie, "It's a Wonderful Life" with Jimmy Stewart at the Building and Loan, you'll get an idea of what was happening with hundreds of people lining up outside the branches of the faltering bank/mortgage lender, Northern Rock, in order to withdraw their deposits and close their accounts. Northern Rock had been using the international capital markets for funding and became a fatality of the global credit squeeze (predicated in many ways by the U.S. mortgage/investor meltdown). They no longer had access to necessary funding and when the news media released the info, there was a run on the bank. Even though the Bank of England agreed to provide emergency financing, guarantee all deposit accounts, and then provide turn-around financing for the beleaguered lender, depositors didn't trust the situation.

Generally conservative Brits were a combination of confused and just plain scared. One woman I spoke to said, "While I don't think the bank will collapse, we don't want our money at risk. We're pensioners." A young couple said they were concerned because they had a mortgage with Northern Rock and didn't want to lose their home. The bottom line: In three business days, depositors had withdrawn the equivalent of 4 billion U.S. dollars.

While I was mesmerized to actually view a "run on a bank," I was also saddened to realize how naive the international population is when it comes to money and mortgage management. Without proper education to the masses, we're likely to keep revisiting financial and mortgage-related debacles again and again in the coming years. Next time, the bank run might not be on foreign soil.

Trend #1: Mortgage Consumer Protection Takes Center Stage

At no other time in U.S. history have we simultaneously had five major housing bills pending on Capitol Hill that focus on protecting the rights of mortgage consumers. They are the Homeownership Preservation & Protection Act (S. 2452), Fannie Mae/Freddie Mac Reform Act (H.R. 3838), Homeownership and Mortgage Equity Protection Act (H.R. 3609), and The Mortgage Reform and Anti-Predatory Lending Act (H.R. 3915). Perhaps of greatest interest is the pending FHA Modernization Act (S. 2338) that would decrease the amount of down payment required on FHA mortgages and convert the mutual mortgage insurance program (MMIP) on FHA loans to a risk-based premium to offset the lender's risk depending on the financial strength of the borrower.

While the outcome for these pending bills is unclear, it's good to know that Congress is pushing to enhance consumer protection in the mortgage process.

Trend #2: A Return to Sensible Lending

As you'll see from chapter 5 on conventional loans, the secondary market is being proactive to return mortgage lending back to a "safe and sane" position. Conventional loan borrowers can expect a few more fees in the form of loan delivery charges and price adjustments, as well as a requirement of 5 percent more down payment when purchasing a property in a "declining market" area. Private mortgage insurance rates have increased as well, with some insurers refusing to write policies in markets where values have softened. Meanwhile, a credit score is, and will continue to be, an increasingly important factor in regard to how much a borrower pays for financing. Price adjustments, (read, "additional fees") will help lenders/investors offset the mortgage risk of a borrower with weaker credit. By tweaking existing programs, it's a positive move to keep lenders in business, investors wanting to purchase mortgage-backed securities, while helping Americans realize and keep the American Dream of homeownership alive.

Trend #3: A Return to Sensible Borrowing

"We have seen the enemy, and it is us!"—Pogo

For housing, it's been the ultimate "age of excess," with consumers using home equity like an overflowing ATM, buying high-end toys and other "stuff" that will be junked long before the mortgage is paid off. Why did this happen? Skyrocketing house prices made it seem like there was no end to the boom. Some played the bubble like a game of Monopoly, only this time, the properties were real. WE believe that, like a trusted friend, home equity would always be there to bail us out. Sobered by the outcome, we hopefully learned and will apply in the future: (1) What goes up, must come down. There are cycles to everything in life, and the real estate market (and its related appreciation) is no exception; (2) Manage your hard-earned equity as you would any other investment. You wouldn't dream of borrowing from your stock portfolio each month to cover your living expenses, so get out of the mind-set of seeing your equity as a cash cow, available whenever a new want surfaces; (3) Never sign any real estate or mortgage document without reading it in full. Never. If you don't understand all of it, don't sign it until you get the answers you need. No matter how much the settlement agent rants and raves about "we've got to fund today," just say "no, not until I receive the answers I need." As a borrower, avail yourself of RESPA's one-business-day right to review all closing documents prior to signing them (as outlined previously in this chapter). It's your right as a consumer. Use it.

No matter how many federal laws are in place to protect consumers, it's impossible to legislate ignorance. Here's to the trend that helps consumers manifest a positive mortgage experience by being informed, inquisitive, and willing to participate as an equally responsible player in the mortgage game.

2

CREDITWORTHINESS

In any homebuying market, buyers need to be creditworthy to be competitive. Without this vital component, a buyer's offer may be knocked out of the running by sellers who want to know that they're selling for the highest price to the buyer most likely to qualify for the purchase.

This chapter will focus on how to access and evaluate your credit report (long before meeting with the lender), the powerful role creditworthiness plays in negotiating for and obtaining a mortgage, and the importance of knowing and working on your credit score long before viewing the first house!

CREDITWORTHINESS: THE BACKBONE OF MORTGAGE LENDING

Q. Judging from the emphasis placed on verifying the type and amount of borrower debt, it seems lenders are very critical of the buyer's creditworthiness.

FIGURE 2.1 *Credit-Reporting Agencies*

Equifax   Experian
Box 740241   Box 2002
Atlanta, GA 30374-0241   Allen, TX 75013-2104
800-685-1111 (8 AM–5 PM ET)   888-397-3742 (24 hours daily)
www.equifax.com   www.experian.com

TransUnion
P.O. Box 2002
Chester, PA 19022-2000
800-888-4213 (24 hours daily)
www.truecredit.com

Good credit is important in securing a home loan. In fact, many lenders will tell you that bad credit is one of the major reasons mortgages are denied. In an era of conspicuous consumption when consumers are using more "plastic," lenders are placing much greater emphasis on how well loan applicants manage the credit they have before granting them more. And because the lender pulls a merged credit report from at least two of the three major credit-reporting agencies (CRA) to compare and evaluate credit, errors and adverse information are more likely to be uncovered. For names, addresses, and URLs of these national companies, see figure 2.1.

A poor credit rating can be the result of a buyer's irresponsibility. More often, however, it arises from unchecked and uncorrected errors on an individual's report.

CHECK YOUR CREDIT IN ADVANCE OF A MORTGAGE APPLICATION

Q. How far in advance of a loan application should someone check his or her credit?

Between 60 and 90 days before beginning the house-hunting process is a good time to examine credit. This can alert the buyer to what creditors have reported, allow unused accounts to be closed, and correct any errors that appear in the information.

THE CREDIT-CHECKING PROCESS

Free Annual Credit Reports Available to Consumers

Q. I heard that consumers can receive a free credit report each year. Is that correct? If so, how do we go about obtaining it?

Under federal law, a consumer can receive his credit report each year free of charge; but it's not just one report, it's a report from each of the three nationwide consumer credit reporting companies— Equifax, Experian, and TransUnion. Made available by the joint efforts of all three reporting companies, the FTC-authorized central website for the free report is www.annualcreditreport.com. Additionally, you can obtain the reports by calling 1-877-322-8228, or by using the form found at the website and mailing it to: Annual Credit Report Request Services, P O Box 105281, Atlanta, GA, 30348-5281.

The site is user-friendly and requires you to use your social security number and a series of security encryption and verification processes to access your credit report information. Because the site is state-of-the-art for safeguarding the consumer's information, using it to access free reports is recommended over merely using links from other potentially less-secure sites on the web. You have the option of accessing a single report from one of the national credit reporting companies at a time (i.e. one report each quarter), or reports from all three at once. The benefit of receiving three reports simultaneously is your ability to compare data between the companies. The alternative approach of accessing one company's report each quarter is beneficial if you're interested in extending your three credit snapshots over the 12-month period of time.

While the formats vary between Equifax, Experian, and TransUnion reports, the information provided is similar. You'll see the obligations you owe, how often you pay those obligations, as well as who has recently checked your credit report. You can also request a credit score from each report you receive for an additional charge. This is a mathematical model that evaluates many types of information in a credit file to determine creditworthiness. Generally, the higher the score, the less risk the person represents to a creditor.

If you'd feel more comfortable accessing each credit report via snail mail, you can do so at: Equifax, P O Box 740256, Atlanta, GA., 30374, 1-800-525-6285, www.equifax.com; Experian, P O Box 9532, Allen, TX, 75013, 1-888-397-3742, www.experian.com; and TransUnion, P O Box 6790, Fullerton, CA., 92834, 1-800-680-7289, www.transunion.com.

WHAT THE CREDIT REPORT SHOWS

Q. If there are three national credit-reporting agencies, do they all report the same information?

Each of the three major credit-reporting agencies are independent companies and may or may not report the same information. That's why the lender pulls a merged or mortgage credit report, showing information from at least two of the three companies when underwriting the mortgage.

All three reporting agencies report information in five categories:

1. *Identification.* This section includes the borrower's name, address, Social Security number, employer, date of birth, and spouse's name, if applicable.
2. *Credit history.* This section lists all open and paid accounts, the current payment history of each creditor reporting to the bureau, and prior payment history (which includes any late payments). By law, adverse information can remain on the report for seven years; bankruptcies can remain for ten years. These negative postings may arbitrarily not come off automatically and their removal should be monitored by the consumer.
3. *Collection.* This section includes any creditors who have turned over an account to a collection agency.
4. *Public records.* All items of public record affecting financial obligations (such as bankruptcies, liens, judgments, divorce decrees, child support adjudications, and so on) are included in this section.
5. *Inquiries.* This section notes who has checked the consumer's credit as far back as 18 to 24 months. Anyone accessing a consumer's credit without a valid business reason could be in violation of the federal Fair Credit Reporting Act, fined up to $5,000, and imprisoned for one year. (Note: The consumer is awarded the fine!)

MAJOR AREAS OF CREDIT EVALUATION

Q. What major credit areas does the lender evaluate before making a loan?

When it comes to determining an applicant's creditworthiness, a lender examines the three *c*'s: character, capacity, and credit:

- *Character* can be evaluated through objective factors such as length of residency at each address, terms of employment, and a report free of financial judgments, liens, and other adverse matters of public record.
- *Capacity* is increasingly important these days, because many consumers carry heavy debts and make many minimum payments on those debts. The lender evaluates the amount of debt compared to income, ways the new obligations may change the debt picture, and the borrower's general economic stability.
- *Credit* is the third measure. The lender evaluates existing credit relationships including bank loans and credit cards. The lender pays close attention to limits, how the current balances relate to those limits, and how long those accounts have been active. For example, a credit card held by the borrower for less than six months but currently at the maximum could indicate that the borrower could have trouble handling additional debt. A lender making the home loan may require a large down payment to lessen the risk.

CREDIT SCORING—THE CREDITWORTHINESS GAUGE

Q. Is credit scoring an improvement over the old method?

Previously, credit interpretation was somewhat subjective, but the introduction of technology and credit scoring has helped take the mystery (and some of the bias) out of evaluating credit.

Credit scoring electronically gives a numerical weighting to various financial factors such as timely payments, debts, and job history, and can help predict the likelihood of mortgage default. While several credit-scoring models exist, many lenders use the Fair, Isaac & Company (FICO) score that ranges from 300 to 850—the lower the score, the higher the risk.

For example, the secondary market requires lenders to obtain an in-file or merged credit report from at least two of the national credit repositories, compare the scores, and average them. If all three scores are obtained, the one in the middle is used. A staple in the mortgage process is the Residential Mortgage Credit Report (RMCR) that additionally investigates rental history and unverified debts using merged information from all three agencies.

Q. How does credit scoring work?

Credit scoring considers a variety of components. For example, errors on a credit report that haven't been removed can cost score points.

Credit scoring also weighs how much available credit the borrower has used. For example, if account balances are 75 percent or more of the credit limit, this can signal high financial leverage and higher risk to the lender. Because the lender compares the amount of debt the borrower carries compared to the amount of income he or she generates, it's important to keep available credit reasonable for the borrower's income level.

Keeping a large number of accounts with zero balances also can lower the credit score because it increases the potential for someone to live beyond his or her means. That's why it's important for the borrower to decide which accounts to keep and close out the rest. In general, the longer the positive credit history, the better the score.

Opening new accounts can lower a score, as can having too many credit inquiries. A score can even be impacted if the borrower transfers a balance to a new lower-interest rate credit card (but the borrower can alert the creditor and the scoring process by making sure the credit-reporting bureau posts this to the credit file).

Q. How many scoring models are there?

Quite a few. In fact, *Fair Isaac Corporation,* www.myfico.com, the company that pioneered this work, designed the initial model for TRW (now known as Experian), which is one of the three national credit agencies. Named after the inventor of this first model, the FICO score was born. In general, it works by applying the following weights to major credit areas:

- *35 percent—Payment history:* Have you paid bills on time?
- *30 percent—Amount owed:* Includes number and types of accounts, total credit lines, and distribution of debts among accounts.
- *15 percent—Length of credit history:* All things considered, longer is generally better.
- *10 percent—New credit:* Applying for several accounts over a relatively short time likely will reduce your score.
- *10 percent—Credit mix:* Your combination of credit cards, retail accounts, finance company accounts, installment loans, and mortgage loans.

The other two credit reporting agencies (CRA), Equifax and TransUnion, use Beacon (the most conservative credit-scoring model) and Empirica, respectively.

Q. What is an acceptable credit score and have there been any tests using them?

Yes, there have been numerous tests to prove their efficacy. FNMA surveyed 1 million loan records and found that 1 in 8 borrowers with a FICO score below 600 was either severely delinquent or in default. Contrarily, only 1 in 1,300 borrowers with scores above 800 had similar mortgage delinquency problems. From these and other surveys, the benchmark of concern is usually with scores of less than 620.

Most lenders who sell their loans into the secondary market use the following parameters when evaluating scores:

- *Scores of 700 and above:* excellent; eligible for enhanced criteria
- *Scores of 680–700:* very good
- *Scores of 640–680:* generally acceptable
- *Scores of 620–660:* marginal
- *Scores below 620:* cautious review required. Borrowers may find themselves locked out of the best loans and terms available. The lender may still be able to make a loan if compensating factors can shore up the borrower's picture. But in general, factors such as lower ratios, extra cash reserves, and/or a lower loan-to-value ratio on the loan won't compensate for unacceptable credit.

Credit scoring has also caused the lending industry to push towards making loans rated at *A–*, *B*, *C*, or *D* to credit-damaged borrowers. Called *customized* or *subprime* lending, these leverage tools will be covered in the next chapter.

CREDIT SCORES VARY BETWEEN CREDIT REPORTING AGENCIES (CRA)

Q. Do credit scores vary between the three national credit repositories?

They often do. A study of credit scores for 500,000 consumers conducted by The Consumer Federation of America, www. consumerfed. org, and the National Credit Reporting Association, www.ncrainc.org, found that credit scores varied between credit repositories by an average of 41 points. Considering that all three firms use the same calculations to produce scores, a 41-point discrepancy could have major negative implications for the consumer.

For example, the study found that for mortgage borrowers with relatively low credit scores, errors in their reports pushed their scores below 620, forcing them to pay an average of 3 percent more interest to obtain a mortgage (the typical rate increase to borrowers whose scores were below 620). This indicates that at least one of the repositories' files contained errors that caused the scores to vary.

This is yet another reason to obtain credit reports from all three repositories to adequately determine exactly what each company is reporting. And don't stop at evaluating just the debts owed on each report. Remember, your score positively rates loans paid in full and long-term accounts that are paid as agreed. Make sure these show on each report as well. Don't forget that credit scoring isn't used solely for obtaining a mortgage. It can impact what you pay for insurance and your ability to rent an apartment, and can even hurt your ability to obtain employment.

IMPROVING YOUR CREDIT SCORE

Q. What are some ways I can raise my credit score?

You can raise your credit score by:

- Repairing errors on your credit report
- Paying all bills on time. Just one late payment in the past 24 months could hurt your FICO score.
- Always paying at least the minimum amount required on each bill
- Reducing debt levels. Potential lenders compare your total debt to your income.
- Never "maxing out" any credit cards
- Keeping creditors aware of your current address. Addresses that don't match your report slow loan applications.
- Never bouncing checks. A single bounced check, if reported to a credit bureau, is likely to stay on your credit report for seven years. So before closing any checking account, make sure all checks have cleared.

Q. Will closing out credit accounts that I no longer use improve my credit score?

Possibly; but I suggest you do so only after consulting a mortgage professional. Here's why. An older "paid as agreed" account may have a more positive impact on your score than a newer account.

If you do end up closing accounts, here's a system I've found that works. Notify the creditor in writing that you wish to close the account. You may want to send the request by certified mail, return receipt requested so that you have confirmation that it was received. Your cut up credit card can be sent as well. Be sure to take a photocopy of the card pasted to your letter before you send it in case you need verification later.

Here's the important part: In the letter, ask the creditor to post the account "closed permanently at customer's request." This clarifies that you voluntarily closed the account and that it wasn't closed by the creditor for adverse reasons. Inform the creditor that you'll check your credit report in 30 days to make sure the account has been closed.

Q. Should a borrower use one of those credit-repair companies to improve a low score?

Absolutely not. They can't do anything that the borrower can't do as well (and it won't cost money, just time). By using the general fix-up tips given in the answers that follow (and then monitoring the report to make sure the correct information is posted), a borrower can improve his or her own credit score, without the aid of companies that profess to rewrite credit history—but can't!

Excellent articles on credit scoring by two of the secondary market buyers can be found at www.fanniemae.com and www.freddiemac.com as well as at all three credit-reporting bureaus' websites.

WHAT CONSTITUTES "GOOD CREDIT"?

Q. If credit is so important, how can a borrower work towards "good credit"?

As seen with the credit-scoring model, good credit doesn't have to be perfect, unblemished credit! In general, a borrower is considered to have good credit if his or her report shows nothing in the past 12 months more detrimental than the following:

- *Revolving credit (credit cards):* no more than two payments 30 days past due, and only one 60 days late in the last two years
- *Installment credit (car loan):* no more than one payment 30 days past due and no payments 60 days or more past due
- *Housing debt (mortgages, rent):* no late payments in past 12 months

Thorough explanations would need to be provided to the lender for any late payments.

ENSURING THE BEST POSSIBLE CREDIT REPORT

Q. What errors could consumers expect to find on their credit reports?

While errors can be found in a variety of forms, frequent mistakes occur in three areas:

1. Misposting because of similar names
2. Multiple entries of the same credit account or previously closed accounts still showing active
3. Accounts that are disputed or improperly reported by the creditor

Q. When is a person's name likely to be confused for another's in credit reporting, and how can one protect against it?

If you're a junior or senior, or have a common name such as Smith, Brown, or Jones, you are likely to have someone else's credit on your report. While names, addresses, and Social Security numbers are generally used to report credit to the correct name, errors still occur. On hearing that someone else's credit was found on his or her report, a homebuyer might remark, "Well, if it's good news, I'll keep it!" The problem is that an additional account, yours or not, could signal extra debt to the lender, which might not be good news for qualifying.

To avoid the name mix-up, it's good to use your full name, including spelled-out middle or maiden names (or both) when applying for credit.

Multiple Credit Entries

Q. Is there anything wrong with multiple entries of the same account showing up on your credit report?

Yes. Depending on the type of mortgage you're seeking, the lender may consider that there's a possible monthly minimum repayment on each card (5 percent of the outstanding balance or $10, whichever is greater if the payment is unknown) for the purpose of loan qualifying. In addition, the lender evaluates not just what is owing but the amount of potential credit available to the borrower.

Removing Errors from the Report

Q. If an error is found on the report, how can it be rectified?

Some of the greatest credit-reporting nightmares come in the form of disputed or improperly reported items. Freeing these errors from your report may be tedious, but it can be accomplished by following these three steps:

1. *File a consumer dispute form* with the reporting bureau, stating that you disagree with the report. A copy is included with each credit report you receive. Additionally, you can find dispute information on each of the three national credit reporting agency websites (in Figure 2.1). By law, it must investigate the complaint in a timely manner (usually in 30 days or less) and report back to the consumer.
2. *Write to the creditor* as well, pointing out the mistake. If the dispute is resolved, have the creditor send letters to all three credit bureaus, asking that they change the information (if they initially received it). By law, the reporting bureau must send a corrected copy of the report to all parties who accessed the report during the time the error appeared.
3. *File an explanation.* If a satisfactory conclusion is not reached with the creditor, the consumer can place an explanation (up to 100 words) on the credit report telling his or her side of the story. This explanation will remain on the report for six months, and the consumer can request the posting be extended for increments of six months.

After correcting an error on a credit report, it's good to request a copy of the corrected report from the credit-reporting agency in approximately 30 days to show that the changes were made.

Q. If there are three major credit-reporting networks, do errors have to be corrected with all three?

Ideally, yes, unless you've obtained a merged report showing information from all of the reporting bureaus. For the best chance at cleaning up an error, submit the change information to all three.

The Credit Appeals Process

Q. If a problem can't be adequately rectified with a credit agency, is there an appeals process?

Because credit-reporting agencies are monitored under the federal Equal Credit Opportunity Act, a consumer could file a complaint with the Federal Trade Commission, Attn.: Correspondence Department, Room 692, Washington, DC 20580, or at www.ftc.gov.

Too Many Credit Inquiries

Q. Could a buyer have a problem if too many credit inquiries appear on his or her credit report?

As seen with credit scoring, a mortgage lender might be hesitant to make a loan to someone who had an abundance of credit inquiries in the past six months. This could serve as a red flag that the party was denied credit, is accumulating open lines of credit to borrow against, or is leveraging assets prior to declaring bankruptcy. This could also indicate that the borrower is checking the credit report repeatedly in anticipation of an adverse posting. Nevertheless, the lender may want a written explanation as to why the inquiries occurred. The exception would be mortgage company queries. Knowing that a potential borrower may be shopping with various lenders for a mortgage, credit inquiries within the past 30 days from lenders are not detrimental to your report.

CHECKING SOMEONE ELSE'S CREDIT

Q. Could just anyone check someone's credit?

While the law requires that there must be a "valid business reason" to check someone's credit, it does not require that the creditor obtain written authorization from the consumer before the report is accessed. In fact, the consumer may not even be aware that his or her credit has been checked! If the consumer later contested that a valid business reason did not exist to check his or her credit, it would be up to the creditor to prove the validity. A federal fine of $5,000 and up to one year in jail applies if the law is breached.

Q. Do credit-reporting agencies have services that alert the consumer when someone accesses his or her credit?

Because of the growing importance and interest of creditworthiness and identity theft, each of the three credit-reporting repositories have special services that alert subscribers when a credit report is requested or when anything adverse is posted to a credit report. In addition, subscribers can receive their own current credit reports by calling a toll-free number and giving a pass code.

SPECIAL CONSIDERATIONS FOR MARRIED AND DIVORCED PERSONS

Q. Can a divorced person have a credit report solely in his or her name, apart from the ex-spouse?

Every person has the right to obtain an individual credit history regardless of marital status. Joint liabilities will appear on both spouses' reports.

Q. Should a divorced person make special arrangements to ensure that his or her credit rating is not adversely affected by the change in marital status?

It's especially important to check credit after a divorce, making sure obligations are sorted out, creditors are notified, and the report is listed solely in the consumer's name. Ideally, this should be implemented before the divorce gavel raps, but usually it is not.

Imagine the nightmare created when someone applies for credit after divorce, only to find that the car and corresponding payment awarded to the former spouse is still showing as a joint obligation! Ideally, the former spouse should requalify for that debt and have the posting removed from the other person's credit report. Again, this is not likely to happen. At the very least, a copy of the divorce decree will be requested by the mortgage lender, showing the allocation of assets and liabilities. This could easily add time to the loan-qualifying process.

Q. Could a person who is married to someone with bad credit get a loan in his or her own name?

A married individual can secure a mortgage in his or her own name provided he or she meets the required income, assets, and creditworthiness guidelines. Again, federal law prohibits discrimination based on marital status; therefore, one spouse's adverse credit cannot be used to deny a loan to the other spouse. We'll cover this in greater detail in the chapter on qualifying that follows.

GETTING A MORTGAGE AFTER MARRED CREDIT

Q. If someone's credit was so bad that they couldn't get a loan, what should they do?

Most lenders will be glad to work with the borrower on exactly what to repair and how. If debt management appears to be a long-term problem, on a case-by-case basis the lender may suggest that the consumer work with a nonprofit organization such as the Consumer Credit Counseling Service. These services are located in almost every major community. The consumer surrenders his or her monthly income and the service pays the creditors. It's vital, however, that the consumer takes this approach only as a last resort and after counsel with several mortgage lenders because some mortgage lenders may view this as "giving up" and as an inability to troubleshoot financial problems.

ESTABLISHING CREDIT

Q. What's the best way for a person with no credit to establish a credit rating?

The answer is, very carefully! The Fair Isaac Company estimates that nearly 25 percent of the credit-eligible consumers in the United States have no reported credit history, also called a "thin" credit file. While amassing large numbers of credit cards may seem to be a great way to establish credit, adding monthly debt to a buyer's long-term debt ratio may hurt loan qualification prospects.

There are several prudent ways to establish credit:

- If a borrower does not believe in credit and pays cash for everything, that practice could be documented to establish creditworthiness. For example, most power companies, utility companies, and small retailers will be glad to verify that the applicant pays in cash and on time when he or she purchases. The more documentation that can be shown to the lender, the better.
- If the buyer is purchasing in several months, the down payment could be put in a bank account and he or she can obtain a loan against it. By placing this money with a lender as collateral, a loan can be made against the funds and repaid to establish credit. Three to six months is a good minimum time frame to show a credible payment pattern.
- Obtaining a major credit card may make sense if the borrower has room for the monthly payment in his or her long-term debt qualifying ratio and will control spending and not run up a huge balance. Consult with a mortgage lender before taking this route.

BE AN INFORMED CONSUMER

With all the knowledge gleaned from your consumer's credit report and scores, you can see why the lender puts such great value on it for making a lending decision. And after the borrower has gathered information, he or she will at least know what everyone else already knew about him or her!

3

QUALIFYING FOR THE MORTGAGE

Before the advent of technology and automated underwriting, it often took days if not weeks to learn if you had a shot at getting a mortgage. The good news is that today, depending on the lender and the type of loan you seek, in a matter of minutes you may hear the (hopefully) good news, "It looks good for qualifying."

But just because technology has streamlined parts of the process doesn't mean that you don't have to come prepared with personal information and some paperwork. Here are tips on what to prepare for and why, and because it's not a perfect world, suggestions for whittling down borrower debt, maximizing available cash, and leverage tips for putting a stronger foot forward with the lender—even if you're a self-employed borrower.

PREAPPROVAL: KNOWING WHAT YOU CAN AFFORD

Q. What's the best way for me to figure out what I can afford?

Your best bet is to have a lender preapprove you for a mortgage. But first, it's important to understand the difference between being preapproved and being prequalified. In the past, most buyers began the home search by being prequalified. That meant sharing with a real estate professional (lender, real estate agent, builder) an overview of their income, their debts, and the amount of cash available for their down payment and closing costs. The professional then applied qualifying ratios. For example, if conventional financing was considered, up to 28 percent of the borrower's monthly gross income could go toward housing expenses (principal, interest, tax, insurance and any private mortgage insurance premium, and/or homeowners fees such as monthly condo association charges). And up to 36 percent of the borrower's monthly gross income could be attributed to the housing expense plus any long-term debts (those that couldn't be paid off in ten months or less).

While prequalifying was better than nothing, it didn't take into consideration the impact of verifying information, and it left both the buyer and the seller with no assurance that financing could be secured. In other words, while it appeared that the borrower might qualify, the lender gave no promise to make the loan.

Preapproval provides a higher level of certainty than prequalifying. It means that unless something changes in your financial picture, the lender will grant you a certain type of mortgage assuming a certain interest rate. It essentially makes you a cash buyer, with the flexibility that goes with it.

Q. What does preapproval require?

Lenders require buyers to present verification of income (W-2 form, pay stubs, bank statements, or income tax returns if a buyer is self-employed). It's a good idea to bring along verification of other assets (brokerage accounts, 401(k)s, etc.).

Using and verifying this information combined with the credit report and credit scoring, the lender can then commit to make the borrower a mortgage amount of X, based on an interest rate of Y. Lenders can provide buyers with "preapproval letters" that can be presented to sellers when the offer to purchase is made. Preapproval not only gives the buyer and seller confidence, it's a great marketing tool for the lender!

Q. What information should a preapproval letter contain?

A solid preapproval letter will contain the following information:

- Amount of loan
- Interest rate
- Address and contact information for the mortgage broker or lending officer
- Date of the preapproval letter (one dated 30 days or more in the past may no longer be reliable)

QUALIFYING RATIOS

Q. Lenders talk a lot about qualifying ratios. How do they work? They seem a bit mysterious!

Don't let the fancy semantics fool you! Ratios are merely percentages. Qualifying ratios simply apply the percentages to the borrower's monthly gross income. And while important, technology and automated underwriting systems (AUS) have made them just one part of the qualifying picture.

Here's what happens. The lender tallies up the annual gross income, divides it by 12 (to determine monthly gross income), and then multiplies it by the percentage allowed for the borrower's housing debt as well as total long-term debt based on the type of loan the borrower is seeking.

Qualifying Example

See figure 3.1, grab a pencil, and we'll work through the form together. (Note: This form reflects conventional qualifying guidelines. Check in the appropriate loan chapters—Chapters 7, 8, and 9—for specific adjustable-rate mortgage [ARM], FHA, and VA qualifying forms.)

FIGURE 3.1 *Conventional Quick Qualify*

What Can You Afford?

	COLUMN A	COLUMN B
Annual Gross Income:	$ _____	
Divide by Number of Months:	÷ 12	
Monthly Gross Income: (Record it in both columns. Perform operations only on figures in the same vertical column.)	= _____	= _____
Lenders will allow 28% of monthly gross income for housing expense:		× .28
Maximum Monthly Housing Expense Allowance (Column B):		= _____
Many lenders allow 36% of monthly gross income for long-term debt:	× .36	
Long-Term Monthly Expense Allowance:	= _____	
Figure out your monthly long-term obligations below, and subtract it from the allowance:	− _____	
Child Support	$ _____	
Auto Loan	+ _____	
Credit Cards	+ _____	
Other	+ _____	
Other	+ _____	
Total Long-Term Obligations	= _____	
Monthly Housing Expense Allowance:	= _____	
Look at the last amount in Columns A and B above. Record the smaller amount:	$ _____	
About 20% of the housing expense allowance is for taxes and insurance, leaving 80% for payment of mortgage (principal and interest):	× .80	
Allowable Monthly Principal and Interest (PI) Expense:	= _____	
Divide this amount by the appropriate monthly payment factor:	÷ _____	
	= _____	
Multiply by 1,000:	× 1,000	
Affordable Mortgage Amount (what the lender will lend):	$ _____	

Step One

Post the amount of your annual gross income in Column A and then divide it by 12 to determine your monthly gross income. Post that answer in Column B as well.

Step Two

The form states that "Lenders will allow 28 percent of monthly gross income for housing expense." In Column B, multiply your monthly gross income by 28 percent and post your answer on the line provided. This represents the maximum monthly housing expense (principal, interest, tax, insurance, private mortgage insurance, and/or monthly homeowners association fees) for which you can qualify.

Step Three

The form states that "Many lenders allow 36 percent of monthly gross income for long-term debt." Multiply your gross monthly income by 36 percent and post that answer in Column A. This represents the maximum amount of your monthly income that can go toward your long-term debt, which includes your housing expense plus debts that can't be paid off in 10 months (or are recurring).

Step Four

Next comes the fun part. Tally up your long-term debt obligations (any debt that can't be paid off in ten months or is recurring, such as child support, auto loans, credit cards, etc.) and subtract the total from the previous answer in Column A. This answer will be posted as your "Monthly housing expense allowance" in Column A.

Step Five

Look at the last amounts in Columns A and B and "Record the smaller amount." (The lender goes with the smaller amount to compensate for the amount of the borrower's debt.)

Step Six

Because you may not yet know exactly what your property taxes and insurance are, estimate that 20 percent of the housing expense allowance

FIGURE 3.2 *Loan Payment Table (Monthly Payment for Each $1,000 Borrowed)*

Interest Rate	5 Years	20 Years	30 Years
14.00%	$ 7.40	$6.06	$4.77
4.50	7.65	6.33	5.07
5.00	7.91	6.60	5.37
5.50	8.17	6.88	5.68
6.00	8.44	7.16	6.00
6.50	8.71	7.46	6.32
7.00	8.99	7.75	6.65
7.50	9.27	8.06	6.99
8.00	9.56	8.36	7.34
8.50	9.85	8.68	7.69
9.00	10.14	9.00	8.05
9.50	10.44	9.32	8.41
10.00	10.75	9.65	8.78

Note: Chart represents principal and interest only.

This table helps you calculate your monthly housing costs (not including property taxes, insurance, and any mortgage insurance premium). Each factor represents the principal and interest cost for each $1,000 borrowed. For example, if you're considering a $100,000 30-year mortgage at 8 percent, you would multiply 100 by $7.34 to equal $734 per month principal and interest payment.

will go for taxes, insurance, and any private mortgage insurance, leaving 80 percent for mortgage principal and interest. Multiply your answer from Step 5 by 80 percent to find this amount.

Step Seven

Next, look at an amortization table (you can find one in figure 3.2). Based on current interest rates, find the monthly payment factor that corresponds to the interest rate and divide it into the last answer you found in Column A. (Example: $900 divided by 6.65, which is the factor for 7 percent interest for a 30-year loan term, gives you $135.340.)

Step Eight

Multiply your last answer by 1,000 because the chart represents principal and interest for each $1,000 of loan amount. (Example: $135.340 × 1,000 = $135,340.) Congratulations! You can afford this much loan!

Q. What if you already know what your ratios are? Can you use them to calculate what you can afford?

Absolutely! All you have to do is back up through the process just completed. For example, the $135,340 loan required a monthly principal and interest payment of $900. To that amount you'd need to add back the 20 percent you took out for taxes, insurance, and private mortgage insurance (if applicable). So the maximum PITI (principal, interest, tax, and insurance) payment would be $1,125.

Q. What amount of monthly income would you need to qualify for that payment?

Using the conventional qualifying ratios, divide $1,125 by 28 percent. This equals $4,017.86. That's the amount of monthly income you'd need to qualify for a $1,125 PITI payment.

Q. So by using your monthly income and the payment you can afford, you can figure out what your ratio is, correct?

That's right. Let's say you have $5,000 in monthly income to qualify for that same $1,125 payment. What would your housing ratio be? To find it, you'd divide the $1,125 payment by the $5,000 monthly income. The answer (and ratio) is 23 percent. This means that with this amount of income, only 23 percent of your monthly income would be going to the PITI payment. That's great! Low ratios are good news because they signal that proportionately only a small amount of your gross monthly income is going for your house payment.

Conversely, a high ratio indicates that you're trying to buy a champagne-budget house on a beer-budget income. The options are to shop for a lower-priced house, find a larger down payment, or obtain a loan that would give you more leverage (like an FHA loan for higher ratios or an adjustable-rate loan with lower interest rates).

Remember that qualifying ratios are merely one test of affordability. That's why it's important to work closely with a good lender who can apply other information (called compensating factors) that may contribute additional positives to your qualifying profile. You can find detailed information about compensating factors by loan type in the chapters that follow.

Q. Because credit scoring plays such a big role in mortgage qualifying, how important are ratios today? Could someone have unacceptable ratios but a strong credit score and still get a loan?

Potentially, yes. As in the past, ratios are just one of the many approval indicators considered by the lender. Borrowers with high ratios who can present compensating factors such as strong credit and/ or large down payments have often been exceptions to the rules and will continue to be.

HIGH PROPERTY TAXES IMPACT QUALIFYING

Q. The last house we owned we paid less than ½ of 1 percent of our home's value in annual property taxes. After moving to another state, we've had to settle for a smaller house than we had before since the property taxes are nearly 3 percent of the home's value annually.

What you're describing is happening to a large percentage of homeowners and, unfortunately, is likely to continue. With strong home appreciation of the past seven years and the rising cost of running municipalities, property taxes have increased, some even doubling. A new rule of thumb is to make sure you can financially afford the property taxes and homeowner's insurance for the long run before making a decision on the home you purchase. This is a prime reason why high property tax areas like Florida coupled with insurance-related occurrences of Mother Nature are driving owners on fixed incomes to other more housing-affordable areas.

Here's an example. Let's say that your last house was assessed at $200,000 and you paid ½ of 1 percent in property taxes. That would be $83.33 per month. But the same $200,000 house with property taxes of 2.5 percent per annum would drive your monthly tax payment up to $416.67, an increase of more than 500 percent! And long after the mortgage is paid off, the property taxes and insurance demand to be paid. If you figure that homeowners in high-cost property tax and insurance areas need to work at least two months or longer each year just to pay these two bills, it may become financially unfeasible for people to keep the homes they've worked a lifetime for.

QUALIFYING THE SELF-EMPLOYED BORROWER

Q. Is it usually tougher for the self-employed buyer to get a mortgage?

It depends on the circumstances and the type of loan desired. Because the self-employed buyer's cash flow and profitability is often tough to predict, guaranteeing income can be difficult to prove to the lender. In addition, the low documentation/no documentation (low-doc/no-doc) loans, many of which were made to self-employed borrowers, have shown significantly more defaults than have standard documentation loans. Self-employed borrowers, designated as anyone who owns 25 percent or greater interest in the business that employs him or her, are challenged by the mortgage loan process for two reasons:

1. *Income tax write-offs whittle down the self-employed borrower's net income.* While this is favorable come April 15, it's a negative factor in qualifying for a mortgage loan. An applicant currently making a $1,200 mortgage payment may find it impossible to qualify for even a $600 loan payment on a new loan. Even after the lender adds back some deductions for the purpose of qualifying (such as IRA deposits and depreciation), the applicant may not qualify.

2. *Self-employed applicants must provide extensive documentation to the lender.* This is a mandate from the secondary market because there is greater room for a borrower to embellish verifications if he or she is employer and employee. In addition to the standard items a loan applicant must furnish, the self-employed borrower may be required to provide the following:
   - Two years of signed copies of complete income tax returns (with all schedules attached), a business balance sheet, and a year-to-date profit-and-loss statement for the sole proprietor
   - If the business is a corporation, an S corporation, or a partnership, signed copies of the past two years of federal business income tax returns (with all schedules attached), a year-to-date profit-and-loss statement, and a business credit report

     Because many self-employed entrepreneurs are not the best bookkeepers, pulling these records together may prove tough, if not impossible, for some applicants.

Q. What red flag areas do lenders monitor to make sure the self-employed borrower is revealing his or her entire financial picture?

Red flags include income and deductions showing only increments of a hundred, for example, $500 or $1,000, on tax returns; a taxpayer in a high tax bracket who prepares his or her own return; and a self-employed borrower who shows no estimated tax payments being paid.

Q. How is the self-employed person's income calculated to qualify for a loan?

A rough formula would be as follows: Using income tax returns, add up the applicant's income after expenses (but before taxes) for the past two years. Then calculate the year-to-date income after expenses (but before taxes) for this year. Finally, divide the total of those sums by the number of months involved to get the average monthly income.

Q. What other requirements must a self-employed person, working on commission, fulfill to qualify?

For the applicant who works on commission, the lender needs W-2 forms and completed, signed tax returns for the past two years. The income is then averaged over the time period reported.

If the borrower's sole compensation is from commission, a year-to-date income statement will also be required. In general, the lender wants to see the amount of income tending to increase.

Creative Financing for the Self-Employed Borrower

Q. What other types of loans might a self-employed borrower use?

Another way the self-employed buyer might qualify would be by using a 75 percent first mortgage, a 10 percent down payment, and having the seller or lender carry 15 percent of the purchase price in second mortgage financing. Called 75/10/15 financing (and discussed in depth in Chapter 11), the borrower may be less scrutinized in taking a 75 percent loan, may sidestep requirements and the cost of private mortgage insurance, and may more readily qualify, because rates and points may be lower.

Q. What kinds of creative financing could a self-employed borrower try?

Seller financing is always an option, even though the seller may require the same credit report or other income verification a lender does.

A second suggestion might be to apply for a business loan rather than a mortgage. If a borrower is well established with a lender who understands his or her business workings, the borrower might use a commercial loan to fund the purchase.

While rates can vary, two points over prime is reasonable interest to expect to pay, with most loans being adjustable rather than fixed rate. Loan amortizations may be short term (10 to 15 years), but the borrower could negotiate a roll-over option with the lender.

A third option would be to take loans against assets, such as certificates of deposit, stock, life insurance, and so on. The benefit is that you keep the asset intact while pulling cash out. This type of mortgage, called *pledged asset,* is discussed in Chapter 5. The leverage techniques section later in this book goes into greater detail on these ideas.

Q. What tips can you give self-employed borrowers to give them a better chance of getting a mortgage?

A lender may waive the year-to-date profit-and-loss statement in the early months of the year, because the year is young and there's not enough history. In addition, a lender who holds other loans of the borrower may limit some documentation, especially if the lender does not sell the loan to the secondary mortgage market and keeps the loan in portfolio (in-house) instead.

LOW-DOC/NO-DOC LOANS

Q. Are low- or no-documentation loans still available?

While the mortgage meltdown did much to eradicate many of the wholesalers funding and the lenders originating low-documentation/ no-documentation loans, there are still some available in the marketplace. Termed "liar loans" since the borrower's information is often embellished in order to get the mortgage approved, low-no-doc loans do have a market niche for legitimate borrowers. For example, someone who makes a lot of money but does not want to divulge the exact amount is a candidate for a low-doc loan. Or perhaps an entrepreneur who has strong assets and credit but does not want to take the time to pull together the tax information and balance sheets for the six companies he owns.

Here's an overview of the types of limited documentation loans available:

- *Stated documentation:* This means that the underwriter will use what the borrower shows on his application without any verification. This type of loan often requires more down payment and a higher rate of interest. But the loan still has to make sense. For example, if a grocery store clerk states that she makes $85,000 per year, the underwriter would want to see other verifying information, that is, other assets or a high credit score.
- *Stated income documentation:* This loan allows the borrower to "state" the income on the loan application for the purpose of calculating qualifying ratios, but everything else is verified including assets, debts, and employment.
- *Stated asset documentation:* Here the assets are "stated" on the application, but everything else is verified. Stated asset loans don't require the borrower to provide the last three months of bank statements.
- *No income documentation:* No income information is placed on the loan application at all; therefore, no ratios are calculated. This loan type has fairly steep down payment, credit, and asset requirements.
- *No asset documentation:* Similar to the no-income doc loan, no assets are listed on the application. Income, however, is verified; but the lender assumes that the borrower has sufficient funds to close the loan.
- *No income, no asset documentation:* This "NINA" loan type lists no income on the application, no pay stubs or income tax returns need to be provided, nor does the borrower have to provide any bank or investments statements for proof of assets. The lender verifies everything else, including credit and employment history.
- *No employment documentation:* The borrower does not disclose any information regarding employment, but the lender verifies everything else.

Only time will tell how many of these alternative underwriting approaches will remain in mainstream lending. But one thing is for sure: those that do remain will require underwriters and borrowers to make much stronger cases for their positions than they've had to make in the past.

SUBPRIME NONPRIME LOANS

Q. I've heard about people with questionable credit who still managed to get a mortgage. How did they do it?

It's likely in today's lending world of customized credit that even after major credit glitches such as bankruptcy and/or foreclosure, a borrower can qualify for some type of mortgage (albeit one with higher interest and/or more points and fees). Instead of the top *A* category loans purchased by the secondary market (usually referred to as *standard* or *prime mortgages*), a borrower may only be able to qualify for a lower-rated loan: *B, C,* or *D,* subprime or nonprime loan.

As it relates to mortgage risk, subprime means a category of loans available to borrowers who have had damaged credit on a regular or extensive basis. Problems can fall into three primary areas of credit blemishes: (1) mortgage credit, (2) consumer credit, and (3) public record postings. For example, the latter category would include someone with a foreclosure or a judgment against him or her.

After scoring and grading the borrower's credit, the lender would place the borrower in the appropriate category. A *B* subprime borrower, for instance, might have two mortgage payments past due in the past 12 months, while a *C* subprime buyer might have had a bankruptcy discharged 14 months ago. (Note the comparison chart found in figure 3.3, which shows the type and amount of derogatory credit, the loan rating, as well as the additional interest [rate premium] a borrower would pay for the loan.)

FIGURE 3.3 *Subprime Loan Rating Chart*

Rating	Description/Allowable Derogatory	Ratios	Equity (LTV)	Rate Premium
A– FNMA EAI, 2, 3	**Mortgage** — Current; 2 × 30, 0 × 60; **Consumer Credit** — Generally excellent, no more than 20% of all other accounts report delinquencies; no bankruptcy; no judgments over $100	42/42	80 – 90	0.00 – 2.50%
B	**Mortgage** — Current; 4 × 30, or 2 × 30 & 1 × 60; **Consumer Credit** — reasonably good; no more than 40% of all other accounts report past delinquencies; no bankruptcy in 24 – 36 months; no judgments over $250	45/50	75 – 90	1.50 – 3.00%

C	**Mortgage** — Slow; 6 × 30, 1 × 60, 1 × 90 —Can be currently past due; **Consumer Credit** — Significant past problems; many accounts late; open judgments; no bankruptcy within last 12–24 months	50/60	70	2.00 – 6.00%
D	**Mortgage** — Currently past due/ foreclosure; **Consumer Credit**— Serious problems, collections, judgments, delinquencies; recent but active bankruptcy	60/60	50 – 60	4.00 – 12.00%

Rates and points vary widely between loan categories. Depending on the loan types and market factors, *B* subprime loans might spread two to three interest rate points above standard fixed-rate 30-year loans, so borrowers are advised to shop diligently before committing to a certain loan program.

Q. Does the amount of the down payment play a role in the type of loan a subprime borrower can obtain?

Yes, it does. A rule of thumb is that the greater the amount of equity (i.e., a larger down payment), the weaker the credit can be. So factoring in the amount of the down payment, it could be possible for a borrower who previously has gone through bankruptcy to be placed in a higher-category subprime mortgage, rather than someone who has been late twice on mortgage payments.

Q. What caused the subprime market to crash?

The subprime/nonprime market crashed for myriad reasons. But, it's important to remember why this market was created in the first place––as a short-term fix to give credit-marred borrowers a chance to obtain a mortgage while they improved their credit and could then refinance. Unfortunately, successful for one purpose, nonprime mortgages became the staple d'jour for the mortgage industry, especially for profit-driven investors.

First introduced in 2002, nonprime mortgages met a welcomed market of consumers who'd had previous bankruptcies or other types of credit damage. The success of this new-found market niche expanded in 2003 and, by 2004, had morphed into an even-larger market share. In fact, unscrupulous lenders were placing borrowers in subprime programs with hefty origination fees even when their credit scores could warrant prime interest rate loans! Borrowers, literally bidding on houses in a frenzied market place, jumped at the chance to secure any financing, no matter what the cost.

In 2005, in an effort to further expand the market, guidelines were reduced allowing limited documentation subprime loans, resulting in the first major strain of defaults and foreclosures. Refinancing options for subprime borrowers dried up, and by early 2006, foreclosures were clearly on an upward spiral. That, coupled with investors who woke up to realize that the yields promised on their mortgage-backed securities were not being delivered, panicked and began making "call back"/restitution claims against the primary lenders. That, in turn, dried up any new funding to that market segment...and the rest is history.

Q. Will nonprime loans remain in the marketplace?

Yes, I believe so. As with any loan program, used in the right way and to meet a certain need, nonprime loans satisfy a market niche. It's more important now than ever for consumers to diligently shop for the best subprime mortgage, not just for interest rates but for costs and fees. In fact, it's best to first meet with a lender who does not originate subprime loans to see if you meet his/her program guidelines for prime mortgages.

TAX-FREE GIFTS

Q. Is it possible for someone to gift money tax-free to use as a down payment?

Yes. Gifts of up to $12,000 per year, per person, can be received without tax consequences. In fact, a couple with two sets of parents could obtain $96,000 annually ($12,000 to each child/daughter or son-in-law from each parent or father/mother-in-law!) If the couple were to bridge the closing over two calendar years (e.g., closing in January of the new year), the couple could accept $96,000 in December and another $96,000 in January, for a whopping $192,000 down payment all tax-free!

Additionally, receiving money from someone can whittle down his or her estate, helping to protect it from the harsh blows of inheritance tax.

TIPS FOR GENERATING EXTRA CASH

Q. What course of action do you suggest for the applicant who finds that he or she does not have enough income and down payment strength to qualify for a loan?

Here are some possible suggestions:

- *Sell an asset* such as a car, boat, or motorcycle—or hold a giant garage sale!
- *Put a lien on an asset.* Borrow against a car, a boat, a life insurance policy, stock, certificates of deposit, or other personal property. (Be careful not to create more long-term debt in the process.) The borrower could also create cash by, with permission, putting a lien on a relative's asset. This is best accomplished when the borrower is a co-owner of the asset, such as stocks, bonds, or certificates of deposits.
- *Refinance an asset* such as personal property (either free and clear or with existing debt on it) to free up cash.
- *Receive a gift letter* for the down payment or closing costs from a relative, or perhaps an employer, depending on the type of loan.
- *Barter a service,* using sweat equity as either part of the down payment or closing costs. For example, a roofer may make roof repairs in lieu of using the seller's cash for repairs.
- *Forgo a vacation* and work instead! This could generate extra income. If a bonus is in the borrower's future, now might be a good time to request it. The borrower may even be willing to take a little less for the privilege of receiving the bonus early.
- *Transfer the use of an item.* For example, a buyer could allow a builder to use his or her backhoe in exchange for the builder paying more points on the loan. (This type of transfer would be regulated by the type of loan selected.)
- *Use receivables coming to the buyer.* Notes carried that pay out over time could be assigned to the seller as part of the purchase price.
- *Use a coborrower or cosigner* to help reduce the loan amount for which the borrower needs to qualify.
- *Borrow against your retirement account:* After determining whether your plan allows and reviewing the financial impact it will have for the long run, it may make sense to help you generate your down payment.
- *Have the seller or other third party place extra funds with the lender* in a pledged account to add extra collateral to the loan and therefore reduce the lender's risk. This is examined in depth in Chapter 5.

TIPS FOR REDUCING DEBT

Q. How can an applicant reduce debt to qualify for a mortgage?

The following suggestions might assist the buyer in debt relief:

- *Pay off a debt.* Use cash or another asset to alleviate the debt or sell an asset that has debt against it.
- *Pay down a debt.* Because the secondary market views long-term debt as anything that can't be paid off in ten months, the borrower could pay down the debt below that point. Lenders can choose to be more restrictive on what's considered long-term debt, so check with the lender.
- *Refinance a high-rate loan.*
- *Consolidate your loans.* Doing this may allow the borrower to take several high-rate loans and wrap them into one lower-interest-rate loan, and even lower the monthly payments by extending the loan term.
- *Destroy credit cards.* The borrower should ask the lender if and how this might benefit the borrower's ability to qualify.

Before changing a cash or debt position, the borrower should consult the lender to see how what's proposed could help or hurt his or her credit picture.

4

COMPARISON SHOPPING

Most people spend several months searching for their dream homes and make a very careful—sometimes painstaking—decision. This only makes sense. After all, for most people, the purchase of a home is by far their biggest investment, the lion's share of which is usually the mortgage. Therefore, it also makes sense to be as diligent in shopping for a mortgage. Choosing the right mortgage can save a borrower thousands on a home purchase.

This chapter provides the tools to use when comparing mortgage choices, starting with the broadest of comparisons—might renting be a better option than buying?—and, then, for those who have the option—is it better to pay cash for the home rather than use mortgage financing?

The mortgage market can be confusing. This chapter will make general comparisons on such issues as points, interest, and lenders. The specifics of loan programs will be discussed later in this book.

RENT OR BUY?

Q. Before someone considers purchasing a home, shouldn't the individual decide if it's the right economic move for him or her?

Absolutely. For most people, a home provides not only a physical shelter but also a tax shelter and a built-in savings plan. Because mortgage interest and property taxes are tax deductible and equity builds as the real estate appreciates, home ownership usually makes good economic sense.

Some circumstances might make renting a more logical option. For example, if it is likely that the buyer would need to sell the property soon, purchasing might be unwise, because recouping down payment and closing costs is unlikely. Or if the real estate sales market is sluggish with values rapidly declining, renting might be a better bet.

Q. Is there financially a way to calculate whether it makes sense to buy, especially if a buyer would own the house only a short time?

Yes. Online lending has brought with it rent-versus-buy calculators! One of my favorites can be found at www.interest.com.

The borrower would supply information about how long the property would be held, the approximate rate of interest charged for a mortgage, the borrower's tax bracket, the expected appreciation (3 percent is conservative), the monthly amount paid to rent a similar house, and the price of the property considered. The calculator will gauge whether it would pay to purchase at this time using a variety of down payment amounts.

Would-be buyers shouldn't overlook the fact that while the rent-versus-buy calculations may indicate that purchasing is a sound financial move, when the owner sells, he or she will need equity to pay a new set of closing costs and hopefully have enough left over to buy a replacement property.

WHAT'S THE COST OF WAITING TO PURCHASE?

Q. Besides potentially higher interest rates, are there any other financial impacts to consider if someone waits to buy a home?

This question is a good one because much of what's lost in waiting to buy can be tallied up in terms of lost appreciation and equity. Here's an example:

Pat Carlisle wants to buy a $300,000 house using a 90 percent loan. If she purchases today at 7 percent interest, her monthly payment will be $1,796 per month principal and interest.

If she waits one year and rates drop 1/2 percent to 6.5 percent, would she have won? No. Based on annual appreciation at even a meager 3 percent, the home Pat wants now costs $309,000, making her 90 percent loan $278,100 and her payments $1,758 principal and interest. She's saved $38 per month by waiting to purchase. Or has she?

What about the $9,000 additional cost of the home? Divided by the monthly savings of $38, it would take her nearly 20 years to recoup the difference! But that's not all. By waiting to purchase, Pat needed $900 more down payment, and a larger loan could mean more closing costs and would be tougher to qualify for. In addition, the lender's loan-underwriting guidelines might have tightened, disqualifying her completely for the loan she needed. And then there's the potential that the type of home she wanted might not be on the market.

We often forget that money is made in real estate with equity buildup and appreciation. These are impacted by length of ownership and compounding. As you can see by Pat's scenario, 3 percent appreciation can make a $300,000 home worth $309,000 next year and $318,270 the following year, compounding on and on. And don't forget the tax advantages of ownership.

Pat's lesson is most first-time homebuyers' lesson: All things considered, if you'll stay in the home long enough to recoup your initial down payment and closing costs, waiting to buy may end up costing you money.

PAY CASH OR GET A MORTGAGE?

Q. Should buyers always take out a loan just to get tax benefits when they purchase a home?

Certainly not. Buyers must first decide what they want to achieve through home ownership, and then determine what financing options are best for their situations. Following are some of the pros and cons of paying cash versus financing a home.

Benefits of Paying Cash

- *The cash buyer pays no mortgage payments.* This is especially important to some buyers who still have nightmares over the number of homes lost to foreclosure during the Great Depression.
- *The person who buys a property with cash pays no mortgage interest.* Mortgage interest can more than double a property's purchase price if the loan runs full term.
- *The cash buyer doesn't spend money, time, or effort obtaining a loan.* Closing costs are minimized to include minor changes such as deed preparation, recording documents, etc.
- *The buyer who pays in cash doesn't need to obtain the property appraisal* required with most mortgage loans.
- *The cash buyer can take out a loan later,* using the value of the property as collateral.
- *Cash can give the buyer greater purchasing power* in the marketplace, because a cash purchase is free of financing contingencies and finance-related costs.

The Downside of Paying Cash

- *The cash buyer uses precious cash to buy the home,* potentially depleting reserves for other purchases and emergencies. By obtaining a mortgage, the borrower employs the first tenet of real estate leverage: purchase using OPM (other people's money), even if it's the lender's!
- *No mortgage interest* means loss of tax advantages. Also, if consumer loans are needed later to finance other purchases, that interest is not tax deductible like mortgage interest.
- *The cash buyer can't take advantage of tax-deductible closing costs.* With a mortgage, a buyer can finance some fees into the loan to provide greater purchasing leverage. Additionally, discount points paid (even by the seller) are tax deductible for the buyer.
- *The cash buyer who does not obtain an appraisal could be purchasing an overpriced property.* Should the property need to be sold in a short time, it might not bring the full price paid.
- *By taking out a loan later, the buyer becomes both the borrower and the seller* for the purpose of paying costs. These additional fees might include title insurance, discount points, and other closing fees.

- *Mortgages applied for later might be considered refinances,* with their interest rates and fees not treated so liberally as with initial mortgages. In addition, this might prohibit the borrower from getting all the cash he or she needs out of the property. The purchaser would also need to anticipate whether he or she could qualify, should a loan be necessary later.

A buyer can find exactly the right financing that provides tax advantages without being so financially burdensome that he or she can't sleep at night. This will be discussed further in this chapter.

MAKING A FINAL DECISION ON THE LOAN AND THE LENDER

Q. Before making a final decision on the loan you choose, what should you consider?

Shopping for a loan is a lot like buying a car—it has to be priced right, be comfortable, and be able to last as long as needed! That's why it's increasingly important to shop not only for the actual loan, but for the lender as well.

There are myriad sources of lenders in the marketplace today. If it's been quite awhile since you've shopped for a lender, you might not be aware that in addition to the traditional bank, savings and loan, or mortgage bank resources for money, there are mortgage brokers who "broker" money. They lend none of their own money, but instead match you up with the type of loan that best suits your needs, often accessing hundreds of loan programs to do so. Buyers with special challenges such as marred credit or a property to finance outside of typical lender guidelines often find the creative options they need from mortgage brokers.

A good lender will set the stage for a positive win-win loan experience. The loan officer not only will provide all the information the borrower needs to make an informed decision about which loan to choose, but will do everything possible to troubleshoot potential obstacles to bring the transaction to a speedy and successful closing. A lender may provide the information to help the buyer compare loan types, as shown in figure 4.1.

FIGURE 4.1 *Financing Options for $105,300*

CONVENTIONAL LOAN, 30-YEAR TERM—5 percent down payment

Monthly Payment
P & I	$ 657
Property taxes	58
Hazard insurance	50
HO dues/condo fees	0
Mortgage insurance	64
Total monthly payment	$ 829

Cash Requirements
Down payment	$ 5,265
Closing costs	1,946
Prepaids	1,510
Total cash to close	$ 8,721
Cash reserves	1,659
Loan amount	100,035
Financed fees	0
Total loan amount	$100,035
Loan to value	95.00%

Note Rate	6.8750%	Origination/Discount	1.00%
APR	7.9377%		

CONVENTIONAL LOAN, 30-YEAR TERM—20 percent down payment

Monthly Payment
P & I	$ 554
Property taxes	58
Hazard insurance	50
HO dues/condo fees	0
Mortgage insurance	0
Total monthly payment	$ 662

Cash Requirements
Down payment	$21,060
Closing costs	1,738
Prepaids	1,293
Total cash to close	24,091
Cash reserves	1,323
Loan amount	84,240
Financed fees	0
Total loan amount	$84,240
Loan to value	80.00%

Note Rate	6.8750%	Origination/Discount	1.00%
APR	6.9864%		

FIGURE 4.1 *Financing Options for $105,300 (Continued)*

FHA LOAN, 30-YEAR TERM

Monthly Payment
P & I	$	693
Property taxes		58
Hazard insurance		50
HO dues/condo fees		0
Mortgage insurance		42
Total monthly payment	$	843

Cash Requirements
Down payment	$	3,388
Closing costs		1,751
Prepaids		1,501
Total cash to close	$	6,640
Cash reserves		0
Loan amount		101,913
Financed fees		2,293
Total loan amount		$104,206
Loan to value		96.78%

Note Rate	7.000%	Origination/Discount	1.00%
APR	7.8296%		

VA LOAN, 30-YEAR TERM

Monthly Payment
P & I	$	715
Property taxes		58
Hazard insurance		50
HO dues/condo fees		0
Mortgage insurance		0
Total monthly payment	$	823

Cash Requirements
Down payment		0
Closing costs		1,739
Prepaids		1,435
Total cash to close	$	3,174
Cash reserves		0
Loan amount		105,300
Financed fees		2,105
Total loan amount		$107,405
Loan to value		100.00%

Note Rate	7.000%	Origination/Discount	1.00%
APR	7.3017%		

These figures are deemed reliable but not guaranteed. This is being provided for informational purposes only and is not a loan commitment.

Reprinted by permission of Shelly Mulberry, Wallick and Volk, P.O. Box 685, 222 E. Eighteenth Street, Cheyenne, WY 82001, 307-771-8364.

Some of the best resources for finding the right lender are friends, family members, and coworkers who have recently financed a home. The smart borrower will ask such questions as:

- *What lender did you use?*
- *What kind of loan did you get?*
- *Were you pleased with the time frames for processing and closing the loan?*
- *How have you been treated since the closing?* Ask questions about payments, receipt of coupon books, ability to pay your mortgage online, and inquiries about other services.
- *Did the lender primarily refinance loans rather than initiate new ones?* This could indicate that a new loan applicant might have to wait in the processing line behind large numbers of loan refinances, which are relatively easier to process. This is particularly impactful during peak refinancing periods when interest rates are low.

As an additional resource, the borrower should ask real estate agents to provide names of lenders they know are reputable. Often this will be based on the types of loans in which lenders specialize, which is great information to have because it can help speed up closing.

Don't overlook the fact that not all lenders make all types of loans. Additionally, a lender may make a certain loan type, but not specialize in it. For example, a lender who handles just one or two VA loans a year might not be the best resource for a marginally qualified borrower who needs little-known underwriting leverage to qualify. Borrowers should ask what the percentage of total volume this type of loan constitutes before making a formal application.

Q. What's the difference between using a mortgage broker and a mortgage banker or other type of lending institution?

Mortgage brokers, as their name denotes, "broker" mortgages. They locate borrowers who need mortgage money and place them with investors who want to make loans. The mortgage broker receives a fee for making a successful match.

Unlike some other types of lenders, mortgage brokers do not work with their own cash—they merely place borrowers with lenders.

One plus in working with mortgage brokers is that they have access to a variety of investors and myriad loan types. They can help marginal borrowers locate financing with investors willing to take more risk.

Mortgage bankers, on the other hand, not only originate loans but also close the loan using their funds. They make their profit by charging fees and points and also by selling the loan in the secondary market.

Mortgage bankers also profit by servicing loans or selling the servicing rights on loans they originate. Servicing is the process of receiving monthly loan payments and collecting and accounting for the taxes and insurance on mortgages. Many large mortgage banker companies today operate separate loan servicing divisions that contribute greatly to corporate profit.

Q. Even though mortgage brokers can shop for the best deals, is it true that they often overcharge consumers?

Any lender you work with should have the mission of getting you the best mortgage. But since mortgage brokers are independent contractors who are free to charge whatever they wish for their services, the consumer needs to know how to maximize their market scouring ability while not overpaying for financing.

Mortgage brokers make their money by adding a markup to the wholesale price quoted by the lender. If the lender quotes a wholesale price of 7 percent with zero points, the mortgage broker might add one point resulting in a retail price to the consumer of 7 percent with one point (1 percent of the amount financed). In general, mortgage brokers try for the largest markup they can on each transaction. Obviously, consumers who are not motivated to shop the competition and/or are unsophisticated borrowers willing to accept a relatively higher interest rate are the ones who could end up overpaying. And there's an additional incentive from the wholesale lender to the mortgage broker—yield spread premiums (YSP). These are side payments, often in amounts of several thousand dollars, made from the lender to the mortgage broker for closing a more profitable, higher-rate loan. Unfortunately, the consumer may not be aware of these premium fees until closing. The key here is to look for the words "Premium Yield Adjustment/POC" (paid outside of closing) on the loan settlement statement. That's a trigger that there's more to the story where fees are involved.

Besides shopping multiple lenders, how can you best protect yourself from overpaying from the start? Hire a mortgage broker to shop for you and set the price for the service in advance in dollars rather than a percent of the loan. Reduce to writing and mutually sign something like the following: "I, John Doe mortgage broker d.b.a. "East Coast Loans, Inc." hereby agree that the total compensation for my services in obtaining a mortgage for Jane Smith, including all amounts paid me by Ms. Smith and the lender who provides the loan, will be $X. (Spell out in dollar amount). If the lender does compensate me more than $X, the difference will be used to reduce Ms. Smith's other settlement costs."

Q. Can the builder of a home force a borrower to apply for a loan with a certain mortgage?

No. This is restraint of trade and is illegal. While it's not a bad idea to consider a lender the builder knows and does a high volume of business with because the loan might receive special attention, that lender should not be the borrower's sole option.

QUESTIONS TO ASK BEFORE CHOOSING A LOAN

Q. Once the lender has received information about the borrower and has discussed possible financing programs, what general loan questions should the borrower ask the lender before choosing the best loan?

Following are some questions a borrower might ask to clarify his or her loan choice:

- *Is the interest rate you're offering me fixed or adjustable and is it the best possible rate based on my credit score and financial buying power?* Your credit score is your history of repaying debt and is the main source lenders use to determine the interest rates they offer you. To obtain the best possible interest rate, you should shop around. A high credit score should result in your being offered a low interest rate.
- *Is there a prepayment penalty on the loan if I pay it off early?* If yes, what is the amount of the penalty and to how many years of the loan would it apply? In order to increase lenders' profitability, many loans today contain prepayment penalties that can be as much as six months' worth of interest and often extend through the first five years of the loan. If you'll plan on paying off or refinancing the loan in the short term, best to sidestep this feature even if it ends up costing you a higher interest rate.

- *Can I pay taxes and insurance outside of the loan payment?* If you're making a down payment of at least 20 percent on a conventional mortgage, it's likely that the lender will allow you to pay your property taxes and insurance outside of the monthly loan payment. As in most instances, if you don't ask, you don't get.

- *Are you locking my interest rate and, if so, for how long?* A rate lock is when the lender or broker "locks in" a stated interest rate for a specific period of time, usually 30 days. This means that if interest rates rise, you still will receive the quoted or "locked" rate. (We'll cover more on lock-ins later in this chapter).

- *If I pay for the appraisal, how do I obtain a copy of it?* If you've paid for it, most lenders will provide you a copy if you ask; however, you may need to make your request in writing immediately after closing.

- *Whom do I contact to obtain the closing documents one business day prior to the closing?* By federal law, you are entitled to obtain a copy of the HUD settlement statement one business day prior to closing. Having this statement ahead of time is designed to give you and your attorney adequate time to review all costs and correct any errors that need to be made prior to document signing. Contact your lender for the HUD statement.

INTEREST RATES, LOAN TERMS, AND DOWN PAYMENTS

Q. Is the interest rate the major consideration when shopping for a loan?

While one of the first options consumers consider when making an affordable home purchase (and erroneously, often where they stop shopping), the interest rate is certainly not the only factor in mortgage financing. Following is a quick checklist of questions the borrower should ask, followed by an explanation of each:

- *What are the borrower's financing goals?* The borrower should estimate the time he or she will own the property. Short-term owners could use an adjustable-rate mortgage (ARM) for short-term savings; elect for a higher interest rate with fewer discount points, which would not be recouped if the property were sold in a short time; or use a loan containing a balloon provision.

    Long-term owners could use a 15- or 10-year fixed-rate loan to build equity quickly and sidestep interest over the life of the loan; or use a permanent buydown to reduce the interest rate for the life of the loan.

- *Will anyone else be participating as a coborrower or cosigner on the loan?* The answer to this question may dictate the type of loan available to the borrower, for not all loans allow multiple borrowers.
- *How much savings does the borrower wish to use as a down payment?* Is that including, or in addition to, the closing costs? This can help determine the size and the type of loan.
- *How much of a monthly payment is the borrower prepared to make?* This answer should be based not only on what the borrower can afford but also on the size of the monthly payment he or she is mentally prepared to make for the long run.
- *What are the borrower's current mortgage or rent payments?* A lender may hesitate to approve a loan with radically larger payments than a consumer is accustomed to paying without the consumer showing a substantial income increase. A severe payment difference may increase financial pressure on the borrower, perhaps enough to cause the borrower to default on the loan.
- *Would the borrower mind if the payment amount fluctuated?* If so, it's probably not wise to take on an ARM or similar interest-sensitive loan.

A 15-Year versus a 30-Year Loan

Q. How does one choose between a 15-year and a 30-year loan?

Many factors go into deciding which loan term best suits a buyer's needs and qualifying abilities. If a borrower qualifies for a 15-year loan, the savings in interest payments is substantial. The monthly principal and interest payment on a 15-year $100,000 loan at 7 percent is approximately $899, compared to $665 on a 30-year term. Payments on the 15-year loan would total $161,790. The 30-year loan would cost a whopping $239,509—nearly $78,000 more!

Q. Are there other financial benefits to using a 15-year versus a 30-year loan?

Interest rates may be lower on the 15-year loan, depending on the lender and the loan program. Because equity builds faster on a 15-year loan, a low down payment may be less of a problem if the borrower has to resell in a short period of time.

Q. If a 15-year mortgage makes such good financial sense, why doesn't everyone get one?

First, not everyone can qualify for a 15-year loan. Because of the shorter amortization time, the monthly payment is larger. Referring to the earlier example comparing costs for the 15- versus 30-year loan: To qualify for a 30-year loan's $665 principal and interest payment, the borrower would have to have $2,375 income per month to meet a lender's 28 percent housing ratio requirements. To qualify for the 15-year loan's $899 payment, however, the borrower would need $3,210 income per month, or $835 more than is needed for the 30-year loan.

Second, some borrowers enjoy the peace of mind that comes with a lower monthly payment, enjoying the cushion were they to fall on tough financial times. In fact, approximately 80 percent of all loans are 30-year loans. Borrowers could make prepayments on the 30-year loan to retire it early if the loan program allowed, but with the 15-year loan they'd be saddled permanently with the higher payment.

The exception to this school of thought is found with homeowners who are refinancing their existing loans. A much larger percentage of those individuals are using 15-year loans, and, in some cases, 10-year loans, to reduce their purchasing costs.

Remember that a borrower who is making a higher monthly payment will not have that money available for other investments. This could mean lost financial opportunities.

Lenders are usually more than happy to project costs to help buyers decide which loan term best suits their needs and means. Total borrowing costs for different loan terms can be compared by using the chart in figure 4.2.

Q. What about a 10-year mortgage? When does it make sense?

Figure 4.2 *Comparing Interest Costs by Loan Term for a $100,000 Mortgage*

Terms	Monthly Payment	Months Paid	Total Cost	Interest Cost
40-year	$ 621.43	480	$298,287	$198,287
30-year	665.30	360	239,509	139,509
20-year	775.30	240	186,072	86,072
15-year	898.83	180	161,790	61,790
10-year	1,161.08	120	139,330	39,330

Ten-year mortgages are ideal for borrowers who want to save interest and retire the loan quickly. But the trade-off is that you need to be able to handle the monster-size payments that can be as much as twice the size of those of a 30-year loan. Additionally, you must qualify well within the ratios and have a stable, well-established monthly income.

Q. On the other end of the continuum, some borrowers are going with 40-year mortgages. Why would anyone want to pay that long on a mortgage?

Forty- and even fifty-year mortgages are fairly recent inventions by the lending community to make monthly payments more affordable and qualifying easier for consumers. With median prices skyrocketing, amortizing a loan for an additional 10 or 20 years help consumers financially qualify for the mortgage they need. But as far as making good economic sense for most homeowners, they tragically miss the mark and should be avoided if at all possible.

As you see if in figure 4.2, the monthly principal and interest payment for the 40-year mortgage is just $43.87 less than it is for the 30-year loan, but you add more than $58,000 in total costs if you held the 40-year loan to maturity. The reality is that most borrowers initially take a 40-year mortgage to qualify for their first home and replace it with a more affordable loan later.

There's a dangerous downside to taking on a 40-year mortgage for the long haul—the lack of equity buildup. During a stagnant real estate market coupled with low property appreciation, saddling yourself with a 40-year mortgage could mean low equity build-up at best during the first 7 to 10 years of the loan. If you had to sell the property during that time, you might find yourself owing as much as the property is worth. This is particularly true if you'd made a meager down payment and/or financed closing costs into the mortgage. That's why it's imperative for short-term owners to counsel upfront with the mortgage professional and apply a worst-case scenario. The statistics speak volumes. At the end of seven years on a 30-year mortgage at 7 percent interest, you'd owe approximately $91,000 compared to nearly $97,000 on the 40-year loan. The $6,000 equity could make the difference between receiving a check at closing or writing one!

PROS AND CONS OF SMALL VERSUS LARGE DOWN PAYMENTS

Q. How does a borrower weigh the advantages of making a small versus a large down payment, other than what the lender might require on a certain loan?

As discussed earlier, it may not be in the short-term buyer's best interest to invest lots of money in the property. Too small of a down payment, however, coupled with low property appreciation, may create a deficit if the owner needs to sell in a very short period of time. If the borrower knows this and is willing to take the risk, he or she should be prepared to make up the shortfall when he or she sells.

A second consideration is that the borrower may want to make a large down payment if it means securing a lower interest rate or sidestepping the costs of fees or PMI. This will be discussed in depth in chapter 6. A large down payment may even loosen some loan underwriting requirements because the lender's risk is reduced.

DETERMINING LOAN COSTS

Q. How does the borrower determine which loan program is most cost-effective, especially where loan costs and fees are involved?

Unlike comparing interest-rate differences that are fairly obvious and straightforward, comparing loan costs and fees can get complicated. This is because it's not just the loan costs that are being compared, but also the loan program terms.

Fixed Rate versus Adjustable Rate

The lender offers a 90 percent conventional, fixed-rate loan at 8 percent interest with total closing costs of $2,500. Costs for a 90 percent ARM at 6 percent interest, however, are $2,900; the loan also can be converted to a fixed-rate loan at any time during the first five years of the loan.

At first glance, it's virtually impossible to tell which is the better buy. The borrower needs to compare financially the two loan programs based on (1) how long he or she anticipates keeping the loan, (2) what

FIGURE 4.3 *Loan Comparison Worksheet*

	Loan Type		
	Conventional	FHA	VA
Sales Price	$ _____	_____	_____
Interest Rate	$ _____	_____	_____
Down Payment	$ _____	_____	_____
Total Loan to Be Amortized	$ _____	_____	_____

Estimated Loan Costs

MIP (Unless FHA Included Above)	$ _____	_____	_____
Loan Origination Fee	$ _____	_____	_____
Assumption Fee	$ _____	_____	_____
Credit Report	$ _____	_____	_____
Appraisal Fee	$ _____	_____	_____
Recording Fee	$ _____	_____	_____
Title (ALTA) Policy (Use Loan Amount)	$ _____	_____	_____
Attorney's Fee	$ _____	_____	_____
Escrow Closing Fee	$ _____	_____	_____
Interest Proration	$ _____	_____	_____
Fire and Hazard Insurance First Year	$ _____	_____	_____
Lender's Application Fee	$ _____	_____	_____
Purchaser's Buydown Points	$ _____	_____	_____
Long-Term Escrow Setup Fee	$ _____	_____	_____
Tax Service Fee	$ _____	_____	_____
Misc., LID, City Code, Reserves	$ _____	_____	_____
Home Inspection Fee	$ _____	_____	_____
Total Estimated Closing Costs	$ _____	_____	_____

Reserves and Prorates

Property Taxes (Minimum Two Months)	$ _____	_____	_____
Fire and Hazard Insurance (Minimum Two Months)	$ _____	_____	_____
Mortgage Insurance	$ _____	_____	_____
Total Reserves and Prorates	$ _____	_____	_____
Total Cash Outlay	$ _____	_____	_____

Estimated Monthly Payment

Principal and Interest	$ _____	_____	_____
Tax Reserves	$ _____	_____	_____
Insurance Reserves	$ _____	_____	_____
MIP Insurance (Unless FHA Included Above)	$ _____	_____	_____
Total Estimated Monthly Payment	$ _____	_____	_____

The undersigned hereby acknowledges receipt of a copy of this estimation.

By _____ Signed _____ Date _____

the conversion fees might be, and (3) how the rate would adjust if the loan were converted to a fixed rate.

Lenders will prepare comparisons such as these if provided with the necessary information to plug into the scenario. This is the best way for borrowers to make sure they are not being led astray based only on bargain interest rates and low closing costs. A loan comparison worksheet is shown in figure 4.3.

NO CLOSING COST LOANS

Q. What are no closing cost loans?

No closing cost loans, available from lenders for new financing or refinancing, are loans in which the lender pays/waives/fronts all closing costs. These nonrecurring closing costs (title and escrow fees, appraisal, and lender's fees) are one-time fees paid when obtaining the loan, and do not include recurring costs (interest, property taxes, and insurance) paid in your monthly payment.

Q. Why would a lender agree to pay a borrower's closing costs?

As with most financing approaches, there are trade-offs (and benefits to the lender). In other words, there's no such thing as a free lunch. The borrower always pays the settlement costs — one way or another. If it's not paid in cash at closing, it's paid in the future by rolling it into the mortgage or accepting a higher interest rate. For example, the lender might offer a 6.75 percent loan with ½ discount point, a 7 percent loan with zero points, or a 7.25 percent mortgage with no closing costs, all for a 30-year fixed-rate mortgage. Your choice could be based on (1) what you can qualify for, (2) what you're trying to achieve financially (i.e., short- versus long-term ownership), (3) the amount of funds you have for closing, and (4) what you're comfortable with paying.

No closing cost loans are good when you're tight on funds for closing or you plan to hold the loan or the property only a short time and don't want to part with closing money you can't recoup. You might also select a no closing cost loan if you want to move quickly to obtain a loan (e.g., when interest rates are falling). These loans are especially attractive when refinancing into a lower interest rate. Because there are no up-front costs, your savings are immediate.

If you're a real risk taker, you might consider refinancing your adjustable-rate mortgage every year with a no closing cost loan—keeping your initial teaser (discounted) rate intact! Rates for this type of loan are often 2 percent or more below 30-year fixed-rate mortgages.

CATEGORIES OF CLOSING COSTS

Q. What are the major categories of loan-related costs?

Loan-related costs vary depending on the type and size of loan. Following are some general loan-related cost categories that pertain to most buyers:

- *Down payment* (minus any earnest money deposit)
- *Out-of-pocket costs:* fees for appraisal, credit report paid, and any loan application fee at the time of the loan application, plus other costs, such as home inspection, paid at the time of the loan application and paid at the time of the closing
- *Title insurance:* a one-time fee that varies among states and with the size of the loan
- *Two months' escrow:* two months' impound of property tax, homeowners insurance, and private mortgage insurance, if the loan so requires
- *PMI initial premium* (if not financed into the loan)
- *First year's homeowners insurance:* a paid receipt showing payment or funds advanced to the lender to pay directly to the insurance company
- *Discount points,* if applicable
- *Prorated loan interest:* interest paid by the day for the closing month, to a maximum of 30 days
- *Two months' cash reserves:* an equivalent of two months of mortgage payments left over in cash as financial padding (required on conventional loans; not given to the lender, just verified to be on hand; can be in savings, a 401(k), IRA, etc.). Depending on the loan type, this requirement can be reduced or waived.

Fees to Negotiate

Q. What loan fees can be negotiated with the lender?

As with many things in this world, closing costs and discount points can be negotiated. But it's tougher for the borrower to obtain large concessions unless there are trade-offs with the lender.

For example, the lender may be much more willing to reduce closing fees or require fewer discount points if the borrower is well qualified and is making a substantial down payment. In addition, if a higher interest rate is being charged, the lender might offer other concessions.

The lender may be willing to entice a borrower with low fees when the company is seeking a larger business market share or introducing a new program. In addition, a lender may give incentives to faithful past customers or to encourage a new borrower who may bring additional business to the lender.

Low fees, however, can be smoke and mirrors—obscuring an overall higher interest rate or other lender benefit. As previously mentioned, asking the lender to compare different financing options is the best approach in determining the true cost of borrowing. This can be accomplished in a matter of minutes, using the lender's computer or financial calculator.

Q. What types of loan costs generally vary widely from lender to lender?

Fees are as different as the lenders who charge them. The major differences can be found in the following three major categories:

1. *Loan origination fees.* Many companies don't charge this fee, but some do. It's usually considered another point (1 percent of the loan amount) and can make a seemingly great loan package a bad choice. If charged, this is also a fee that may not be explained thoroughly up front.
2. *Separate application fees.* Most companies include the application fee in the out-of-pocket expense quote; others consider this a separate fee (of several hundred dollars), which may not be explained until the borrower applies for the loan. Borrowers should ask about this when calling to check for rates and costs because the amount can vary significantly among lenders.
3. *Miscellaneous fees* (often called *fluff fees, garbage fees,* or *junk fees*). As the names denote, these are the most extraneous and

negotiable of the bunch! They include document preparation fees, courier charges, notary fees, administrative fees, document review fees, etc. The gravest problem here is that these fees do not have to be factored into calculating the annual percentage rate (APR) quoted to the borrower. So it's totally possible that a lender quoting a low interest rate is actually making up for it by charging tons of garbage fees! Spend time reviewing the good faith estimate provided to you by the lender before committing to a certain loan program.

DISCOUNT POINTS

Q. What are discount points and how are they used?

One point is equal to 1 percent of the loan amount. Points are used to increase the lender's financial yield on the loan. For example, if the lender has the choice between making a loan at 7 percent and one at 7.5 percent interest, it's pretty obvious which one it would choose.

Points bridge the gap between interest rates, allowing the lender to make the loan at a lower interest rate. While the value of points can vary depending on financial markets, most lenders consider that it takes roughly four to six points to lower the interest rate by 1 percent. This can be illustrated through the following example:

If a lender quotes that it will take two points (2 percent) to lower a 7 percent interest rate to 6.5 percent on a $280,000 loan, that's $280,000 × 2 percent, or $5,600 at closing to bridge the financial gap in interest by ½ percent.

Most loan types allow the seller and the buyer to negotiate payment of points in the purchase agreement. See chapters on specific loan types for further clarification.

Determining How Many Points to Pay

Q. If the lender gives the borrower the option of how many points to pay for a certain rate of interest, what's the best way to decide?

The prime factor to consider is the time the borrower will own the property and keep the loan. The following is a formula to help determine the "dollars and sense": Calculate the difference in the monthly payment amounts and the difference in the cost of the points. Divide the amount paid in points by the amount saved by the lower monthly payment to obtain a breakeven mark for holding the property. Here is an example:

> Mr. Fredericks is getting a $90,000 mortgage for 30 years. The lender tells him that there are two choices: He can pay 7.5 percent interest with zero points for a payment of $629.30 per month, or obtain a 7 percent loan with two points for a payment of $598.78 per month.
>
> The mortgage payment difference is $30.52. The difference in points is $1,800. So to calculate the breakeven point he would take the expense ($1,800) and divide it by the monthly payment savings ($30.52). It would take Mr. Fredericks nearly 57 months to break even. Obviously, if he won't keep the house or the loan that long, it doesn't make financial sense to pay the extra points to obtain the lower interest rate.

Keep in mind that this example is a relatively simplistic analysis and doesn't take into consideration the time value of money (including the lost financial opportunity of not investing the money), tax ramifications, or the long-term savings of the lower interest rate.

Q. Can a borrower negotiate points with a lender?

Possibly. Lenders determine points primarily based on the price they have to pay for funds, the type of loan involved, and other lender competition in the marketplace. If the lender does decide to charge fewer points, one or more of the following offsetting factors could be in the picture:

- *Is the borrower willing to pay a premium rate of interest?* Remember, points bridge the gap in the lender's financial yield on the loan, so this shortfall may need to be recouped somewhere.
- *How strong is the borrower?* If the lender could risk losing the applicant by not being competitive enough on the points, a concession might be necessary.

Remember, points are merely one piece of the borrowing puzzle. No amount of discount point concessions is worth dealing with a slow loan processor or an unscrupulous lender.

Q. Are points tax deductible on mortgage loans?

For the purpose of acquiring residential real estate, discount points are tax deductible in the year they are paid. The IRS specifies that for points to be deducted, they must not exceed points generally charged in the area.

In March of 1994, the IRS surprised everyone when it changed its policy to reflect who could deduct points on mortgages (retroactive to January 1, 1991). The ruling allows buyers to deduct points on mortgages—even if paid by sellers. Previously, points were deductible only if the buyer paid them at closing.

The change comes after the IRS decided that the buyer really pays the points, even if the seller helps share the expense. The rationale was that the seller typically increases the sales price to include the points.

Points paid in refinancing are handled differently. Owners who refinance must deduct points over the life of the loan, not all at once.

For example, if a borrower paid $3,600 worth of points when refinancing to obtain a 30-year loan with a lower interest rate, he or she could deduct only $10 for each of the next 360 months, or $120 per year. For this reason it may help to minimize points paid to refinance a loan.

USING BUYDOWNS

Q. How does someone buy down an interest rate?

Buydowns are prepaid interest used to reduce the interest rate on a loan temporarily or permanently. The buyer or other party pays this money at closing, allowing him or her to qualify at the lower interest rate and reduce the monthly payment.

Buydowns can bring the interest rate down for a short period (called a temporary buydown) or permanently lower the interest rate for the life of the loan. One of the more familiar approaches is the 3-2-1 buydown, where the interest rate is 3 percent lower than the note rate of the loan for the first year, 2 percent lower during the second year of the loan, and 1 percent lower during the third year of the loan, after which it stays at the note rate—the interest the borrower agreed to pay—for the life of the loan.

Q. We've heard of builders offering buydowns as incentives to potential buyers. How does this work and are there any downsides for borrowers?

Using buydowns in financing can help borrowers grow into the mortgage payment during the first few critic.. , ownership.

Here's how a buydown mortgage works. In your example, the builder is willing to pay discount points (with one point equal to one percent of the loan amount) to buy the initial interest rate down. Let's say that the going rate for a 30-year, fixed-rate loan is 6 percent. Using a typical 2-1 buy-down, the rate would be 4 percent (2 percent less for the first year) and 5 percent (one percent less for the second year). At year three, the rate becomes the full 6 percent and remains there for the remaining terms of the mortgage. Unlike an adjustable-rate mortgage that rises or falls to keep pace with changing interest rates, a buydown mortgage stays the same after the initial two-year period.

Let's compare the payments between the standard-rate mortgage compared to the buydown. On a $150,000 loan at 6 percent interest, the basic monthly payment of principal and interest only would be $899. At 4 percent during the first year of the mortgage, it would be a significant $183 less per month at $716, increasing to $805 at 5 percent interest the following year. That means that for the first year you would save $2,196 in payments and $1,128 during the second year. By the time you reached the interest rate of 6 percent at the beginning of the third year, your total payment savings we be $3,324. That's savings that can go a long way toward landscaping, window coverings, and furnishings for your new home.

The only downside of a buydown mortgage is not being financially prepared to weather the payment increases during the first three years of the loan. If you're worried that your income won't keep pace with the rising payments, you're best advised to save the difference between the buydown payment and the third-year payment each month in an interest-bearing account and/or purchase a less expensive home resulting in more affordable payments.

DETERMINING LOCK INS

Q. When would it make sense for the borrower to lock in the interest rate?

With fluctuating interest rates, this has turned out to be the real estate $64,000 question. Locking in an interest rate means that if interest rates rise during a specific time frame (usually 45 to 60 days), the rate quoted will remain the same. Again, this depends on a variety of factors.

Following are basic questions about how advantageous it is to lock into an interest rate:

- *If the borrower doesn't lock in and the rate increases, could he or she still qualify for the loan?* Logic dictates that if a bump in the rate will disqualify the borrower, locking in is not only prudent, it's advised!
- *How long is the lock in and how far away is the closing?* A 45-day lock in will be useless if closing is projected for 60 days.
- *Is there a fee for locking in?* When is it paid? Is it refundable? This often applies to fees for extended-rate lock ins that extend an interest rate guarantee to more than 60 days. It's therefore wise for the borrower to know what's being paid, when it's paid, and under what circumstances, if any, it can be refunded because most fees are nonrefundable.
- *If rates drop, would the rate lock float downward?* Many lenders use this provision, called a floatdown, to stay competitive when interest rates drop. During times of falling interest rates, loan shoppers should make sure they have this floatdown provision.
- *How long will the borrower keep the loan?* Should he or she pay more points up front to get the lower interest rate, or less points and go with a higher interest rate? (Isn't it amazing how many decisions are based on how long someone will keep the loan and the property?) Again, the standard answer is: Short-term ownership favors less points paid at closing and higher interest rates. Long-term ownership favors more points paid at closing to receive lower interest rates.

The borrower can check several sources before deciding to lock in the interest rate:

- *Borrowers should check the lender's lock requirements which can vary greatly.* Some charge nothing and require submission of a limited amount of information. Others charge a fee that is returned to the borrower only if the loan closes or if the borrower is rejected. If you jump to another lender in favor of a better deal, you'd lose the fee. This type of no-nonsense lender might also require submission of a full loan application. In general, the tougher the lenders' lock requirements, the more likely the lender will honor the lock if interest rates rise. It's a sign that he's serious about his reputation, profitability and wants to stay in the mortgage game for the long haul.

- *Ask for a written letter of lock commitment from the lender.* It's one thing for a lender to tell you that she's locked in the rate when it isn't (termed a "fake lock") so that if market rates don't increase, she pockets the difference between the price quoted for the lock period and the price available for delivery in a few days time.
- *Be wary if the lender balks at locking in an ultra-low interest rate without strict stipulations such as large up-front fees and/or a completed loan application.* If a lender can't guarantee/lock in a low rate, it may not exist. This type of unscrupulous lender is hoping that rates will go down so he can honor the rate or tell the borrower that rates went up after the application was received.
- *What have been the lender's interest rate trends on that particular type of loan and what is projected?*
- *Check financial indicators:* the federal discount rate—the rate at which banks borrow money from the Federal Reserve; actions of the Federal Reserve Board (which tightens or loosens monies in circulation); and especially the 10-year Treasury note market, which has a big impact on determining short-term interest rates. These can be monitored through local newspapers such as the in-depth coverage in *The Wall Street Journal,* found online at www.wsj. com. Also check online resources such as www. interest.com and www.hsh.com.
- *Remember the role international events play in interest rates.* In our global economy, international crises play even bigger parts in the volatility of U.S. interest rates. In fact, many lenders advise that if negative world news is brewing, it probably makes sense to lock in the rate.

Q. If I lock in an interest rate with a lender who doesn't allow floatdowns, is there anything wrong with jumping to another lender to obtain a better interest rate on a loan?

Potentially. This is likely to happen when interest rates first start to up tick but can be Russian roulette for buyers. It's going to take time to apply and be approved with another lender, and because you've contracted with the seller to close on or before a particular date, should that date arrive and you aren't prepared to close, the seller would be free to walk away from the transaction. You may be better off to attempt to negotiate with the first lender than chance losing the seller and the purchase. And because he or she wants to close the loan in progress, you just may find a middle ground.

JUST SAY NO TO MORTGAGE LIFE INSURANCE

Q. We're in our late 30s, have two children, and just purchased our first home. We're being bombarded with requests to take out life insurance to pay off our mortgage if either of us dies. Is this a good idea?

The official-looking insurance request forms that come in the mail after you've gotten a mortgage may make you wonder if this insurance is one more requirement for getting/keeping your mortgage. But look again. Not only is this type of insurance optional, it's potentially a financial rip-off.

First, mortgage term insurance requires you to make equal monthly payments over the life of the loan, even though the mortgage pay-off/insurance settlement amount decreases over time. For example, a claim filed by your spouse this year would pay off say a $200,000 loan; but a claim filed in year 20 of the mortgage would only pay off $100,000—the outstanding mortgage amount at that time.

Second, policies are often replete with "teaser" terms to entice you to take the insurance, but they are benefits that may never materialize. Let's say that a policy claims to return part or all of your paid premiums once your mortgage is paid off. But if you read the fine print you find that it requires you to make all 30-years worth of payments as criteria for the rebate! And since most homeowner's move or refinance every six or so years, very few consumers see their premiums returned.

A better, more financially sound solution to mortgage term insurance is life insurance purchased through your insurance agent. Not only do you get to choose how much insurance you need and want, you also get to shop around for the best rates. The amount your family would be paid remains the same no matter how much you owe on the house. And if you move, the policy won't be affected.

So the next time you open your mail to read "last chance to ensure that your loved ones will keep a roof over their heads" you'll know just what to do—take good aim at the circular file, and toss!

5

CONVENTIONAL LOANS

A conventional loan is any mortgage that is neither insured nor guaranteed by the government. Contrary to popular belief, there's no shortage of affordable fixed-rate loans in the wake of the mortgage meltdown. Consumers still have a plethora of affordable programs available to them for first and second homes as well as investment property.

In this chapter, we'll investigate the advantages and disadvantages of conventional lending and uncover little-known facts regarding underwriting that can help the borrower obtain the loan.

PROS AND CONS OF CONVENTIONAL FIXED-RATE LOANS

Q. What are the advantages to the borrower of a fixed-rate conventional loan?

The advantages are:

- The interest rate is set for the life of the loan. This prevents escalating interest and payments.
- Some lenders may be willing to keep the loan in their own lending portfolio, thus allowing more underwriting flexibility.
- Lenders may negotiate or eliminate certain loan fees.
- Lenders may allow comortgagors.
- A lender may allow collateral other than or in addition to the real property being mortgaged.
- A lender may be willing to finance personal property with the real estate loan, such as appliances and/or furniture. Such "package loans" may be made when a newly constructed property is sold furnished by the builder.
- Appraisals need to meet only the lender's guidelines (if the loan is held in portfolio) or the secondary market's (if applicable), instead of the strict appraisal standards of the FHA and the VA.
- If PMI is required, its premiums are usually less expensive than with ARM programs or FHA mortgage insurance.
- For a borrower who may have difficulty obtaining PMI, the lender may self-insure the loan, increasing the interest rate to compensate for any potential loss.
- The lender can fund a portion of the closing costs in exchange for a higher interest rate. *Premium pricing* is discussed later in this chapter.

Q. What are the disadvantages to the borrower of the conventional fixed-rate loan?

The disadvantages are:

- The interest rate is set for the life of the loan. If interest rates fall, the borrower's rate does not.
- Interest rates are set by each lender and can exceed those of the FHA and the VA.

- Origination fees and other loan costs are determined by each lender and can therefore be higher than those costs in similar programs.
- Most loans with greater than an 80 percent loan-to-value ratio will require the borrower to purchase PMI.
- Conventional loans may require the same, if not larger, down payments than those of government programs.
- Some lenders may require nonrefundable application and processing fees at the time of the loan application.
- Lenders may not allow some creative financing options for the buyer.

Q. Who makes the rules regarding what a lender can and can't do in conventional mortgage lending?

It depends. A lender who wants to sell loans into the secondary mortgage market has one set of rules. If those borrowers require PMI, there's another set of rules. In addition, local lenders' boards of directors might be even more restrictive.

Because a majority of all conventional loans are sold to the secondary market, those guidelines often apply and become the benchmark for conventional mortgages.

PROFILE OF A
CONVENTIONAL-LOAN BORROWER

Q. Is there a standard profile of a borrower who could best benefit by using a conventional fixed-rate loan?

In general, a conventional-loan buyer

- has at least a 3 to 5 percent down payment, or is making the purchase with a gift of 20 percent or more from a third party; or has strong enough credit to offset the down payment requirement.
- has money for closing costs, and reserves.
- has good to excellent credit.
- can qualify for a loan using a standard ratio and market-rate interest.
- doesn't usually need a lot of special loan underwriting considerations.

- desires a fixed-rate mortgage (for financial and/or emotional stability).
- has fairly light debts in proportion to his or her income.
- might ask the lender to keep the loan in portfolio (particularly if he or she has been a longtime customer, or is using a large down payment).
- can wait the standard 30 to 45 days it takes to close the loan.
- has room in his or her qualifying and loan payments for PMI insurance.

If this profile fits you, a conventional loan may best suit your needs.

SECONDARY MARKET GUIDELINES

Q. Does the secondary market have any maximum loan limits for loans it purchases?

Yes. These are reevaluated each year and termed "conforming mortgages." For example, in 2008, a single-family one-unit dwelling had maximum loan limits of $417,000, ($625,500, or 50 percent higher in Alaska, Guam, and the U.S. Virgin Islands). Mortgages on single-family multiple-unit dwellings were capped at $801,950 ($1,202,925 in Alaska, Guam, and the U.S. Virgin Islands).

Loans in excess of these secondary market loan ceilings can still be made by the lender. These are called jumbo or nonconforming loans and are sold separately to investors rather than through the usual secondary market channels. Because these loans are not the standard size, the borrower may have to pay approximately ½ percent or more additional interest and other lender incentives such as additional points to obtain a nonconforming mortgage. You'll find a list of underwriting guidelines for nonconforming mortgages at figure 5.1.

In an unprecedented occurrence, The Economic Stimulus Act of 2008 established a temporary increase to conventional loan limits in high-cost areas as defined by the U.S. Department of Housing and Urban Development (HUD). These jumbo-conforming mortgages are available only through 2008 in high-cost areas and are calculated as 125 percent of the area median home price as determined by HUD, not to exceed $729,750 except in Alaska, Hawaii, Guam, and the U.S. Virgin Islands. For further information regarding maximum loan amounts for your area, go to www.efanniemae.com, The Office of Federal Housing Enterprise Oversight, www.ofheo.gov, or www.hud.gov.

Conforming Loans

Q. If a borrower's loan was sold to FNMA or FHLMC in the secondary market, what kind of qualifying ratios would be required?

Qualifying ratios are based on the type of loan program and its underwriting guidelines. (NOTE: The following information applies only to conforming loans. See figure 5.2.)

Qualifying ratios. The standard, or benchmark qualifying ratios for most conventional mortgages (with the exception of affordable housing programs) are that PITI should not exceed 28 percent of the borrower's gross monthly income; and that PITI plus long-term debt (any debt that extends 10 months or more) should not exceed 36 percent of the borrower's gross monthly income. That said, today's extensive use of automated underwriting systems (AUS) with Fannie Mae's proprietary product, Desktop Underwriter® (DU), and Freddie Mac's Loan Prospector® system (LP) make the use of strict ratios less important. Giving statistical weight to a wide variety of borrower strengths such as credit score and amount of down payment, lenders make decisions based on the borrower's complete profile, not solely ratios.

Loan-to-value ratios. The maximum loan-to-value ratio is 95 percent on single-family residences (excluding affordable housing programs), 95 percent on second homes, and 75 percent on investor loans.

FIGURE 5.1 *Loan Underwriting Guidelines for Jumbo, or Nonconforming, Loans*

Investor	Jumbo		Nonconforming		
	LTV Matrix				
Transaction	LTV	CLTV	Property Type	Maximum Loan	Maximum Financing
Owner-Occupied Purchase Rate/Term Refinance	95% 90% 80% 70% 60%	90% 90% 90% 90% 90%	1 Family, Condo 1-2 Family, Condo 1-4 Family, Condo 1 Family, Condo 1 Family, Condo	Check with local lender	
Owner-Occupied Cash	75%	75%	1-2 Family, Condo	Check with local lender	
2nd Home Purchase Rate/Term Refinance	90% 80% 75%	90% 90% 90%	1 Family, Condo 1 Family, Condo 1 Family, Condo	Check with local lender	
2nd Home Cash-Out Refinance	70%	70%	1 Family, Condo	Check with local lender	
Investor Purchase Rate/Term Refinance	70%	70%	1-4 Family, Condo	Check with local lender	
Programs Offered	30- and 15-Year Fixed Rate				
Buydowns	Allowed. 2-1 and 1-1				
Eligible Properties	SFD, SFA, PUDs, Condos must meet FNMA Guidelines — Max 4 stories				
Secondary Financing	Maximum LTV for 1st Mortgage is 80% (i.e. 80-10-10 is i.e.) 2nd Mortgage Maturity must be at least 5 years; payments must cover minimum interest.				
Refinancing	Up to 95% LTV Over 90% cannot include Closing Costs or Prepaid Items. Existing 2nd Mortgages must be "seasoned" for 12 Months or payoff is considered "cash out" Amount of Cash Out is limited to 75% LTV				
Private Mortgage Insurance	Required for > 80% LTV. 35% Coverage for 95% LTV; 22% for 90%; 12% for 85%				
Assumability	No — Conventional Loans all have a due-on-transfer clause				
	Income Restrictions				
Qualifying Ratios	90.01 — 95.00% LTV — 28/36 < 90% — 33/38 Buydowns Qualify at Start Rate				
Documentation Types	Full, Alternative and Reduced Documentation				
	Reduced Documentation LTVs				
	LTV	CLTV	Property Type	Maximum Loan	Maximum Financing
	70% 65% 60%	90% 90% 90%	1 Family, Condo 1 Family, Condo 1 Family, Condo	Check with local lender	
Non-Occupant Co-Borrowers	Max LTV for using non-occupant co-borrower's income for qualifying is 90% LTV. Occupant Borrower must still have 38/45 Ratios and have 5% of own funds invested.				
Self-Employment	Minimum 2 Years — Self-Employed/Commissioned				
Trailing Spouse	Not Allowed				
	Asset Restrictions				
Seller Contributions	95% LTV — 3% 90% LTV — 6%		Investor — 2%		
Cash Reserves	95% LTV — 3 Months PITI 90% or Less — 2 Months				
Borrowed Funds	Must be secured. Secured loans must be counted in ratios.				
Gifts	80.01 — 95% LTV borrower must have 5% of own funds invested into transaction. < 80% LTV — No Limit. Source, transfer and receipt must be documented. Donor must be "family" member.				
	Credit/Borrower Restrictions				
Credit Scores	680 Minimum				
Multiple Properties	Borrower may have no more than 4 properties financed.				
Non-Resident Aliens	Not Allowed				
Derogatory Credit	0 × 30 last 24 Months on Mortgage. NO Bankruptcies, Foreclosures, or Major Derogatory Credit Allowed.				

FIGURE 5.2 *FNMA and FHLMC Loan Underwriting Guidelines for Conforming Loans*

Investor	**FNMA/FHLMC**				**Conforming**		
LTV Matrix							
LTV/Occupancy	Owner Occupied		2nd Home	Investor	Property Type	Loan Amount	(AK, HI)
Transaction	LTV	CLTV	LTV	CLTV			
Purchase or Rate and Term Refinance	95%	90%	90%	70%	Single Family, Condo	$333,700	$500,550
	90%	90%	N/A	70%	2 Unit	$427,150	$640,725
	80%	80%	N/A	70%	3 Unit	$516,300	$774,450
	80%	80%	N/A	70%	4 Unit	$641,650	$962,475
Cash-Out	75%	75%	70%	65%	Single Family, Condo	$250,275	$375,412
Refinancing	Streamline or Limited Qualifying to 95% LTV if current loan is FNMA Serviced – Over 90% cannot include Closing Costs or Prepaid Items. Existing 2nd Mortgages must be "seasoned" for 12 Months or payoff is considered "cash out"						
Eligible Properties	Single Family Detached (SFD), Single Family Attached (SFA), 2-4 Unit Residential, Planned Unit Developments (PUDs), Condominium – New PUDs, all condos have eligibility criteria – See Property Types for Eligibility						
Multiple Properties	Owner Occupied No Limit Investment/2nd – no more than 4 finance						
Mortgage Insurance	Conventional Loans all have a due on transfer clause – this precludes assumption						
Programs Offered	95%	All Occupancy Types			30, 20, 15, 10 Year Fixed		
	95%	Owner/2nd Only			7 & 5 Yr 2 Step, 2-1 Buydown, Interest Only, 3/1, 6/2, 7/1 ARM		
	90%	Owner/2nd Only			1 Year ARM, 7/23 & 5/25, 3-2-1 Buydown		
Documentation Types	Full/Alternative – Income Verification may be waived by DU/LP						
Income/Borrower Restrictions							
Qualifying Ratios	95% LTV – 28/36 or DU/LP 75% LTV – 33/38 or DU/LP				ARMs Qualify at 2nd Year Rate Buydowns Qualify at Start Rate		
Employment History	Minimum 2 Years History, 2 Years in same business for Self-Employed						
Trailing Spouse	Corporate Sponsored Relocation Only. 80% LTV Max, 6 Months Reserves, 25-50% of Spouses Income may be used if it can be documented that former employment is available in new location.						
Non-Resident Aliens	No Restrictions – must have 24 month work, asset and credit history.						
Non-Occupant Co-Borrowers	Max LTV for using non-occupant co-borrower's income for qualifying is 90% LTV. Occupant Borrower must still have 38/45 Ratios and have 5% of own funds invested.						
Asset Restrictions							
Seller Contributions	95% LTV – 3% 90% LTV – 6% 75% LTV – 8%				Investor – 2%		
Cash Reserves	95% LTV – 3 Months PITI 90% or Less – 2 Months				2 Months – May be Waived Under Affordable Gold, Community Homebuyer		
Gift Letters	80.01 – 95% LTV borrower must have 5% of own funds invested into transaction. < 80% LTV – No Limit. Source, transfer and receipt must be documented. Donor must be "family" member.						
Secondary Financing	Maximum LTV for 1st Mortgage is 75% (i.e. 75-15-10 is o.k.) 2nd Mortgage Maturity must be at least 5 years; payments must cover minimum interest. 2nd may not be ARM if 1st is ARM. 1st Mortgage may not be a balloon.						
Borrowed Funds	Must be secured/counted for qualifying						
Credit Restrictions							
Credit Scores	Bureau Scores are applied. With two scores take the average, with three scores take the middle. Scoring regimen is not absolute but follows the following guideline.				Eligible for Enhanced Criteria Cautious Not Eligible for Max Financing	Over 700 660 – 620 below 620	
Mortgage History	0 × 30 days late for last 12 Months						
Major Derogatory Credit	Must have 2 years RE-ESTABLISHED history. Time Elapsed since resolution Bankruptcy – Chapter 7 – 4 Years; Chapter 13 – 2 Years; Foreclosure 4 years.						

AFFORDABLE HOUSING PROGRAMS

Q. With all the focus on the lack of home affordability, are there any loan programs geared to help lower-income borrowers purchase a home?

Yes. In fact, financial institutions have jumped on the bandwagon to serve lower-income borrowers, not wanting to appear discriminatory against them (read, "penalized"). These efforts have created a proliferation of first time homebuyer/affordable housing programs offered by the secondary market and private institutions. The following general categories of programs offer relaxed guidelines, making it more feasible for borrowers to qualify.

FNMA Community Homebuyers Programs

Down Payment Options and Program Enhancements:
- 3/2 option allows 3 percent down payment and 2 percent gift, grant or loan from a nonprofit institution. Limited to households whose income falls within 100 percent of median family income for the Standard Metropolitan Statistical Area (SMSA) where the property is located
- 5 percent down payment with family income within 115 percent of median income in SMSA
- 97 percent loan-to-value with 3 percent down payment
- 100 percent loan-to-value with 0 percent down payment
- Reserves may be waived
- 33/38 qualifying ratios

FHLMC

Down Payment Options and Program Enhancements:
Same as FNMA Community Homebuyer except
- 40/40 qualifying ratios
- 97 percent LTV with lower PMI coverage
- 100 percent LTV with lower PMI coverage

Community Lending Guidelines

Under federal deposit insurance guidelines, certain savings banks can make "community" loans on mortgages if the loan has no teaser/discounted rate:

- 95/5/0 (zero down payment) transactions with 5 percent coming from either unsecured or borrowed funds
- 5 percent down payment with 5 percent seller contribution
- Other limited down payment options

A qualifying sheet for conventional loans to help assist in calculating loan payments is shown in figure 5.3.

Adjustable-rate mortgage qualifying ratios are shown in chapter 7.

Guidelines for Condominiums and Town House Purchases

Q. What about loans for condominiums and town houses? Are they underwritten the same way as is detached housing?

Lenders will generally lend up to 95 percent loan-to-value ratio for fixed-rate loans on owner-occupied condominiums and town houses. As with single-family detached dwellings, qualifying for an adjustable-rate mortgage will be based on the loan's second-year rate.

There are no specified minimum square-footage restrictions in the secondary market because lending is based solely on the unit's marketability. The development project must be FNMA- or FHLMC-accepted or have lender warranties. In addition, the project cannot have heavier investor concentration (nonowner-occupied units) than a certain percentage of the total—usually approximately 40 percent for established projects and 30 percent for new developments.

What Counts as Long-Term Debt?

Q. The secondary market considers long-term debt as any debt that can't be paid off in 10 months. Could the lender choose to be more restrictive?

Yes, if the lender found the borrower marginally qualified or determined that payments were a substantial percentage of the borrower's gross income and could affect the repayment of the loan. An example would be a marginally qualified buyer, making a small down payment, who has a $450 car payment with five payments remaining.

The lender could also choose to be more restrictive if defaults in the area are high. A cautious lender could allocate a minimum payment of 5 percent of the outstanding balance for the purpose of calculating long-term debt. Payments of short-term obligations or others that don't have set monthly payments could be allocated at least the interest due monthly.

FIGURE 5.3 *Conventional Loan Qualification Form*

Sales Price   (1) _____

   Less Loan Amount(2) _____ Equals Required Down Payment $ _____

Estimated Closing Costs Plus Estimated Prepaid Escrow   + _____

   Total Closing Cost $ _____

Less Cash on Deposit   − _____
Required Cash to Close $ _____
_____

   (2) _____ Divided by (1) _____ Equals LTV _____ %

Gross Income (Mortgagor) _____ and (Comortgagor) _____ = $ _____ (A)
Proposed Housing Expense

    Principal and Interest $ _____

    Other Financing   _____

    Hazard Insurance   _____

    Taxes   _____

    Mortgage Insurance   _____

    Homeowners Association Fees   _____

    Other: _____   _____

Total Housing Payment   _____ (B)

Total Obligations (Beyond Ten Months)   _____ (C)

Total Housing Payment (B) Plus Monthly Obligations (C)   _____ (D)

   (B) _____ Divided by (A) _____ = _____ %   Housing Ratio

   (D) _____ Divided by (A) _____ = _____ %   Total Debt Ratio

Contributions Help the Buyer Qualify

Q. What contributions does the secondary market allow the seller to make?

A contribution, also called a *financing concession,* is the payment of a cost that is typically paid by the buyer but instead is paid by the seller or a third party.

Such items can include transfer taxes, cost of title insurance policies and surveys, recording fees, tax stamps, attorneys' fees, and any seller-paid buydown or seller-paid financing costs.

Seller contributions that can be made over and above the following limits are those that occurred when market interest rates shifted and the seller used points to buy down the interest rate. Lender-paid buydowns and lender-funded transaction costs do not have to be counted against what the seller can contribute to the buyer.

If contributions exceed the following limits, any excess will be subtracted from the sales price before the loan amount is calculated:

Occupancy	LTV/TLTV	Maximum Financing Concessions Based on Value
Primary residence and second home	75% or less	9%
	Greater than 75% up to and including 90%	6%
	Greater than 90%	3%
Investment property	All	2%

Because the Government National Mortgage Association (GNMA, or Ginnie Mae) deals with government-insured and guaranteed loans, these underwriting guidelines are covered in chapters 8 and 9.

Guidelines for the Property

Q. What are the standard property guidelines for the secondary market?

Although properties are approved on a case-by-case basis, properties must generally meet the following guidelines:

- The property should be in an area with properties of comparable value and quality.

- Streets must be dedicated and properly maintained.
- Land value cannot be excessive compared to the improvements on the property.

An estimate of value from an appraiser is used to substantiate all loans sold to the secondary market.

USING COMPENSATING FACTORS WHEN RATIOS DON'T FIT

Q. If a borrower's ratios exceed the standard guidelines, could he or she ever qualify for a loan?

Possibly. While secondary market qualifying guidelines set the standard for granting loans called *benchmark ratios,* that is 28/36, there can be exceptions to the rules. Examples might include a borrower with a history of handling a higher-than-average rent payment—especially if other long-term debt is relatively low—or a borrower who consistently saves a high percentage of his or her annual income. These are what the secondary market terms *compensating factors* and include borrowers who

- have a strong credit score (for example, a 720 or higher FICO score).
- make a large down payment.
- purchase a property that qualifies as energy-efficient. This can result in the lender approving larger housing and long-term-debt ratios.
- demonstrate the ability to devote a greater portion of their incomes to housing expenses (especially if they've paid rent equal to or exceeding the payment they want to qualify for).
- show a consistent pattern of saving, maintain a good credit history, or have a debt-free position.
- demonstrate a potential for increased earnings because of education or job training.
- have short-term income (Social Security income, child support, etc.) that traditionally is not counted in qualifying because it would not continue three years or more beyond the date of the mortgage application.
- purchase a home because of corporate relocation of the primary wage earner, and the secondary wage earner (with a previous work history) is expected to find employment (called a trailing spouse).
- have substantial net worth.

- receive rent from related persons living in the house.
- have financial reserves that can be used to carry the mortgage debt, part of which must be in the form of liquid assets equal to at least two months of PITI payments.
- demonstrate that they are able to carry a substantial housing payment, the new housing expenses don't exceed their old expenses, and they have a good prior mortgage payment record and acceptable credit.
- have a total long-term-debt ratio of 30 percent or less, excellent payment histories on prior mortgages or rent, and acceptable credit.

Having one or more of these compensating factors can serve as strong leverage for the borrower who needs a little extra oomph when qualifying for a loan. If the loan is being processed using an automated underwriting system (AUS), these considerations will be factored into the process.

LITTLE-KNOWN FACTS ABOUT UNDERWRITING

Q. Are there ever any differentiations between what local lenders allow and what the secondary market will accept?

There certainly are. In fact, if the borrower knows what to ask for, some of the following little-known facts can be used to help put loans together:

- The secondary market will allow the seller to take the borrower's existing property or an asset other than real estate in trade as part of the down payment on the property, as long as the borrower has made a 5 percent cash down payment on the new loan.
- The seller can give the purchaser credit toward the down payment for a portion of previous rent payments made under a rental purchase agreement. The minimum original term of the rental must be 12 months, and only those rents that exceeded the market rent, as determined by an appraiser, can be counted. For example, if the market rent is $800, but the purchaser actually paid $900, the monthly credit toward purchase would be $100.
- A borrower can pool his or her funds with funds received as a

gift from a relative who lives with him or her to come up with the minimum 5 percent cash down payment. But the giver of the funds does not have to qualify, nor does he or she take title. Both parties must reside in the new residence. In addition to these funds, the borrower could receive an additional down payment gift from a relative or a gift or grant from a church, municipality, or nonprofit organization.

- When the loan-to-value ratio for a mortgage is 80 percent or less, the full down payment may come from a gift from a relative or a gift or grant from a church, municipality, or nonprofit organization. This means that one of these parties would make the entire 20 percent down payment and the borrower would not have to make any other down payment from his or her own funds.

Q. How can a prospective borrower take advantage of all these great underwriting exceptions and little-known facts?

If a lender doesn't qualify the borrower, or claims that borrower resources are marginal for the loan size, the borrower could use this information to negotiate additional purchasing leverage. It can't hurt! You can find in-depth information about conventional loan programs and underwriting at both www.fanniemae.com and www. freddiemac.com, or subscribe to an online service at www.allregs.com.

Q. Does the secondary market limit making loans based on the amount of properties held by an owner?

Yes, with clarification. The secondary market will allow a borrower to have any number of properties with financing on them as long as the property currently being purchased will be a principal residence.

The borrower can have no more than four properties currently financed if the new property being purchased is a second home or an investment property.

These guidelines apply to all properties held by the borrower, not just those purchased by the secondary market, but do not apply to properties that are free and clear with no outstanding financing.

BORROWERS WITH BANKRUPTCY OR FORECLOSURE HISTORIES

Q. Can someone who has previously declared bankruptcy apply for a loan to be sold to the secondary market?

A bankruptcy must have been fully discharged for a minimum of four years and the borrower must have reestablished good credit. In rare situations, this time frame might be trimmed to two years if it's proven that the bankruptcy was caused by extenuating circumstances (extensive hospital bills, etc).

Q. Can borrowers who have had previous foreclosures get conventional loans?

The secondary market usually won't purchase loans of borrowers who have had mortgage foreclosures within the past four years. As with all other types of adverse credit, the lender will require a thorough explanation.

TYPES OF QUALIFYING INCOME AND VERIFICATION

Q. What kind of income will conventional lenders accept and how is it verified?

In general, the lender wants to determine the probability and stability of the borrower's income sources. This means verifying two years of history for all income, full-time or part-time. Self-employed applicants need two years in the same business to qualify.

If a borrower is employed by a relative or family-owned business, federal income tax returns must be provided to the lender.

Following is a checklist of additional income sources that might be considered:

- Part-time income can be counted, provided it has been uninterrupted for the past two years and is anticipated to continue; seasonal work is acceptable and the borrower requires reasonable assurance that he or she will be hired back for the next season.
- Overtime and bonus income that has occurred for the past two years and that will probably continue can be counted. (If the employer doesn't say that the overtime will end, it can be considered to

continue.) The lender will average the past two years of such income; if this income is more than 25 percent of the borrower's total income, income tax returns must be provided.

- Raises guaranteed to occur within 60 days of the loan closing may be included for the purpose of qualifying.

Other income sources could include:

- Retirement income
- Military income
- Veteran's benefits
- Social Security income
- Alimony
- Child support
- Notes receivable
- Interest and dividend income
- Employer-subsidized mortgage payments
- Trust income
- Unemployment benefits
- Rental income
- Automobile allowances and expense account payments

USING GIFTED FUNDS AS LEVERAGE

Q. It's great that a borrower can use down payment funds given by a relative or institution, but what kind of documentation has to be shown to the lender?

A gift from a relative must be evidenced by a letter signed by the donor. It must specify the dollar amount of the gift and the date the funds were transferred; list the donor's name, address, telephone number, and relationship to the borrower; and include the donor's signed statement that no repayment is expected.

The lender must verify that the funds are in the donor's account or have been transferred to the borrower's account. This could mean obtaining a copy of the donor's withdrawal slip and the borrower's deposit slip, or a copy of the donor's canceled check.

If funds haven't been transferred prior to settlement, the donor can give the closing agent a certified check for the amount of the gift. Because funds borrowed by a donor as a gift to a buyer might later put a strain on the buyer to repay the amount, some lenders will want to check the donor's account history to determine the original source of the gift (for example, to ensure that the donor has been accumulating it in a savings account). The donor should be advised that this investigation could occur so that he or she won't be personally offended if it does.

If a gift or grant comes from a church, municipality, or nonprofit organization, it must be evidenced by a copy of an award, gift letter, or the legal agreement that specifies the grant or gift's terms and conditions. In addition, the lender must include a copy of the documents showing the transfer of the funds.

CITIZENSHIP IS NOT A REQUIREMENT

Q. Does a borrower have to be a U.S. citizen to qualify for a loan to be sold to the secondary market?

No, mortgages can be made to resident aliens. A lawful, permanent U.S. resident can qualify under the same terms and conditions as a U.S. citizen. He or she must prove residency with a Certificate of Resident Alien Status or green card.

Mortgages can be made to nonpermanent resident aliens as well, as long as the borrower occupies the property as a primary residence and a 24-month history of work and credit history plus assets can be shown.

REFINANCING WITH CONVENTIONAL LOANS

Q. What kinds of refinancing guidelines does the secondary market use?

Guidelines for Changing Loan Interest Rate or Term

- Loan-to-value ratio on owner-occupied properties can't exceed 95 percent.
- When subordinate financing (a second mortgage) is less than one year old, FNMA will not allow it to be paid off from the proceeds of a "no cashout" refinance.
- A junior lien (second mortgage) obtained through FHLMC must have had at least one year of payments from the origination date of the mortgage to be refinanced. If not, it is considered a cashout and all applicable guidelines apply.

- Loan-to-value ratios on investment property cannot exceed 75 percent.

Guidelines for Pulling Equity (Cash) Out

- On owner-occupied refinancing, the maximum loan-to-value ratio cannot exceed 90 percent.
- On second-home refinancing, the maximum loan-to-value ratio cannot exceed 90 percent.
- On investor property refinancing, the maximum loan-to-value ratio cannot exceed 70 percent.

CLOSING COSTS

Q. Does the secondary market require the borrower to pay certain closing costs?

The secondary market requires that the borrower pay the following prepaid settlement costs:

- Interest charges and real estate taxes for any period after the settlement date
- Hazard insurance premiums
- Impounds for PMI, unless it is financed as part of the mortgage amount

Other costs may be paid by the buyer or seller, based on what they've negotiated. As discussed previously, however, costs paid for the buyer by the seller would be considered contribution amounts and maximum limits would apply before being subtracted from the appraised value of the property, prior to calculating the maximum loan available.

Exceptions to contributions are third parties who are not participants in the sale, including the buyer's relatives or an employer. There are no restrictions on the amounts they can pay, but the funds might need to be tracked as gifted monies. The borrower should check with the lender regarding specific examples of nonparticipant funds that could be used. For examples of buyer and seller cost estimate sheets, see figures 5.4 and 5.5 on the next two pages.

FIGURE 5.4 *Buyer Cost Estimate Sheet*

Buyer _____

Property Address _____

Sale Price .... $ _____
First Mortgage Balance to Be Assumed .... $ _____
Second Mortgage or Contract to Be Assumed .... $ _____
Contract .... $ _____
Down Payment .... $ _____

Estimated Loan Costs
Service Charge/Origination Fee .... $ _____
Assumption Fee .... $ _____
Credit Report .... $ _____
Appraisal Fee .... $ _____
Recording Fees .... $ _____
ATA Policy (Title Insurance) .... $ _____
Escrow Fee .... $ _____
Escrow Preparation Fee .... $ _____
Interest Proration .... $ _____
Tax Preparation Fee .... $ _____
Fire Insurance .... $ _____
Home Inspection Fee .... $ _____
Discount Points (if applicable) .... $ _____
Initial Mortgage Insurance Premium* .... $ _____
Total Estimated Closing Costs .... $ _____

Reserves and Prorates
Property Taxes .... $ _____
Fire Insurance .... $ _____
Mortgage Insurance† .... $ _____
Total Reserves and Prorates .... $ _____
Total Estimated Cash Outlay .... $ _____

Type of Loan _____ for _____ years
Rate of Interest _____ % (Approximately)
Principal, Interest .... $ _____
Taxes Reserves .... $ _____
Insurance Reserves .... $ _____
Total Monthly Payment .... $ _____

The undersigned purchaser hereby acknowledges receipt of a copy of this estimate and it is hereby understood that it is an estimate only.

Buyer _____

Buyer _____   Date _____

*VA loans do not incur this cost. For FHA loans, use FHA one-time premium (if not financed).
†FHA and VA loans do not incur this cost.

FIGURE 5.5 *Seller Cost Estimate Sheet*

Prepared for _____ Address _____

Prepared by _____ Estimated Closing Date _____

Selling Price .... $ _____

Approximate Indebtedness
    First Loan ....@ _____ % $ _____
    Second Loan ....@ _____ % $ _____
    Other ....@ _____ % $ _____

Gross Equity... $ _____

Seller's Estimated Costs
    Brokerage Fee ....$ _____
    Title Insurance Policy (Sales Price)...................$ _____
    Long-Term Escrow Set-Up Fee ....$ _____
    Escrow Closing Fee...$ _____
    Mortgage Discount ....$ _____
    Contract Preparation ....$ _____
    Attorneys' Fees...$ _____
    Appraisal Fee ....$ _____
    Interest to Closing ....$ _____
    Property Tax Proration ....$ _____
    Payoff Penalty...$ _____
    Recording Fees...$ _____
    Reconveyance Fee ....$ _____
    Required Repairs ....$ _____
    City Inspection..$ _____
    Local Improvement Districts (LIDs) Assessment.............$ _____
    Misc...$ _____
    _____ ....$ _____

If Income Property
    Prorated Rents..$ _____
    Security or Cleaning Deposits.............................$ _____

Less Total Estimated Costs .... $ _____

Subtotal .... $ _____

Estimated Credits
    Reserve Account...$ _____
    _____ ....$ _____

Plus Total Credits .... $ _____
Estimated Seller's Proceeds .... $ _____
Less Loan Carried by Seller... $ _____
Estimated Net Cash Proceeds .... $ _____

Seller _____ Date _____

THE IMPACT OF THE MORTGAGE MELTDOWN ON TODAY'S BORROWERS

Q. After the fall from grace in the mortgage market, what can borrowers expect with conventional loans?

The conventional mortgage market has changed considerably in the past year. In fact, someone who obtained a mortgage in the years preceding the melt down, might find it tough to qualify today for the same loan. Many exotic mortgages have disappeared while others remaining have been trimmed or guidelines drastically changed. In general, the market is getting back to basics after an environment when almost anyone who could fog a mirror could obtain a mortgage. The conventional market is reinventing itself so as not to repeat the disaster of the past several years. With foreclosures escalating and the national credit markets in a tailspin, conventional lenders (under guidelines from Fannie Mae and Freddie Mac and their oversight agent, the OFHEO) want to stabilize lending and safeguard it moving forward. To this end, conventional lenders have changed some practices and employed new closing fees that, unfortunately, will be borne by borrowers.

Adverse Market Delivery Charge

Q. What are these new fees called and how much would they cost, say on a $200,000 purchase?

There are three of them, so we'll cover each separately.

The first new conventional mortgage charge is an adverse market delivery charge. Its objective is to sweeten the pot for lenders/investors due to trepidation in the lending market. The cost per mortgage originated is .25 percent of the amount financed. Fortunately, the borrower can decide whether to pay the cost at closing or add it onto the loan. On a $200,000 purchase using an 80 percent loan-to-value ratio loan, the cost would be $400.

Loan-Level Price Adjustments (LLPA) Expanded

Up to this point in time, this second fee, loan-level price adjustment (LLPA), has been used in the secondary market primarily for high-leverage loans including those with 40-year terms. But due to the precarious market, Fannie Mae and Freddie Mac are passing it on to a much wider base of mortgage borrowers. LLPA is a fee designed to reduce lender/investor risk based on a combination of the borrower's loan-to-value ratio on the mortgage, credit score, and any secondary financing involved, multiple-unit properties, or other risk factor including the payment of interest-only. In other words, the borrower will pay an adjustment fee based on the type and amount of risk the borrower may pose to the lender/investor. Lenders have long been cautious of hefty levels of risk-layering in mortgages. For example, a borrower with a marginal credit score (one risk) purchases a home using an interest-only mortgage (a second risk) and makes only the minimum down payment on that product (third risk). With loan-level price adjustment fees, the lender will be paid additionally by the borrower for the risk.

We'll use the $200,000 purchase price in an example. Let's say that you want to obtain an 85 percent loan-to-value ratio loan and your credit score is 670. Using the secondary market guidelines, for a loan-to-value ratio loan between 81 percent and 85 percent, and a borrower with a credit score between 661 and 679, you would pay 1.25 percent of the mortgage amount for this new post-delivery fee. That's $2,000 on a $160,000 loan. A weaker credit score of less than 620 on the same loan-to-value ratio loan could more than double that amount to $4,400. While the secondary market is using this new risk-reduction approach to make mortgages more investor-friendly and marketable, it's hoped that chunking-up fees won't financially overleverage some borrowers.

Higher Down Payments Apply in Declining Markets

The third cost change impacts you if you purchase a home in an area where the economy has negative economic growth factors, termed a *declining market* (as detailed by Metropolitan Statistical Area/MSA reports, www.ofheo.gov). Such a purchase will require you to make an additional 5 percent down payment at closing. This is due to the fact that widespread house price depreciation is likely to continue for the near future with more than 200 Metropolitan Statistical Areas declining, including the District of Columbia. In order to avoid upside-down investments moving forward, the secondary market will require the 5 percent padding as a hedge on any loan-to-value ratio loan greater than 80 percent. For example, if you qualify for a 90 percent loan on a $200,000 purchase price /appraised value, you'll be required to make a 15 percent down payment instead of the typical 10 percent. On $200,000, that's an extra $10,000.

The best advice for borrowers today is to carefully choose a lender who can explain every aspect, nuance, and cost of the mortgages being considered based on your objectives for buying the property and time frames for keeping it. Without that help, you might be paying for costs that make no sense for what you're trying to achieve.

Secondary Market Assists Lenders with Workout Assistance

Q. Is the secondary market doing anything to help lenders facilitate workouts for borrowers who are behind on their payments?

Yes, among other ventures mentioned previously in this book, Fannie Mae has designed a new option, HomeSaver Advance™ for lenders to use with delinquent borrowers. Loan servicers can offer a borrower the ability to cure the payment default on the mortgage by agreeing to an unsecured, personal loan. The rationale is that since many delinquencies are caused by short-term hardships, this is one way for the consumer to cure the default and prevent foreclosure.

Q. Besides 10-year, 15-year, 20-year, 30-year, and 40-year amortization schedules, what other types of conventional loan programs will the secondary market accept?

Besides the dozens of types of ARMs that the secondary market will purchase, some of which are discussed in chapter 7, lenders can originate myriad programs.

Programs vary from somewhat common construction-permanent financing to infrequently used leasehold estate loans, and everything in between. There are loans for cooperative housing, energy improvement, rehabilitation of properties, and manufactured housing.

Biweekly, growing equity, and balloon mortgage programs offer borrowers differing degrees of leverage to help them purchase; these concepts will be discussed in-depth in chapter 10.

Both FNMA and FHLMC in the secondary market offer a variety of home affordability programs. The following is an overview of some of the loan programs available.

AFFORDABLE HOUSING PROGRAMS

Affordable housing programs were created by the federal government's Community Redevelopment Act to provide affordable housing to a larger sector of Americans.

As mentioned previously, qualifying ratios are easier, cash reserves to close are less, and compensating factors can be used (such as a history of paying high rent). In addition, Mortgage Credit Certificate tax credits may be used with some programs to whittle down the PITI and allow buyers to qualify for more home.

Depending on the affordable housing program, buyers receive education on aspects of home affordability, including energy efficiency and home maintenance. Most programs cap the price of the home as well as set the maximum income allowable to qualify.

Community Homebuyer Programs

These loans were the pioneers of the affordable housing movement. Designed to assist low-income and moderate-income first-time homebuyers, 100 percent mortgages, interest-only products and other flexible underwriting guidelines are hallmarks. Check out Fannie Mae's "My Community Mortgage" product at www.efanniemae.com, and Freddie Mac's "Home Possible" products at www.freddiemac.com. No cash reserves are necessary, and homebuyer education is required (but can be waived under certain circumstances).

MORE FIRST-TIME BUYER LOANS

97 percent mortgages

Geared to first-time buyers who can financially handle the monthly payment but haven't accumulated the down payment, these programs allow the buyers to borrow the down payment—even on a credit card!

100 percent loans. The "100" means 100 percent financing with no down payment required, only a 3 percent contribution to closing costs! In fact, the seller can even contribute to help cover the closing costs.

Interest-only mortgages. An interest-only program helps a borrower qualify for a larger loan amount—for the first 15 years of the loan. At year 16 it becomes fully amortized until the end of the 30-year term. The borrower can prepay any amount without penalty at any time and immediately reduce future monthly payments during the interest-only period.

OTHER CONVENTIONAL-MORTGAGE PROGRAMS

Pledged-Asset Mortgage

These programs allow homebuyers to borrow up to 100 percent of the sales price (or appraised value, if less) of a home when they pledge a stable financial asset (typically certificates of deposit). Assets can come from the borrower or a family member and can range from a minimum 10 percent pledge from the borrower to a maximum 30 percent pledge from a family member. The borrower is required to make a down payment of between 3 and 5 percent (depending on the loan program chosen).

Balloon Mortgages

Balloons are short-term mortgages with some features of a fixed-rate mortgage. First, they provide level monthly payments that amortize over a stated period of time (e.g., 30 years), but provide for a balloon payment that is due at the end of an earlier specified term (e.g., 5, 7, 10, or 15 years). Depending on the program chosen, at the end of the balloon term (e.g., 5 years), the borrower can convert the loan into a fully amortized market-rate loan (e.g., for 25 years) in either fixed-rate or adjustable-rate formats.

Construction-permanent mortgage. This loan can be used to lock in fixed interest rates on both the construction and the permanent mortgage financing. A borrower can save because he or she has just one set of closing costs (not normally the case with many construction loans). Fixed rates as well as fixed-period adjustables of three, five, or seven years are available.

Renovation mortgage. This product serves a dual purpose. A borrower can use it to purchase a home and repair or improve it simultaneously with just one loan—with a first-mortgage interest rate that's lower than typical home equity or second-mortgage rates. Maximum loans of up to 95 percent of the "as completed" value are available.

Online Programs

The wide array of mortgages, including qualifying guidelines, can be found online at www.efanniemae.com and www.freddiemac.com.

6

PRIVATE MORTGAGE INSURANCE ON CONVENTIONAL LOANS

Lender guidelines and the rules of the secondary market restrict the ability of lenders to make high loan-to-value mortgages without some guarantee against borrower default. Private mortgage insurance (PMI) allows lenders to increase their loan-to-value ratios and still sell their mortgages in the secondary market. If the PMI company approves the loan, it will issue a commitment to insure the lender. With this guarantee, the lender can increase the loan amount and the borrower receives the benefit of a smaller down payment.

The biggest challenge for most first-time homebuyers is raising the money for the down payment. Private mortgage insurance is therefore one key to affordable housing, making the dream of home ownership possible for many.

This chapter explains the cost of PMI and how it impacts the mortgage. The focus is on how PMI companies work with lenders of conventional loans. (The Federal Housing Administration has its own insurance program, which is covered in chapter 8. VA loans, described in chapter 9, are guaranteed.)

THE BASICS OF PRIVATE
MORTGAGE INSURANCE

Q. Is there any way a lender would make a loan to a buyer who might be considered a marginal risk?

The lender might require that the buyer purchase PMI to indemnify the lender for any loss caused by default during the early years of the loan. Typically, any loan-to-value ratio greater than 80 percent (particularly if the loan is to be sold in the secondary market) will require the purchaser to include PMI as a requirement of securing the loan. Private mortgage insurance originated in the 1950s with the first large carrier, Mortgage Guaranty Insurance Corporation (MGIC), referred to as *magic*. For this reason, early PMI methods were deemed to "magically" assist in getting lender approval on an otherwise unacceptable loan package. Today, however, there are eight PMI insurance underwriting companies in the United States. (See figure 6.1 for contact information.)

Q. How does PMI work?

PMI companies write insurance protecting approximately the top 20 percent of the mortgage against default, depending on the lender's and investor's requirements, the loan-to-value ratio, and the particular loan program involved. (For a claim illustration, see figure 6.2.) Should a default occur, the lender sells the property to liquidate the debt and is reimbursed by the PMI company for any remaining amount up to the policy value.

FIGURE 6.1 *Private Mortgage Insurance Companies*

Genworth Mortgage Insurance
  Corporation
P.O. Box 177800
Raleigh, NC 27615
800-444-5664
Fax: 919-846-4260

Mortgage Guaranty Insurance
  Corporation
250 E. Kilbourn Avenue
MGIC Plaza
Milwaukee, WI 53201
800-558-9900
Fax: 1-888-601-4440
www.mgic.com

PMI Mortgage Insurance Company
3003 Oak Road
Walnut Creek, CA 94597
800-288-1970
Fax: 415-291-6175
www.pmi-us.com

Republic Mortgage Insurance Company
P.O. Box 2514
Winston-Salem, NC 27102-9954
800-999-7642
Fax: 919-661-0049
www.rmic.com

Triad Guaranty Insurance Corporation
P.O. Box 25623
Winston-Salem, NC 27114
800-451-4872
Fax: 919-723-0343
www.tgic.com

AIG United Guaranty Corporation
P.O. Box 21567
Greensboro, NC 27420
800-334-8966
Fax: 919-230-1946
www.ugcorp.com

Q. What does PMI cost?

Costs vary from insurer to insurer, as well as from plan to plan. For example, a highly leveraged adjustable-rate mortgage would require the borrower to pay a higher premium to obtain coverage. Depending on their credit scores, buyers with a 5 percent down payment on a conventional fixed-rate loan can expect to pay a premium of approximately 0.63 percent of the annual loan amount ($105 monthly for a $200,000 purchase price). But the PMI premium would drop to around 0.40 percent of the annual loan amount (or $67 monthly) if a 10 percent down payment was made on the loan.

Q. How is private mortgage insurance paid?

PMI fees can be paid in several ways, depending on the PMI company used. Borrowers can choose to pay the first-year premium at the closing; then an annual renewal premium is collected monthly as part of the house payment. Or the borrower can choose to pay no premium at the closing, but add on a slightly higher premium monthly to the

FIGURE 6.2 *PMI Claim Illustration*

Original purchase price	$100,000
Original loan (10 percent down)	90,000
Principal balance due	88,915
Accumulated interest	
(excluding any penalty interest or late charges)	7,850
Subtotal	$ 96,765
Attorneys' fees	$ 2,420
Property taxes	1,140
Hazard insurance (premiums advanced)	710
Property maintenance (preservation expenses)	350
Disbursement and foreclosure cost	525
Subtotal	$101,910
Less escrow balances and rent received	240
Total claim	$100,670

Generally, after a lender has instituted foreclosure and acquired evidence of marketable title to the property, a claim can be submitted. On receiving the claim, the insurer will decide whether to pay the entire claim and take title to the property or pay the coverage amount stated in the policy. The insurer will typically take title only in those cases when acquisition and sale by the insurer is likely to reduce the insurer's loss. When the insurer does take title, the lender will receive the full amount of the claim.

On receiving this claim, the insurer will attempt to determine the likely resale price. The expenses resulting from a sale would include the real estate agent's commission and other settlement costs, which on average would run at about 10 to 15 percent of the sales price. The insurer obtains this and other information to decide what option to take. From the lender's perspective, if the policy was written with 25 percent coverage, the claim payment option made by the insurer would have been $25,168, which means the lender could sell the property for approximately $80,000 and not suffer loss.

principal, interest, tax, and insurance payment. Buyers who want to sidestep paying PMI at the closing but not increase their monthly house payment can finance a lump-sum PMI premium into their loan. With this type of payment plan, should the PMI be canceled before the loan term expires (through refinancing, paying off the loan, or removal by the loan servicer), the buyers may obtain a rebate of the premium.

Q. How does the buyer apply for PMI?

Although the buyer typically bears the cost of PMI, the lender is the PMI company's client and shops for the PMI on behalf of the borrower. Many lenders deal with only a few PMI companies because the lenders know the guidelines for those insurers as well as the financial stability of those companies. This can be a problem when one of the lender's prime companies turns down a loan because the borrower doesn't fit its risk parameters. An unenterprising lender might follow suit and deny approval on the loan application without consulting even a second PMI company. Pandemonium results: The buyer is upset, wondering what's wrong with him or her; the lender is apologetic while responding that the borrower didn't meet the underwriting guidelines.

From the lender's point of view, it desires the very best quality as well as an assurance that the PMI company will stand behind its loan guarantee commitment. And today, when tough times abound for many types of insurance companies, lenders are putting an even higher priority on the strength and credibility of the PMI companies with which they do business. In fact, hundreds of thousands of dollars in PMI claims could be uncollectible should a PMI company declare bankruptcy.

The lender has an increasingly difficult task to be fair to the borrower while shopping for the most effective method to soften liability. Sometimes, it may appear that a lender has no justification for doing what it does—but looking deeper, the justification is undoubtedly there.

Q. What can the buyer or agent do if PMI is denied by one insurer?

If PMI is denied by one insurer, consider the following possibilities:

- The borrower can ask the lender to submit the application to another (or several other) PMI insurers. A list of those licensed to do business in the borrower's state can be obtained from the lender or the state's insurance commission. Note, however, that the first question asked by the subsequent PMI company may be, "Has this party ever been denied insurance?" It's difficult to tell just how much impact the answer to this question has on consideration of the application. If the lender refuses to shop for another insurer, the borrower may not only be teaming up with the wrong PMI company, but the lender also may leave much to be desired.
- Although somewhat of a rarity today, the borrower can ask the lender to hold the loan in portfolio and not require PMI (primarily a strong requirement of the secondary market). The buyer might

entice the lender to keep the loan by transferring accounts held with other lenders or by increasing the note rate (a form of self-insurance for the lender).

- The borrower can explore ways to decrease the loan-to-value ratio so that PMI will not be required by the secondary market. Here is an example:

A gift letter donor could be located for the down payment, leaving the borrower's funds to be used as an additional amount down; or the borrower could team up with a relative or friend to create leverage as coborrowers. A lender might be willing to make the borrower a 10 percent second mortgage in tandem with an 80 percent first mortgage, using a 10 percent down payment from the buyer (called *piggyback financing*). The borrower benefits by not paying PMI. However, the second mortgage creates a second lien on the property with payments often at a higher interest rate than that on the first mortgage. And, of course, the borrower must financially qualify to repay both loans.

Additionally, the buyer might ask that a seller carry back part of the financing (structured much in the same way as piggyback financing). The lender will want to see a copy of the security document for the seller financing so that its impact can be considered in the loan underwriting of the first mortgage, especially regarding large monthly payments or balloon payments.

HIGH FORECLOSURES TIGHTEN PMI GUIDELINES

Q. Have mortgage default problems had a large impact on the private mortgage insurance industry?

Absolutely. Similar to other industry segments, PMI companies have suffered significant financial losses due to increased defaults and are revamping policies and guidelines to ward off future problems. Effective in the first quarter of 2008, two of the primary players have not only declined to insure mortgages of more than 97 percent loan-to-value, but have increased the amount of down payment required to insure investor properties among other changes. Continuing PMI industry research and loss mitigation will continue to design new guidelines for withstanding downturns in distressed markets. Private mortgage insurance has proven to be and will continue to be one of America's best long-term solutions to housing affordability.

COMPARING PMI TO A PIGGYBACK SECOND MORTGAGE

Q. How would financing the entire PMI premium into the loan differ from using a second mortgage in a piggyback situation with an 80 percent first mortgage, a 10 percent down payment, and a 10 percent second mortgage?

Let's crunch the numbers and find out: $200,000 purchase price; a down payment of 10 percent; first mortgage at 6.5 percent for 30 years; second mortgage at 8 percent for 15 years; financed PMI premium of 2.1 percent.

	80-10-10	Financed PMI
Mortgage insurance premium		2.1%
Loan amount, 1st mortgage	$160,000	$180,000
Loan amount, 2nd mortgage	$ 20,000	-0-
Financed premium	-0-	$ 3,780
Total loan amount	$180,000	$183,780
P & I, 1st mortgage	$ 1,011	$ 1,162
P & I, 2nd mortgage	$ 191	-0-
Monthly payment	$ 1,202	$ 1,162

Financing the premium would cost the borrower less than taking on a second mortgage. First, the monthly payment is $40 lower. Second, you aren't stuck with a second mortgage—that lasts 15 years! And last, but not least, once the private mortgage insurance is removed, the borrower will receive a rebate of the financed single premium of several thousand dollars (based on the date of the PMI removal). And, as you'll learn in the next answer, private mortgage insurance is tax deductible. Check out great articles and PMI calculators at www.privatemi.com (the PMI trade association), www.mgic.com, and www.pmi-us.com.

PMI IS TAX DEDUCTIBLE

Q. I heard that the tax deductibility of private mortgage insurance was in effect for 2007. Has that been extended?

Yes. A new law on that topic extended the tax deductibility of private mortgage insurance on federal income tax returns through 2010.

Borrowers with household incomes of $100,000 or less will be able to deduct the full cost of the mortgage insurance premiums paid during those tax years.

PMI APPROVAL GUIDELINES

Q. Does PMI insure only first mortgages on owner-occupied housing?

No. Some PMI insurers will take on second-mortgage risks as well as insure investor properties. Be prepared, however, to pay some heftier premiums.

Q. How could a buyer best be apprised of the PMI guidelines and regulations?

The borrower should ask the lender the following questions while applying for PMI insurance:

1. How many companies' programs will be shopped?
2. How does the selected policy compare overall to others in the marketplace, evaluating the following criteria:
   - Rates
   - Size of policy (particular loan-to-value ratio insured)
   - Documents from the lender outlining the procedure for requesting removal of PMI

Q. What can the borrower expect the PMI company to look for in approving him or her for PMI insurance?

PMI companies look at many of the same questions posed by the lender, plus the following questions. Giving the "wrong" answer to these has proven to increase the risk factors of default on the loan. Here are some red flag questions from PMI insurers:

- *Are payment increases scheduled in the loan, and if so, is it feasible that the borrower can meet them?*
- *Does the loan have a discounted "teaser" rate, such as on some ARMs?*
- *Are there any temporary buydowns that may mean increased interest and payments later on?*
- *Is the loan-to-value ratio high (for the type of loan used, as well as for the marketplace)?*

- *To what financial degree is the seller contributing?* (Most PMI companies allow up to 3 percent of the sales price for a loan with a loan-to-value ratio more than 90 percent, 6 percent when the loan-to-value ratio is less than 90 percent and under, and up to 3 percent on investor properties. Although the appraiser is expected to adjust for seller contributions, the amounts specified are the maximum amounts allowable by most PMI insurers.)
- *How much cash does the borrower have on hand?* (PMI companies are putting much more emphasis on reserves as a cushion against delinquent payments.)
- *Is the economy of the area sound?* Due to the mortgage meltdown of 2007, many PMI insurers have tightened underwriting guidelines in areas with high foreclosures.
- *Is there an oversupply of housing in the area?* (This might indicate declining market values.)
- *How stable is the borrower's employment?*
- *Is the borrower a professional or unskilled laborer?* (While this may appear to be a form of discrimination, blue-collar workers statistically have higher levels of loan defaults.)
- *Is the borrower using a gift letter to fund any part of the purchase?*

Q. What part does the property play in receiving PMI approval?

Cautious of the impact weak properties have in contributing to defaults, PMI companies continue to scrutinize properties. The following questions address some appraisal hot buttons:

- *How is the neighborhood rated?* (Unexplained or unacceptable appraisal explanations of fair and poor neighborhoods indicate factors that may weaken the borrower's commitment to the property. This may negatively affect the insurability of the loan.)
- *Who appraised the property?* (Most PMI companies reserve the right to declare appraisers and appraisals unacceptable.)
- *How does the property compare to others in the area?* (If a property is valued at 90 percent or more of the highest property value in the neighborhood, it is considered a high-risk property. It typically may have overimprovements and thus a longer marketing time in case of foreclosure.)
- *Is the property physically sound and in good repair?* (A low rating in this category may cause the property to be uninsurable.)
- *What are the comparable properties used in the appraisal, and where are they located?* (Typically, PMI companies will allow no more

than one of the three required comparables to be supplied by the lender or developer from its own files unless justified by the appraiser. In addition, except for rural locations, at least two of the three required comparables must be located within one mile of the appraised property, or the difference in location must be fully explained. This one-mile range normally encompasses the neighborhood of the property.)

- *Was there a sales concession?* (This might be personal property, such as a car or boat, that is included by the seller to consummate the transaction. The value of the item will be deducted from the sales price and appraised value by the PMI company if it has not been deducted by the appraiser.)

Q. So PMI has its own set of qualifying guidelines, one for the borrower and one for the property?

Yes. If the borrower or the property doesn't fit in one PMI company's guidelines, the lender should take a proactive position to, if possible, find one that accepts the risk.

While qualifying for PMI may seem to be an extra hoop for the borrower to jump through, the application and paperwork is handled entirely by the lender. And considering the number of borrowers who couldn't purchase at all because they lack a 20 percent down payment, the minimal effort and cost that PMI insurance adds doesn't seem like a very great price to pay.

REMOVING PMI FROM A MORTGAGE

Q. Can PMI ever be removed?

Potentially. For loans originated after July 29, 1999, federal law requires the lender to remove the PMI once the borrower has 22 percent equity and payments are current on the loan.

This law, enforced by the Department of Housing and Urban Development (HUD), also requires that lenders inform consumers of this at the time of the loan commitment and on an annual basis.

Consumers can petition the lender at any time to request that PMI be removed. On a case-by-case basis, most lenders require the borrower to provide the lender with a fee appraisal showing that the borrower has at least 20 percent equity in the property (through appreciation and/or principal reduction), that the payments have been made on time, and that the property's value has remained stable.

One word of caution: If you petition the lender/loan servicer to remove PMI using a fee appraisal as documentation, be sure the appraiser is approved by the lender. The lender has the right to accept (or not) the appraiser to evaluate the property. If the appraiser is not lender approved, the borrower could end up paying for another appraisal to meet the lender's guidelines.

The federal law governing PMI excludes loans originated as Community Homebuyer and other highly leveraged loans such as FHA loans where mortgage insurance is required to remain for the life of the loan. You can locate PMI cancellation calculators online at www.privatemi.com.

7

THE ADJUSTABLE-RATE MORTGAGE (ARM)

The adjustable-rate mortgage (ARM) products of the early 1980s gave ARMs an initial black eye in the financial marketplace. Many of these early loans were actually renegotiable rate mortgages (RRMs), meaning that on an anniversary date, the mortgagor would have to renegotiate with the mortgagee. This was no easy task due to rising inflation and skyrocketing interest rates. Many consumers couldn't qualify for the higher loan rates, sometimes forcing them to sell the property or face foreclosure.

But ARM products improved over the next two decades offering caps on mortgage adjustments, mandatory rate disclosures, and even the ability to convert the ARM to a fixed-rate mortgage in some programs. In other words, ARMs fulfilled the purpose for which they were designed: short-term financial leverage where the rewards helped offset the risks involved.

As of this writing, it appears we've come full circle. While ARMS are still a practical vehicle for short-term owners and those wishing to minimize monthly payments, a new breed of exotic mortgage products like interest-only ARMs and payment option ARMs make the renegotiating days of the 1980s look tame by comparison. But products are not really to blame. Any loan used for the wrong reasons to help consumers financially leverage into a mortgage they can't afford for the long run, wrapped in a detailed agreement they don't understand, could be viewed as "a bad mortgage." This chapter will outline when and why adjustable mortgages make sense, how much you could save by choosing one, and how to select the best loan to fit your individual needs.

PROS AND CONS OF ADJUSTABLE-RATE MORTGAGES

Q. What are the advantages of ARMs?

The advantages are:

- Lower interest rates than for fixed-rate mortgages allow the buyer to qualify more easily for the loan or leverage into a more expensive property than he or she could otherwise afford.
- Rates adjust based on increases and decreases in the particular index used, which is a gauge of inflation in the economy. (Indexes are discussed later in this chapter.) This creates an equitable situation for lender and borrower alike because the lender's costs are covered, while (hopefully) the borrower's wage increases cover the rise in payment amounts.
- A variety of indexes are available on which to base the ARM.
- The borrower can choose from various adjustment periods, such as six months, one year, three years, five years, seven years, or ten years.
- Some ARMs can be converted to fixed-rate mortgages during a specific time frame in the loan.
- Initial lower-than-market "teaser" rates may drastically reduce the borrower's monthly payment in the first year of the loan.
- Adjustable-rate mortgages are good to use in times of low inflation as well as for short-term ownership.
- Depending on the loan program selected, an ARM may be assumable.

Q. What are the disadvantages of ARMs?

The disadvantages are:

- Depending on the loan program, the buyer may qualify at the second-year rate, not the initial rate.
- There are no interest-rate guarantees because indexes fluctuate with the economy.
- The buyer's financial situation may change after the loan is cast, making payment increases financially prohibitive for the borrower.
- The buyer may overleverage, using an unrealistically low initial teaser rate to get the loan without being able to make the later, higher, payments.
- The loan may contain a negative amortization clause, allowing any shortfall of interest not paid monthly to be added back on to the principal balance. (This could cause a resale nightmare should the buyer have to move while the loan is showing negative amortization. It may also create an unsalable property, with the loan balance exceeding the market value.)
- The buyer may not fully understand ARMs and may not be aware that the lender's program is using an unfavorable index as a base.
- The lender may be charging an unusually high margin, the lender's cost of doing business plus profit, which is added to the index to create the interest rate. This margin is set at the loan origination and remains constant for the life of the loan.
- Convertible ARMs may have high interest rates or margins as a bonus to the lender. If the buyer chooses not to convert to a fixed-rate mortgage, this premium may defeat any cost savings with the ARM or perhaps make the program less cost-effective than a fixed-rate program might have been.

BASICS OF ADJUSTABLE-RATE MORTGAGES

Q. What's the best way to learn how ARMs work?

To understand an ARM, you must have a working knowledge of its components. Those components are:

- *Index:* A financial indicator that rises and falls, based primarily on economic fluctuations. It is usually an indicator of inflation and thus is the basis of all future interest adjustments on the loan. Mortgage lenders currently use a variety of indexes.

- *Margin:* A lender's loan cost plus profit. The margin is added to the index to determine the interest rate because the index is the cost of funds and the margin is the lender's cost of doing business plus profit.
- *Initial interest:* The rate during the initial period of the loan, which is sometimes lower than the note rate. This initial interest may be a teaser rate, an unusually low rate used to entice buyers and allow them to more readily qualify for the loan.
- *Note rate:* The actual interest rate charged for a particular loan program.
- *Adjustment period:* The interval at which the interest is scheduled to change during the life of the loan (e.g., annually).
- *Interest-rate caps:* Limit placed on the up-and-down movement of the interest rate, specified per period adjustment and lifetime adjustment (e.g., a cap of 2 and 6 means 2 percent interest increase maximum per adjustment with a 6 percent interest increase maximum over the life of the loan).
- *Negative amortization:* Occurs when a payment is insufficient to cover the interest on a loan. The shortfall amount is added back onto the principal balance.
- *Convertibility:* The option to change from an ARM to a fixed-rate loan. A conversion fee may be charged.
- *Carryover:* Interest-rate increases in excess of the amount allowed by the caps that can be applied at later interest rate adjustments (a component that most newer ARMS don't contain).

Q. How are rates set for ARMs?

Rates are made up of two components: the index and the margin. The index is an indicator of inflation and can come from a variety of sources. The margin is the cost of doing business for the lender, including profit, and is added on to the index to make the interest rate. This formula is used to determine each interest-rate adjustment.

Q. What are teaser (discount) rates? Are they a good idea?

A teaser rate is an unrealistically low introductory rate, less than what the current index plus margin would total. Lenders may offer these to introduce a new program to the marketplace or to boost business. The benefit to the buyer is the lower initial interest and payments (although some lenders qualify the buyer at the fully indexed—postintroductory—rate). The danger is that when the payments do adjust, their increase may cause "payment shock" to the borrower, who may fall behind or default on the loan. The borrower should go into this type of payment schedule with eyes wide open. Particularly if loan qualification is marginal, the borrower must realize how the full-rate mortgage payments will fit in the family budget.

INDEXES

Q. What indexes does a lender use for ARMs?

Although lenders can choose from a wide variety, it is not always possible for the consumer to request a certain index be used with the loan program desired. The lender offers types of loans that the secondary market has agreed to purchase, which includes a predetermined index.

But a consumer could research various ARMs offered by several lenders to determine which programs contain the best combination of indexes and program benefits. The informed buyer should be aware of the most common indexes (listed in alphabetical order):

CDs. This is an index recently developed by FNMA that represents the median rates paid by banks for six-month certificates of deposit. The CD indexes are very volatile and generally considered to react quickly to change in the market, which is good if rates are falling but not good if rates are rising.

Cost of Deposits Index (CODI). This index is based on rates that banks pay on three-month certificates of deposits. It's characterized by being slow to move—both up and down.

Cost of Funds Index (COFI). Associated with the 11th Federal Home Loan Bank Board in San Francisco, California, this index is derived monthly and represents the aggregate rate at which California Savings and Loans pay on deposits. You can find the latest index information at http://www.fhlbsf.com. In recent years it has remained steady and is perhaps the least volatile of all indexes. It's particularly good to use on the upswing of inflation (when rates are expected to rise) because it's one of the slowest indexes to adjust. Most COFI loans don't have caps, however, so if rates rise dramatically, so will monthly payments. Many COFI loans also allow negative amortization. Make sure that you comparison shop features between ARMs before selecting one.

Cost of Savings Index (COSI). This index is tied to the average interest rate paid out to consumers, known as the *cost of savings*. In other words, it's the average rate consumers receive on interest-bearing accounts. The rate is very low but a margin is placed on top of the index.

FNMA 60-Day Mandatory Delivery. This is an index for loans that will convert to fixed-rate loans for the remaining term at a future date such as balloons or convertible ARMs. It's based on FNMA's actual required yield for 30-year fixed-rate mortgages due to be delivered within 60 days.

LIBOR (London Inter Bank Offered Rate). This is the rate at which different money center banks in London loan each other money. LIBOR is much like the prime rate. It's great when rates are low, but when it moves, it does so rapidly. Because of its volatility, it's possibly the riskiest index for borrowers.

National Mortgage Contract Rate (NMCR). This index is based on the average monthly contract rate charged by all lenders on mortgage loans for previously occupied homes. It's good to use this index at the low point in its cycle. It adjusts very slowly and therefore is preferential to buyers. In addition to averaging fixed-rate loan interest rates, other ARM indexes are also averaged and added into this index, allowing it to stay low. Unlike most other indexes, the contract interest-rate index typically carries no additional margin.

Prime Rate. The prime rate published in *The Wall Street Journal* (http://www.wsj.com) is a compiled number from money center banks and represents the rate at which they lend to their best customers. The prime rate is not a very volatile index; however, it generally rises quickly but declines very slowly.

Treasury Bill Constant Maturity (TCM a.k.a. CMT). Treasury bills are the most common index. They offer a large array of maturities spanning from 90 days to 10 years. Most ARMs are linked to the one-year TCM. The securities themselves are traded minute to minute; however, the Constant Maturity is a yield computation that takes some of the volatility out of the index.

For current treasury securities index rates, contact a local lender, *The Wall Street Journal,* or *USA Today,* or request *H.15* (a weekly newsletter) from Publications Services, Mail Stop 138, Board of Governors, Federal Reserve System, Washington, DC 20551. Online resources such as www.hsh.com and www.interest.com provide up-to-the minute quotes.

DISCLOSURE PROVIDED BY LENDERS

Q. How does the lender help the prospective borrower understand the choices available in ARMs?

The lender must give the borrower written disclosure about ARMs either at the time a loan application form is provided or before the consumer pays a nonrefundable fee, whichever comes first.

The lender must make educational material available to the consumer. Many lenders use the *Consumer Handbook on Adjustable-Rate Mortgages,* published jointly by the Federal Reserve and the FHLBB. A copy of this handbook can be found online at www.ftc.gov.

Additionally, lenders must provide ARM buyers with a loan program disclosure for each adjustable-rate program they're considering. The disclosure information must reveal that the interest rate or loan term can change, identify the index used and the source of information for that index, and explain how the index adjusts and when. A statement must be included advising the consumer to ask about the current margin, interest rate, and discount points.

One last piece of information ARM buyers will review will be the example for each index illustrating how payments on a $10,000 loan would have changed historically. Obviously, because your loan will be in multiples of $10,000, make sure you apply the correct numbers when considering adjustments.

Q. What are the requirements for notifying the consumer about ARM interest-rate changes during the life of the loan?

During the term of the outstanding ARM loan, notice must be given to the borrower of an adjusted payment amount, interest rate, index rate, and loan balance. This notification must be made once every year there is a rate adjustment, regardless of whether there is a payment change. The notice must be mailed not less than 45 days before the new payment amount is due. Furthermore, the disclosure must indicate the extent to which any increase in the interest rate has not been fully implemented (e.g., the index rate plus margin would exceed the cap). The notice also must state the payment required to fully amortize the loan if it is different from that being charged.

MARGINS

Q. If a consumer shopped for the most stable and reasonable index, would that loan result in the lowest interest rate?

Not necessarily. The index could be a dream, while the loan's margin could be a nightmare! Even though searching for the best index is important, shopping for the lowest margin can make a difference of thousands of dollars over the life of a loan.

Q. Who sets an ARM's margin and how does it affect the interest rate?

As stated previously, the lender determines the margin because it is the combination of its costs of making the loan plus profit. The margin is set at the time of the loan application and remains constant for the life of the loan. The index rate plus the margin combine to make the note or accrual rate, also called the fully indexed rate. So even if the index is favorable, a high margin could counteract any expected interest savings.

In the comparative example in Figure 7.1, the one-year treasury index is 3.75 percent. This index, added to the lender's margin of 2.75 percent, would make a note or accrual rate of 6.5 percent. (This note rate isn't necessarily the first-year rate charged by the lender, however, because it may have offered a lower or teaser rate to attract borrowers.) In the example, the lender gave the borrower the 6.5 percent initial interest rate—which is effective until the first interest-rate adjustment—resulting in a monthly payment of $632.08.

When it's time for the annual review of the interest rate on the loan, the borrower finds that the index has increased 2 percent, to 5.75 percent. After adding the margin of 2.75 percent to the index, the interest rate escalates to 8.5 percent, and the payment jumps to $766.83.

While the index may wax and wane, the margin remains fixed for the life of the loan. So, all other points being equal, the loan with the higher margin will end up costing the buyer more.

FIGURE 7.1 *Mortgage Comparison—Adjustable-Rate versus Fixed-Rate*

	Fixed-Rate Mortgage	Adjustable-Rate Mortgage
Mortgage Amount	$100,000	$100,000
Interest Rate	9%	6.5%
Year 1	9%	8.5%
Year 2	9%	10.5%
Year 3		
Year 4		
Year 5		
Loan Term	30 years	30 years
Adjustment Period	N/A	1 year
Maximum Cap Per Period	N/A	2%
Lifetime Cap	N/A	6%

	Fixed	Adjustable	Cumulative Savings Adjustable Mortgage Over Fixed
1. Interest Rate, Year One	8%	6.5%	
2. Monthly Payment × 12	$ 9,655	$ 7,585	
3. Total Payments Made, End of Year One ($2 above)	$ 9,655	$ 7,585	2,070
4. Interest Rate, Year Two	9%	8.5%	
5. Monthly Payment × 12	$ 9,655	$ 9,193	
6. Total Cumulative Payments, End of Year Two (lines 3 + 5)	$19,310	$16,778	2,532
7. Interest Rate, Year Three	9%	10.5%	
8. Monthly Payment × 12	$ 9,655	$10,879	
9. Total Cumulative Payments, End of Year Three (lines 6 + 8)	$28,965	$27,657	1,308

Q. Would a buyer ever benefit by taking a program with a higher margin?

Perhaps, if that program had other redeeming characteristics such as low caps, a good index, or a convertibility option to change the ARM into a fixed-rate mortgage. The benefits to the borrower should financially outweigh the higher margin.

Q. What percent could you expect to be charged for a margin?

Lenders quote margins anywhere from 1 to 4 percent.

Q. What factors would cause a lender to charge different margins on various programs?

Some programs might allow an ARM to be converted into a fixed-rate mortgage while other programs might charge higher margins for the privilege of using a more stable index. Or a lender might have a loan program that makes other concessions that it needs to cover in the form of a higher ongoing charge (margin).

INTEREST AND PAYMENT CAPS

Q. What would prevent the fully indexed rate from hitting astronomical heights?

Caps. Caps are limits, specified per loan adjustment period (called adjustment caps) as well as for the life of the loan (called lifetime caps), that prevent interest rates from going through the ceiling. Just as they protect the upward movement, so, too, they prevent the rate from falling to levels where the loan is no longer cost-effective for the lender.

Q. Besides knowing what the caps are, what else does a borrower need to know about caps?

It's important to know what they apply to—the introductory rate or the note rate? And, particularly if you're using a teaser rate, do the rate caps apply to the first adjustment?

Q. Where do most lenders set caps?

The range swings are as wide as 1 to 3 percent for adjustment period caps, and from 5 to 6 percent for lifetime caps. Some loans, however, may have flat rates stated for lifetime caps in lieu of interval amounts (e.g., the rate cannot drop below 8 percent or exceed 14 percent during the life of the loan).

Q. How do payment caps work?

Just like the rate cap, a payment cap limits the amount a monthly payment can increase per adjustment period. A normal range of payment caps is anywhere between 5 to 12 percent, with 7.5 percent being the most common, because it takes a payment change of approximately 7.5 percent to offset 1 percent of interest increase in a loan. It's also possible to have rate caps and payment caps in the same loan.

Q. What kinds of questions should borrowers ask themselves before getting into an ARM with a payment cap?

First of all, do borrowers anticipate that their incomes will increase to cover the additional monthly payments? They should also ask themselves how much they could afford to have the loan increase—in other words, what is their financial threshold?

Next, they should ask whether the loan has a maximum amount of negative amortization allowed. This is important so that leverage can be controlled, particularly any in excess of the property value. They should also consider whether the property's value will increase enough to offset any negative amortization.

Finally, but perhaps most important, borrowers should measure the gap between the initial interest rate and the payment cap. The greater the difference, the greater the risk of potential negative amortization, if allowed on the loan.

Obviously, payment caps, just as ARMs, need to be evaluated based on the desires and capabilities of the individual borrower.

NEGATIVE AMORTIZATION, CARRYOVER, AND ADJUSTMENT PERIODS

Q. Why would anyone want a loan with negative amortization in it?

If handled prudently, negative amortization doesn't have to be a time bomb. For example, if the property is appreciating and the borrowers are not able to increase monthly payments over time to make up for the interest shortfall, it may not have any adverse effects. Remember, too, negative amortization is a form of leverage. Used wisely, it's good business; used haphazardly, it's a keg of dynamite.

Q. Obviously, most lenders aren't crazy about negative amortization. How do they handle it?

Lenders deal with negative amortization in several ways. They limit the amount that can accrue on a loan, usually to a ceiling of 125 percent of the original loan balance. If the lender deems it necessary, it can ask to increase the monthly payments, extend the loan's term, or ask that the borrower make a cash payment to reduce the balance.

Q. How much impact would rate trends have on the adjustment period chosen?

Quite a lot. With rising rates, the longer the adjustment period, the better. However, lenders may charge higher rates on longer-adjusting programs, so this should be a consideration. Most lenders prefer the one-year adjustment term and will usually reflect this preference in their rates and fees.

If rates appear to be falling, a quicker adjustment period may help to bring down the rate. Remember, too, as discussed previously, the particular index chosen has an impact on how rapidly the changes occur.

CONVERTIBILITY OPTIONS

Q. Wouldn't it be best for the borrower to choose an ARM that could be converted to a fixed rate, in case interest rates went wild?

Although the convertibility option may appear initially appealing, it's not for everyone. The convertibility option allows the borrower to convert the rate from adjustable status to a fixed rate, but not without a cost. Loan options are like items in a cafeteria line—the more you chose, the more you pay. The same is true of ARM options. The cost will be reflected in a higher lender's margin, a higher interest rate, or steeper origination fees.

Q. When would a borrower benefit from a convertibility option in an ARM?

First, a conversion option makes sense when interest rates are high but the borrower feels that they will go down. A borrower can benefit initially by the adjustable rate being lower than a fixed rate; and, when rates do fall, he or she can lock into a reasonable fixed-rate program without requalifying or paying the costs of refinancing.

Second, convertibility options make sense when an ARM is chosen for its attractive initial rates, but the borrower feels that rates in general are edging up. This may apply to a borrower who needs the initial qualifying leverage of the lower rate, but may be leery of being locked long term into an adjustable-rate program. It's not just the cost of the convertibility option that is being weighed, but also the overall cost of the ARM loan package (including origination fees, margins, and the particular index), compared to the costs of the fixed-rate package.

Q. How long does a borrower have to exercise the conversion option?

The conversion option period varies from loan to loan. The most common period is between months 13 and 60. Most loans state a maximum time during which the conversion may take place. If not exercised, the option is lost.

Q. Can a borrower predict what the new fixed rate will be when he or she exercises the convertibility option?

It depends. A few lenders may quote a predetermined rate, but most will wait to compute the new rate until the option is taken. Contrary to popular belief, when an ARM is converted to a fixed-rate mortgage, most borrowers do not receive the lender's current 30-year interest rate for fixed-rate loans. Adjustable-rate mortgages sold into the secondary market base the new rate on the 30-day commitment price of the index plus an additional percentage (e.g., $5/8$, percent). These commitment rates are typically higher than what you would expect to pay if you initially chose a fixed-rate loan. So this rate, coupled with an additional $5/8$, percent, may lessen the attractiveness of the conversion to a fixed-rate loan, and of the convertibility option in general.

Q. When should a borrower ask what the cost of converting a loan from an ARM to a fixed-rate mortgage will be?

The borrower should ask this question up front at the time of loan application. There should be no reason why a definitive answer regarding conversion fees can't be given at that time.

THE QUALIFYING PROCESS

Q. In general, isn't it easier to qualify for an ARM?

Because interest rates for ARMs tend to be lower than for fixed-rate loans, this is typically true. In general, secondary market guidelines require that for ARMS with an initial fixed period of three years or more, borrowers can be qualified using the initial note rate. But for initial loan periods of six months or one year, the second-year rate should be used. The rationale is that payment adjustments early on in the mortgage can increase the lender's risk.

Q. What loan-to-value ratios can a borrower get on an ARM and what are the qualifying ratios?

Traditionally, a borrower can get up to a 90 percent loan-to-value loan with qualifying ratios of 28 percent housing debt and up to 36 percent long-term debt.

If the interest rate on the loan is temporarily reduced by buying down the interest rate, the long-term-debt ratio for qualifying will be 33 percent.

As with all qualifying ratios, lenders could allow these ratios to be exceeded if fully documented with compensating factors. For example, a borrower who has a history of above-average income growth or a recent college graduate who has obtained professional employment with high growth potential might be allowed to exceed traditional ratios. For more information on qualification, see figure 7.2.

PROGRAM TYPES

Q. How many different types of ARMs are there?

Because ARMs are designed to fit borrowers' financial situations, more ARMs exist than can be enumerated here.

A wide variety of terms, caps, and options on ARMs with some of the most common products are in the following list. The first number in the cap is the maximum amount of interest-rate adjustment per period, and the second number is the cap on how high the interest could go over the life of the loan:

- Cost of funds index, six-month adjustments; caps of 1 and 6 percent, with a convertibility option to fixed rate
- One-year treasury securities index, with caps of 2 and 5 percent, with or without convertibility option
- 3-1, 5-1, or 7-1 ARMs, fixed rate for the first respective number of years, then adjusts annually thereafter, with a cap of 2 percent per adjustment

Q. How does the two-step mortgage work?

It may help to think of the two-step mortgage as a 30-year fixed-rate loan with one rate adjustment during its life. Tied to the ten-year U.S. Treasury index, the two-step has a fixed-interest rate for the first five or seven years, depending on the program chosen. After that, the interest rate is adjusted once to a new fixed rate, where it remains for the life of the loan.

Because the initial scheduled payment is lower, the two-step can help a borrower qualify for a larger loan than might have been allowed for a 30-year fixed loan. It's also good for short-term ownership.

FIGURE 7.2 *ARM Qualification Sheet*

Sales Price   (1) _____

  Less Loan Amount   (2) _____ Equals Required Down Payment $ _____

Estimated Closing Costs Plus Estimated Prepaid Escrow   + _____

  Total Closing Cost $ _____

Less Cash on Deposit   − _____

Required Cash to Close $ _____

  (2) _____ Divided by (1) _____ Equals LTV _____ %

Gross Income (Mortgagor) _____ and (Comortgagor) _____ = $ _____ (A)

Proposed Housing Expense

    Principal and Interest $ _____

    Other Financing   _____

    Hazard Insurance   _____

    Taxes   _____

    Mortgage Insurance   _____

    Homeowners Association Fees   _____

    Other: _____   _____

Total Housing Payment $ _____ (B)

Total Obligations (Beyond Ten Months)   _____ (C)

Total Housing Payment (B), Plus Monthly Obligations (C) = $ _____ (D)

  (B) _____ Divided by (A) _____ = _____ % Housing Ratio

  (D) _____ Divided by (A) _____ = _____ % Total Debt Ratio

Q. What's an interest-only ARM?

It's exactly what its name implies—an adjustable rate mortgage where you pay only interest for a specified period of time, usually between 3 and 10 years. The benefit is that you have smaller monthly payments. But after the initial period, your payments will increase since you'll be paying principal and interest for the remaining time of the loan term.

For example, monthly interest-only payments for five years on a $200,000 30-year mortgage at 6 percent would be $1,000. After the initial period (even without an interest rate increase) your payment would increase by more than $500 since you're paying principal and interest—over the next 25 years. The longer the interest-only period of the loan, the higher your monthly payments will be once you start to repay principal.

Q. Is there a certain type of buyer and real estate market when interest-only ARMs might work?

Short-term owners may benefit with interest-only ARMs as well as when purchasing property in a market of strong appreciation and rising property values. Without those components, compounded by the absence of principal reduction in the early years of the loan, a borrower could find herself owing more against the property than the house could sell for.

Q. What's a payment option ARM?

A payment option ARM (aka option Arm) is an adjustable-rate mortgage that allows you to choose among several payment options each month. Options typically include variations of the following:

- A traditional payment of principal and interest which lowers your loan balance each month. Payments are typically based on amortization schedules of 15, 30 or 40 years.
- An interest-only payment that pays the interest due for the month but doesn't reduce the principal balance.
- A minimum (a.k.a. limited) payment that is less than the amount of interest due that month with, obviously, no principal reduction. Interest shortfall will be added to the principal of the loan on a monthly basis, increasing the amount of interest you'll pay over the life of the loan, termed "negative amortization," or paying interest on interest. If you're paying the minimum payment during the final months of the loan, a balloon payment may be required to pay the loan in full.

The option ARM is good for borrowers who want the absolute lowest payment available since this program allows 40-year amortizations.

Q. What's a hybrid ARM?

It is a combination of fixed-rate and adjustable rate program options. The borrower receives a lower fixed-rate in the early years of the loan (selecting from three, five, seven, or ten-year periods, termed 3/1, 5/1, 7/1, and 10/1) followed by the balance of the loan term as an ARM adjusting annually. The good news is that hybrids allow buyers to purchase more home than they can afford thanks to the initially lower interest rate. Unfortunately, that can turn out to be the bad news as well. Now that hybrids are resetting as ARMs, payments can rise beyond the financial reach of many borrowers.

For example, let's say a buyer takes out a 30-year hybrid loan at a fixed rate of 5.19 percent for five years, thereafter converting to an adjustable rate with an interest rate cap of five percentage points. The homeowner's initial payment would be $1,097 principal and interest, but could skyrocket by 55 percent to a whopping $1,698 after the reset with an interest rate of more than 10 percent. This is the reality of why borrowers are in trouble and foreclosures continue to climb.

Q. Besides knowing where the payment could adjust after the reset, are there other terms and conditions a borrower should watch out for with hybrids?

You need to thoroughly understand when the loan will reset, the cap (if any) on the interest rate adjustments, as well any prepayment penalty involved on the loan if you refinance/pay off before a certain period of time (often three to five years). Additionally, since hybrids save the borrower money in the early years of the loan, lenders often charge higher mortgage-origination fees and points. Comparison shopping between lenders is strongly suggested for this program.

Q. What type of borrower do hybrids work for?

If the buyer is reasonably sure that he'll be a short-term owner staying less time than the term of the reset, he can often save money with a hybrid. For example, comparing a $200,000 30-year fixed-rate mortgage at 6.1 percent to a 7/1 hybrid with a start rate of 5.6 percent, the borrower would save nearly $8,000 in interest in the first seven-years of the loan.

Q. What's a hybrid option ARM and how is it different from a traditional option ARM loan?

A hybrid option ARM combines the benefit of a fixed-rate for a predetermined time (i.e. three, five, seven, or ten years) with the ability to make various payment options each month. These include a fully amortized payment with principal and interest, an interest-only option, or a minimum payment that does not cover the amount of interest owing for that month. In the case of the latter, the shortfall is added back onto the loan as is the case with the traditional option ARM.

TAKE ACTION IN ADVANCE OF A RESET

Q. Aren't interest-only, option ARMS, and hybrids the loans that contributed to delinquent mortgage payments and buyers getting into financial trouble? If someone has this type of loan, can they do anything to make sure things don't backfire?

The loans weren't bad; it's more that they were chosen by ill-informed consumers who wanted the lowest-possible payments, to purchase more home than they could afford, in the hope that the housing market would continue to boom with double-digit annualized appreciation. In other words, they wanted all of the financial rewards without any of the risks. Lenders and investors loved the higher profit margins in making/buying exotic loans, so everyone benefited—for the short term. The best thing a consumer can do if he has any type of loan with a reset in it is to: (1) Check out the terms and conditions of the mortgage found on the promissory note as part of the closing documents; (2) Determine if your goals are still realistic to make the required interest-rate adjustments (you'll sell the property prior to the payment adjustment, you'll financially be able to weather the maximum amount of the payment increase, etc) and (3) Make any adjustments to your game plan well in advance of the reset. For some, it could mean refinancing as soon as possible. For others, it could mean keeping the loan until the prepayment penalty clause in the loan expires. The primary reason that people fall delinquent with rate reset loans is that they don't prepare in advance of need. Do triage now and you won't become a mortgage delinquency statistic.

CALCULATION ERRORS

Q. Do errors ever occur in adjusting rates?

Yes, they do. In fact, surveys estimate that between 20 and 30 percent of all adjustable-rate mortgages contain calculation errors. Each borrower must monitor adjustments on his or her individual loan and query the lender if it appears an error has been made.

Each loan has its own set of variables, including the date the loan is to be recalculated, the index to use, and how the interest is to be rounded off. An error in one or all of these areas could change the interest rate charged.

It's wise for the borrower to check his or her loan documents to determine when adjustments are calculated and then check the particular index used on that date. This can be found in *The Wall Street Journal,* www.wsj.com, *USA Today,* www.usatoday.com, and most major newspapers. If the borrower checks index information on the renewal/adjustment date and compares that information to what the lender sent when notifying of an upcoming adjustment, the borrower can help guard against errors. If the information is different, the current loan servicer (where payments are mailed) should be contacted. Most lenders have a review process in place to field and answer borrower inquiries about payment adjustments.

A comprehensive online tutorial for checking the accuracy of an adjustable-rate loan can be found at www.hsh.com.

DETERMINE ARM SAVINGS

Q. When is the best time to use an ARM?

As seen in this chapter, interest rate differentials alone are not enough to justify using an ARM over a fixed-rate loan. The deciding factor should be determined by analyzing the savings between loan programs. As a very broad rule of thumb, if the borrower can save at least $2\frac{1}{2}$, percent in interest by using an ARM, and will hold the property for less than four years, it may pay to go with the ARM. Obviously, the smaller the gap between the fixed and adjustable rates, the less attractive adjustable rates become.

Remember, however, there are a lot of variables to compare in selecting a loan, including the up-front costs of borrowing on each loan considered.

The smaller the gap between rates, the less attractive adjustable rates become.

QUESTIONS TO ASK BEFORE
TAKING OUT AN ARM

Q. What questions about the loan should the consumer be able to answer before taking on an ARM?

- *What is the history of the particular index used by the lender?* (Ask to see historical documentation.)
- *Where do economists think interest rates are currently headed?* If up, your interest savings may not be as great as you thought. If down, you may have an even bigger win than anticipated. (Be sure to compare the answer to this question to the previous discussion about index selection.)
- *What are the terms of the loan? When does the ARM payment adjust? How will the new rate be figured? What is the maximum to which the payment could rise, and the minimum to which it could fall?*
- *What is the lender's margin?* (Because this remains constant for the life of the loan, it has as much, if not more, impact on where the rate adjusts to as does the index.)
- *Is there a convertibility option? If so, what does it really cost?* (Take into consideration any higher interest rate on the loan as well as conversion fees.) Remember to ask how the fixed rate will be determined at the time of conversion. To answer these questions, the borrower should obtain a completed copy of the ARM loan disclosure statement. A borrower who has difficulty weighing the options should seek the expertise of a financial advisor.
- *How long will the property be held?* Remember, ARMs are usually most advantageous with short-term ownership (approximately less than four years if inflation is on the move).
- *Will the ARM be assumable when the property is sold? If so, what are current assumption fees, as well as policies and procedures for assuming this type of loan?*
- *What are the up-front costs of the loan? Do they offset any potential interest savings? Is there any creative way to finance these into the loan to eliminate out-of-pocket cash at closing? If so, how will that affect the monthly payment and any future resale value?*

Q. Which loan provides the best adjustable-rate program?

That's like asking how long someone's legs need to be (long enough to reach the ground). If a particular ARM program suits a buyer's needs, then that's the best loan. The following questions help to determine which type of ARM best suits a borrower's needs:

- *What are the borrower's goals in buying this property?* If rapid equity buildup is desired, the borrower should stay away from any product allowing negative amortization; if the goal is a first-home purchase on tight qualification, perhaps a low introductory rate or rate adjustments that occur every three or five years should be used. The index and margin will also be important.
- *How long do the borrowers plan on owning the property?* Short-term owners should consider a loan with a slow-moving upward index, low up-front loan origination fees, low down payment, and no negative amortization.

  Long-term property owners may be wise to avoid ARMs completely. If an ARM is selected, however, these buyers should select one with a good convertibility option with low conversion fees. Index and margin are very important to long-term owners, who also could use more leverage going in (including negative amortization) because they have more time to recover equity.
- *Who else will participate in the purchase?* If there is only one purchaser, then virtually all ARM programs are available. Many ARM programs sold into the secondary market may not allow coborrowers. Among those that do, each has its own strict guidelines. Check each investor (FNMA, GNMA, and FHLMC) for its own underwriting requirements.
- *How much down payment does the borrower wish to use?* If the borrower wishes to make only a small down payment, high-rate PMI insurance will be required, as will squeaky-clean credit, a strong income base, and cash reserves of at least two or three months. This type of purchaser will have limited negotiating power with the lender, because of extreme leverage.
- *How much of a monthly payment is the borrower prepared to make?* Consider affordability and desirability issues. For most ARMs, the housing ratio (depending on which investor buys the loan) must use an approximate maximum of 28 percent of gross income. The total debt ratio, including all debts of ten months or more plus PITI payment, cannot exceed 36 percent of the gross income.

- *Would the borrower mind fluctuating payment amounts?* If the answer is yes, the borrower is not suited for any type of ARM. If the answer is no, the borrower could choose his or her financially and emotionally preferred frequency of payment adjustment (e.g., every year, three years, five years, or ten years) and choose the type of loan to match.
- *What are the borrower's short-term and long-term liabilities?* Balances are needed to determine this, as well as repayment schedules. If the borrower has many credit accounts and small liabilities, he or she may not be able to qualify for a high loan-to-value ARM, or may have to pay off and close some accounts to qualify. If the borrower has few debts, but is short on down payment or cash reserves, he or she should consider obtaining a gift letter or borrowing from a low-interest source, such as life insurance or a credit union.

Figure 7.3 includes a mortgage checklist from the Federal Reserve Bank that is helpful in choosing the best ARM program to fit a buyer's needs.

One last note: Many borrowers forget about using ARMs when interest rates for conventional fixed-rate loans are low. By offering borrowers extra purchasing power tailored to their individual financial situations, ARMs give added benefits that fixed-rate loans don't offer. Borrowers should not overlook them when shopping for affordable loans.

FIGURE 7.3 *ARM Checklist*

	Mortgage A	Mortgage B
Ask your lender to help fill out this checklist.		
Mortgage Amount	$	$
Basic Features for Comparison		
Fixed Rate Annual Percentage Rate	_____%	_____%
(This is the cost of your credit as a yearly rate, which includes both interest and other charges.)	_____	_____
ARM Annual Percentage Rate	_____	_____
Adjustment Period	_____	_____
Index Used and Current Rate Margin	_____	_____
Initial Payment without Discount	_____	_____
Initial Payment with Discount (If Any)	_____	_____
How Long Will Discount Last?	_____	_____
Interest Rate Caps: Periodic	_____	_____
Overall	_____	_____
Payment Caps	_____	_____
Negative Amortization	_____	_____
Convertibility or Prepayment Privilege	_____	_____
Initial Fees and Charges	_____	_____
Monthly Payment Amounts		
What will my monthly payment be after 12 months if the index rate:		
stays the same?	_____	_____
goes up 2 percent?	_____	_____
goes down 2 percent?	_____	_____
What will my monthly payment be after three years if the index rate:		
stays the same?	_____	_____
goes up 2 percent?	_____	_____
goes down 2 percent?	_____	_____
Take into account any caps on your mortgage and remember it may run 30 years.		

8

FEDERAL HOUSING
ADMINISTRATION LOANS

T his chapter contains basic information about FHA single-family mortgages. Because this information was gleaned from standard FHA guidelines, practices could vary slightly in certain states and cities.

The FHA was established in 1934 under the National Housing Act. It is part of the federal Department of Housing and Urban Development (HUD). Its birth paved the way to mortgage affordability for many Americans who had previously been locked out of home ownership because of a combination of high interest rates and short-term loans, making payments costly. Programs of the FHA expanded loan terms to 30 years at interest rates typically below those of conventional loans.

FHA was also instrumental in determining the first set of construction and appraisal standards for inspecting property prior to loan approval. Many of the quality and safety standards that the housing industry uses today are by-products of early FHA guidelines.

Before 1983, FHA retained the right to control rate ceiling maximums on FHA loans. Interestingly, however, though interest rates are no longer capped, FHA loan rates have remained generally lower than conventional rates. This is the result of supply and demand, default protection to the lender, and discount points, because

- low down payments on FHA loans, as well as fairly liberal underwriting guidelines, make FHA loans attractive, thus creating demand.
- the lender is insured against borrower default for the life of the loan; the lender can offset the lower interest received for the security of loan repayment in case of default.
- discount points charged by the lender help sweeten the pot financially, increasing the desired yield to the lender.

At the time of this writing, the Bush administration is proposing an "FHA Revitalization" bill that would permanently increase allowable maximum loan amounts, eliminate the down payment requirement and extend loan terms to a maximum of 40 years. Additionally, there's consideration to change the current flat-rate premium structure of the Mutual Mortgage Insurance (MMI) to that of a risk-based model. This would allow premiums to be based on the borrower's financial strength, with riskier buyers paying higher premiums. Since these changes could occur at any time, check with your local lender for program guidelines.

LEVELS OF FEDERAL HOUSING ADMINISTRATION LOANS

While FHA national loan underwriting guidelines establish basic guidelines for loan administration, regional FHA offices and local lenders can choose to be more restrictive.

For example, if loan defaults in a local lender's market have been edging up, that lender might choose to be more cautious about taking risks.

That's why it's important for the borrower to shop not only for the type of FHA loan, but for the lender who will make it. In general, lenders who do a high volume of FHA loans will be aware of little-known exceptions and underwriting allowances that make the loan possible.

PROS AND CONS OF FHA LOANS

Q. What are the advantages of using FHA financing?

Following are some of the many advantages FHA loans afford borrowers:

- There is a low down payment requirement. On the standard Section 203(b) of the homeowner's program, the down payment is 3 percent, up to the maximum loan amount allowable in the particular region.
- The entire down payment can be gifted or borrowed from a relative.
- Unlike conventional loans, there are no reserve requirements of two months' PITI payments at closing.
- Loan rates are typically lower than for market-rate conventional fixed-rate loans.
- A seller or other third party is allowed to participate in paying the buyer's closing costs.
- Any outstanding loans originated prior to December 1, 1986, are simply assumable, meaning that the purchaser does not need to formally qualify. Other FHA loans are assumable with qualifying.
- Loans are assumed at the note rate under which they were originated, with the exception of FHA ARMs, which are assumed at the loan's current rate of interest.
- FHA loans have no prepayment penalty when the loan is retired (if FHA is given a 30-day notice to prepay).
- Because a new FHA loan pays off existing encumbrances, the seller receives all of his or her equity, less costs of sale.
- Qualifying guidelines assist the average buyer in the marketplace; some underwriting guidelines are less restrictive than those of conventional fixed-rate loans.
- The lender is insured against loss for the life of the FHA loan.
- It is possible to place subsequent mortgages after an FHA first mortgage. New financing could even be placed around an FHA mortgage originated before December 1, 1986.
- A second mortgage can be initiated simultaneously with a new FHA first mortgage.

Q. What are the disadvantages of using an FHA loan?

- Loans originated after December 1, 1986, are no longer assumable without qualifying.
- On loans originated before December 1, 1986, purchasers who do not receive a release of liability when selling may be secondarily liable should the loan default.
- Buyers and sellers may object to paying discount points or other closing costs attributed to FHA financing.
- Because a seller may be requested to pay fairly heavy costs to assist a buyer, the seller may want to sell only if the full price is received.
- A mortgage insurance premium (MIP) is required up front, or can be financed into the loan, and an annual renewal premium is charged, payable in the monthly payment.
- A 1 percent loan origination fee is charged on FHA loans.
- Appraisal guidelines for FHA loans may be more stringent than those of conventional mortgage appraisals.
- Loan processing for FHA loans may take longer than for conventional loans.
- Generally, borrowers are allowed only one FHA loan at a time.

THE BASICS

Q. What is the basic FHA loan called?

The primary single-family program is the Section 203(b) loan, which provides financing for a one- to four-family owner-occupied dwelling. This includes a condominium, Planned Unit Development (PUD), and new construction financing, all of which must be on the FHA's approved list. Loans are available in rural and urban areas and offer terms for 10 to 30 years.

Q. Are FHA loans only for low-income buyers?

That's a common misconception. Although some FHA-subsidized programs assist low-income families, FHA's mission is to insure lenders on housing loans made to borrowers who do not meet the necessary down payment requirements or other conditions of conventional mortgages. With FHA loans, borrowers still need to meet monthly income guidelines sufficient to support housing obligations. Because the loans are insured by HUD, however, the lender is protected against the borrower's default and can offer more liberal terms and competitive interest than a buyer might otherwise be able to obtain.

Q. Who is the typical FHA buyer?

Although each buyer's qualifications and profile will be unique, following are some general characteristics. The FHA borrower

- is only moderately qualified and needs a qualifying interest rate lower than required for a market-rate conventional loan.
- needs leverage in qualifying, with a lower down payment or gifted funds.
- is working with a seller or other third party to pay part or all of the closing costs and prepaids.
- requires a loan that is assumable.
- desires an insured loan (with possibly some of the mortgage insurance eventually rebated if the loan is paid off early).
- wants to place a second mortgage initially behind the FHA first mortgage, or later during ownership of the property.
- is interested in leveraged programs of ARMs, GPMs, or GEMs.

Q. What are the general buyer qualifications for FHA loans?

A borrower must have a satisfactory credit record, the down payment required (or gifted funds available for the down payment), cash needed to close, and steady, verified income to make the monthly payments without difficulty.

Q. Is there a good online site for consumers to access answers regarding FHA loans?

Yes. While the main HUD portal of www.hud.gov may seem the natural point of beginning, it's deep and wide and you may forget your question before you find the page you need! For consumers, my favorite link would be www.faq.fha.gov (aka www.answers.hud.gov) where you can find answers to commonly asked questions or ask a question of your own. Answers by phone are available Monday through Friday, 8AM to 8PM ET, at 1-800-CallFHA, (1-800-225-5342).

Citizenship Is Not Mandatory

Q. Is U.S. citizenship mandatory for obtaining an FHA loan?

While the borrower must reside on the property, U.S. citizenship is not a requirement for obtaining an FHA loan. Under the Equal Credit Opportunity Act, lawful permanent residents of the United States are entitled to the same credit benefits as any American citizen and may not be discriminated against because of national origin. Permanent and nonpermanent resident alien borrowers must show an established employment history and evidence that employment will continue.

Borrowers Restricted to One FHA Loan at a Time

Q. Why are FHA buyers restricted to one loan at a time?

In the past, FHA experimented with allowing borrowers to have multiple, simultaneous FHA loans if the first loan did not have a high loan-to-value ratio. If the borrowers wanted to purchase again with an FHA loan, they could pay down the balance on the first home to 75 percent loan-to-appraised value.

Foreclosures ensued, so now borrowers are allowed only one FHA loan at a time. Exceptions to this rule include the borrower who relocates from another area and can only qualify by using an FHA loan, or whose family size has increased so that the present home no longer meets his or her needs. Additionally, if a co-borrower will remain in the property, the vacating borrower is eligible to apply for an FHA loan on another property.

QUALIFICATION GUIDELINES

Maximum Mortgage Limits and Loan-to-Value Ratios

Q. Are there national guidelines that dictate what size FHA loan a borrower can obtain?

Yes. FHA limits maximum loan amounts based on a percentage of the conforming FHLMC limits as well as area median prices. The Economic Stimulus Act of 2008 increases limits for FHA mortgages approved on or before December 31, 2008 to the following: the lesser of 125 percent of the area median price (on a county-by-county basis);

or $729,750, which is 175 percent of the FHLMC conforming loan limit. This means that all FHA limits will be increased across the board. For areas with low median prices, the maximum will go to $271,050. In areas with high area median prices, the maximum can go as high as $729,750. These are substantial increases from years past (up approximately 30 percent or more), but the catch is that these maximums are (at the time of this writing) in effect only through calendar year 2008.

Q. How is the FHA 203(b) maximum mortgage amount calculated?

The borrower first must determine if he or she is in a low closing cost or high closing cost area. This information can be obtained by contacting a real estate agent or the lender, or by visiting HUD on the Web at www.hud.gov and accessing the table for the appropriate state and region. See figure 8.1 for a state roster. Using that information, apply the following formulas.

Maximum loan-to-value percentages for low closing costs states are

- 98.75 percent for properties with values/sales prices equal to or less than $50,000.
- 97.65 percent for properties with values/sales prices in excess of $50,000 up to $125,000.
- 97.15 percent for properties with values/sales prices in excess of $125,000.

Maximum loan-to-value percentages for high closing costs states are

- 98.75 percent for properties with values/sales prices equal to or less than $50,000.
- 97.75 percent for properties with values/sales prices in excess of $50,000.

FIGURE 8.1 *Closing Costs and Loan-to-Value Ratios*

Low Closing Costs States	High Closing Cost States
Arizona, California, Colorado, Guam, Idaho, Illinois, Indiana, New Mexico, Nevada, Oregon, Utah, Virgin Islands, Washington, Wisconsin, Wyoming	All others
98.75% if < $50,000 97.65% if $50,000 – $125,000 97.15% if > $125,000	98.75% if < $50,000 97.75% if > $50,000

Q. Can borrowers finance closing costs into the loan?

Yes. The following scenarios provide various examples of how this can be accomplished.

Use the Mortgage Credit Analysis Worksheet found in Figure 8.2 to work out the calculations. Later you can use this worksheet to pencil in your own qualifying information.

Scenario 1: Buyer Responsible for Closing Costs

Q. How would the maximum mortgage amount be calculated on a $100,000 property purchase (and appraisal) if the buyer is paying $1,000 in closing costs in a high closing cost area?

First, calculate the maximum mortgage ($100,000 × 97.75 percent = $97,750). The borrower needs at least 3 percent ($3,000) cash into the purchase (excluding prepaid expenses such as taxes and insurance).

The borrower's acquisition cost is $101,000 ($100,000 plus $1,000 of closing costs that are his or her responsibility). The $101,000 less the maximum mortgage of $97,750 requires a cash down payment of $3,250. Because this represents at least 3 percent of the sales/appraised price, no further calculation is necessary.

FIGURE 8.2 *Mortgage Credit Analysis Worksheet*

Mortgage Credit Analysis Worksheet Purchase Money Mortgages	**U.S. Department of Housing and Urban Development** Office of Housing Federal Housing Commissioner	OMB Approval No. 2502–0059 (Expires 11/30/2010)

See back of page for Public Burden and Sensitive Information statements

All numbered entries in $ except where noted.

Case number	Section of the Housing Act	Check one ☐ Existing Construction ☐ Proposed Construction

1a. Borrower's name	2a. Social Security Number

1b. Co-Borrower's name	2b. Social Security Number

3a. Mortgage without Upfront MIP	3b. Total UFMIP	3c. Mortgage with UFMIP	4. Appraised Value (without CC)	5. a. Total Closing Costs (CC) _____ b. Less Paid by Seller _____ c. Equals Borrower's CC _____

6. Current housing expenses	7. Term of loan ___ years	8. Interest rate ___ %	9. Adj. buy-down interest rate ___ %	

10. Statutory Investment Requirements
- a. Contract Sales Price
- b. Borrower-Paid Closing Costs (from 5c)
- c. Unadjusted Acquisition (10a + 10b)
- d. Statutory Investment Requirement (10a x 0.03)

11. Maximum Mortgage Calculation
- a. Lesser of Sales Price (10a) or Value (from 4)
- b. Required Adjustments (+/-)
- c. Mortgage Basis (11a + 11b)
- d. Mort Amt. (11c x LTV Factor ___% or Less)

12. Cash Investment Requirements
- a. Minimum Down Payment (10c-11d) (This amount must equal or exceed 10d)
- b. Prepaid Expenses
- c. Discount Points
- d. Repairs/Improvements (Non-Financeable)
- e. Upfront MIP Paid in Cash
- f. Non-Realty and Other Items
- g. Total Cash to Close (Sum of 12a thru 12f)
- h. Amount Paid (Earnest Money, etc.)
- I. Amount of Gift Funds [Source _____)
- j. Assets Available
- k. 2nd Mort (if applicable) [Source _____)
- l. Cash Reserves (Sum 12h thru 12k, minus 12g)

13. Monthly Effective Income
- a. Borrower's base pay
- b. Borrower's other earnings (explain)
- c. Co-borrower's base pay
- d. Co-borrower's other earnings (explain)
- e. Net income from real estate
- f. Gross monthly income

Remarks (attach additional paper if needed)

14. Debts & Obligations — Monthly Payment | Unpaid Balance
- a. Total installment debt
- b. Child support, etc.
- c. Other
- d. Total monthly payments

15. Future monthly payments
- a. Principal & interest – 1st mortgage
- b. Monthly MIP
- c. Homeowners Association Fee
- d. Ground rent
- e. Principal & interest – 2nd mortgage
- f. Hazard insurance
- g. Taxes & special assessments
- h. Total mortgage payment
- i. Recurring expenses (from 14d)
- j. Total fixed payment

16. Ratios
- a. Loan-to-value (11d divided by 11a) . %
- b. Mortgage Payment–to–income (15h divided by 13f) . %
- c. Total fixed payment–to–income (15j divided by 13f) . %

17. Borrower rating (enter "A" for acceptable or "R" for reject)
- a. Credit characteristics
- b. Adequacy of effective income
- c. Stability of effective income
- d. Adequacy of available assets

18. Borrower's CAIVRS Number | Co-borrower's CAIVRS Number

LDP/GSA (page no. & date) | LDP/GSA (page no. & date)

Attachment A Information
A1. Contract Sales Price of Property (line 10a above)
A2. 6% of line A1
A3. Total Seller Contribution
A4. Excess Contribution

Final application decision ☐ **A**pprove ☐ **R**eject	Examiner's signature & date X	Underwriter's signature & date X	CHUMS ID Number

Previous editions are obsolete

form **HUD-92900–PUR** (10/98) ref. Handbook 4155.1

Scenario 2: Seller Pays the Closing Costs; Buyer Receives Premium Pricing

Q. What if the property sold and appraised for $100,000, but the seller was paying part of the closing costs, and the balance was paid by the lender, increasing the interest rate (called premium pricing)?

Oops—you didn't tell us if it was a high or low closing cost area! (Let's use high cost.) The maximum mortgage calculation ($100,000 × 97.75 percent) equals $97,750. Because this loan amount represents less than a 3 percent cash down payment ($2,250), the maximum mortgage must be reduced to $97,000 to ensure that there's a minimum of $3,000 down (exclusive of prepaid expenses). The required investment must be from the borrower's own funds, a bona fide gift, a loan from a family member, or from a government agency. It may not come from an increase in the interest rate of the loan (premium pricing) or from sources such as the seller, builder, or real estate agent.

Scenario 3: Buyer Responsible for Closing Costs; Seller Contributes a Decorating Allowance

Q. What about a property (in a high closing cost area) that sells for $100,000, appraises for $103,250, with the buyer paying $2,000 in closing costs, and the seller contributes a decorating allowance of $1,000?

Decorating allowances and other inducements to purchase, as well as sales concessions exceeding 6 percent, must be subtracted from the lesser of the sales price or value before calculating the maximum mortgage amount. So first subtract the decorating allowance from the sales price ($100,000 – $1,000 = $99,000) and then multiply that amount by 97.75 percent. This results in a maximum mortgage of $96,773. In this case, the decorating allowance penalized the borrower, requiring him or her to make a larger down payment.

Q. Can the 3 percent borrower cash requirement consist of discount points or prepaid amounts?

No. The 3 percent must be exclusive of both discount points and any prepaid amounts.

GIFTS

Q. Could the borrower use gifts for the down payment on an FHA loan?

Yes. Gifts for down payments can come from a relative of the borrower, the borrower's employer or labor union, a charitable organization, a governmental agency, or a close friend with a clearly defined interest in the borrower. Parties to the transaction (real estate agents, a builder, etc.) are not allowed to gift down payments to buyers without the donated amount being first subtracted from the sales price (before the maximum allowable loan is figured).

Q. I heard that someone gave money to a couple as a wedding gift for a down payment on an FHA loan. Could this be done?

Yes. In 1997, bridal registry accounts were initiated by FHA to allow friends and relatives to contribute to an account for down payment and closing costs. In fact, similar accounts can be set up for other occasions besides weddings (e.g., graduation gifts) for anyone who's a potential homebuyer.

Here's how it works. Prospective homebuyers contact lenders who originate FHA loans to set up individual federally insured depository accounts in the parties' names. Funds may be deposited by friends and relatives directly into the account, or given by cash or check to the parties for deposit.

Depending on how lenders wish to market the homeowner bridal registry program, they can provide information about the program directly to friends and relatives of the potential homebuyers using FHA's promotional brochure or one designed by the lender. In addition, lenders can provide gift cards with the gift giver's name to document the gift. Not only will the program help buyers obtain a down payment, the monies will be tracked and accounted for using FHA guidelines, ready as part of the loan documentation when the buyers are ready to apply for the loan.

The funds remain under the control of the individuals for whom they're deposited. The funds can be withdrawn at any time and aren't required to be used to purchase a home. (What a neat way to help pay the wedding expenses!) In addition, engaged couples don't have to be married before they can use the monies to close on a home loan.

BORROWING THE DOWN PAYMENT

Q. Can a buyer borrow the down payment for an FHA loan?

Yes. Buyers can borrow the down payment secured against assets such as stocks, bonds, automobiles, and real estate (other than the property being purchased).

In addition, loans could be secured against deposited funds such as life insurance policies and loans against 401(k)s. If repayment of the loan against the asset can be obtained by converting the asset to cash, the repayment for the purpose of loan qualification would not be required.

CLOSING COSTS

Q. How could a seller financially assist a buyer?

The seller can pay discount points, buydowns, and other financial supplements (called *financing concessions*) for the borrower up to a maximum of 6 percent of the sales price. Past that point, deductions will be made dollar for dollar from the sales price before the maximum loan amount is figured.

Any charge considered a seller-paid closing cost for the buyer will be subtracted likewise from the sales price as well as contributed to the 6 percent ceiling.

NO CASH RESERVES REQUIRED

Q. Does the borrower need two months of reserve PITI payments in cash as with other loans?

There is no reserves requirement set by FHA on single-family, one-unit dwellings. The lender could impose reserves of three months of PITI on multifamily occupied dwellings, such as two-unit to four-unit properties.

QUALIFYING INCOME

Q. What are the qualifying income criteria for standard FHA loans?

It's a common misconception that buyers who do not fit within the exact qualifying ratios will not receive FHA loans. Although the following ratios are guidelines, they are not absolutes. The loan underwriter will carefully weigh each individual situation before making a lending decision.

Housing Ratio

The following monthly expenses should not exceed 31 percent of the borrower's monthly gross income: PITI (including MIP); any homeowners association or condo fees; and any local improvement district (LID) or improvement assessments.

Total Debt Ratio

The following monthly expenses should not exceed 43 percent of the borrower's monthly gross income: total mortgage payment, auto payments, installment charges, loans, child support, alimony, or other obligations to run more than ten months. Refer to the worksheet found in figure 8.2.

Compensating Factors

Q. What exceptions could the lender make on these ratios?

Strong consideration to exceed the ratios could be given an applicant who uses a large down payment and has substantial cash reserves after closing, a history of light use of credit, excellent job history, and no other large debt payments such as a car loan.

Also considered as compensating factors would be the borrower's track record of managing a large house payment, a new house payment that will increase only slightly, or compensation or income not reflected in qualifying, but which could directly assist repayment of the mortgage. Changing circumstances, such as child support with only two years of payments left to pay, may also be considered. Purchasing a home because of job relocation with the trailing spouse expected to return to work could count as a compensating factor.

In addition, a property that meets energy-efficiency guidelines can allow the borrower's ratios to be increased by 2 percent on both the housing and total debt ratios.

Q. On which of the two ratios—housing or long-term debt—is the lender usually the more flexible?

Lenders are usually more flexible on the housing ratio. The rationale is that if the borrower's long-term-debt ratio is 43 percent or less, the borrower could perhaps handle a larger house payment.

Documenting Income

Q. What kind of income qualifications must the borrower prove to qualify for an FHA loan?

As with all mortgages, the borrower must prove stability of income. While the FHA does not mandate a minimum length of time a borrower must have held a position, the lender must verify the most recent two full years of employment. If part of this history included school or military time, the borrower must provide evidence supporting this, such as college transcripts or discharge papers. Allowances for seasonal employment—such as are typical in the building trades—may be made.

Changing jobs need not be viewed as negative if the changes were in the same line of work, advanced the borrower's position, and were accompanied by income increases.

Q. Are pay increases counted in qualifying income?

Pay increases, such as performance raises, bonuses, and cost-of-living adjustments, can be included as income if they will begin within 60 days of the loan closing and can be verified by the employer.

Q. Will overtime and bonus income count toward FHA qualifying?

Overtime and bonus income may be used to qualify if the borrower has received this type of income for the past two years and will in all likelihood continue to do so. The lender will use an average figure based on the past two-year history.

Q. Does part-time income count?

Because HUD recognizes that many low-income and moderate-income families rely on part-time and seasonal income, FHA lenders may include part-time and seasonal income in qualifying if the borrower has worked the job uninterrupted for the past two years and appears likely to continue. Seasonal employment is viewed the same way, focusing on the rehire for the next season. Other situations that do not meet the two-year history can be seen only as compensating factors by the lender.

Q. How does the lender verify commission income?

Commission income is averaged over the previous two years, and the borrower must provide his or her last two years' tax returns along with a recent pay stub to verify this income. A borrower showing income decreases from year to year will need to show significant compensating factors to receive loan approval.

Q. Do retirement and Social Security benefits count as income?

Yes, but this type of income must be verified from the source (usually the former employer or the Social Security Administration) or through federal tax returns. If any benefits expire within the first full three years, this income will be considered only as a compensating factor.

Q. How is alimony or child support verified?

Alimony and child support must be projected to continue for at least the first three years of the mortgage. The borrower must provide a copy of the divorce decree and evidence that payments have been made for the past 12 months. An exception to this 12-month guideline would be if the payer's ability and willingness to pay is adequately documented by the lender.

Self-Employed Borrowers

Q. Are self-employed borrowers qualified for FHA in the same tedious way they are for conventional loans?

More or less, but the FHA may make an exception for self-employed borrowers who have been employed less than two years but more than one year. The self-employed borrower may qualify for an FHA loan if he or she has at least two years of previous employment in the same line of work or a combination of one year employment and one year formal training.

DETERMINING DEBT FOR LOAN QUALIFYING

Q. How does the lender view debt for FHA loan qualifying?

The borrower's liabilities included in the long-term-debt ratio for qualifying include installment loans, revolving charge accounts, real estate loans, alimony, child support, and all other continuing obligations. The basic guideline is that any debt that extends ten months or more must be considered in the qualifying ratios. Debts lasting less than ten months need not be counted unless they substantially affect the borrower's ability to repay the mortgage in the early months of the loan. An example of a debt that might be counted would be a substantial car payment with four payments remaining.

Q. Does child care count as a borrower debt?

No, it does not count as a borrower debt.

Q. Are cosigned loans counted as debt for qualifying?

If the individual applying is a cosigner on a car loan, student loan, or any other obligation including a mortgage, the lender requires verification that the primary obligor has been making payments on a regular basis and has no history of delinquent payments on the loan over the past 12 months.

Q. What are the other special guidelines that relate to debt for an FHA loan?

If a borrower has a debt projected to begin within 12 months of the mortgage closing, such as student loan repayment, the lender must include the anticipated monthly obligation in the underwriting analysis. An exception would be if the borrower provides written evidence that the debt will be deferred to a period outside of this timeframe. Balloon notes that come due within one year of the loan closing must be considered as debt.

ALTERNATIVE DOCUMENTATION

Q. Is quick processing available with FHA, similar to that on conventional loans?

Lenders can use the alternative documentation method, which expedites processing. The borrower is required to provide the following to use this method:

- Bank statements for the most recent three months
- W-2 forms for the past two years
- Paystubs covering the most recent 30-day period, with the borrower's name and Social Security number

The lender will verify employment by telephoning the employer prior to closing, confirming the buyer's position and salary range.

If all of these cannot be obtained, standard processing is required.

PREVIOUSLY BANKRUPT BORROWERS

Q. Can borrowers who have previously declared bankruptcy purchase a home using an FHA loan?

Yes. In fact, FHA's evaluation of previous bankrupt borrowers has been one of the most liberal in the mortgage-lending industry. A lender may allow a bankrupt borrower to secure a mortgage loan if the Chapter 7 bankruptcy has been discharged for at least three years and credit has been satisfactorily reestablished, and it appears that the problems surrounding the bankruptcy are unlikely to recur. Additional positive factors for granting a mortgage in less than three years would be that the bankruptcy was caused by extenuating circumstances beyond the borrower's control.

Borrowers who have filed bankruptcy under Chapter 13 must be one year into the payout and have trustee approval to add the debt.

In either case, borrowers must provide detailed letters of explanation and supporting documentation to the lender.

BORROWERS WITH PREVIOUS FORECLOSURE

Q. Can consumers with previous foreclosures obtain an FHA loan?

Yes, provided that the foreclosure was discharged at least three years ago.

PROPERTY GUIDELINES

Q. What kinds of property certifications must be conducted to secure an FHA loan?

The FHA will require termite inspections if applicable, testing of wells for bacteria and chemical analysis, and other property certifications based on the borrower's geographic area.

Q. Are there any safeguards that govern the condition of property insured by the FHA?

In 1998, HUD launched a Homebuyer Protection Plan designed to reinvent the FHA's home-appraisal process and create a new level of consumer confidence in the homebuying process.

Under the plan, homes purchased with FHA-insured mortgages

- require a more thorough basic survey of the physical condition of the home to uncover potential problems.
- require appraisers, for the first time, to disclose property defects to potential buyers.
- impose stricter accountability on appraisers and tougher sanctions for those who act improperly (ranging from barring them from doing FHA appraisals to fines to potential prison sentences).
- allow homebuyers to finance up to $300 in home inspection costs into their mortgage loan.

Q. Does the FHA have to comply with the Energy Policy Act of 1992 on new construction?

For both FHA and VA loans, new construction begun after October 24, 1993, must comply with the 1992 Model Energy Code (MEC) of the Council of American Building Officials (CABO). A written certificate must be obtained from the builder stating that minimum energy standards have been met before the loan can be approved.

Q. Are any credits allowed for energy-efficient homes?

In addition to being able to increase both qualifying ratios by 2 percent, buyers can have the cost of energy-efficient improvements financed into the mortgage. The allowable amount is the greater of 5 percent of the property's value (not to exceed $8,000).

LEVERAGE

Q. Are coborrowers allowed on FHA loans?

Coborrowers are allowed on FHA loans. By definition, coborrowers take title to the property and obligate themselves on the mortgage note, but do not live in the property. The loan-to-value ratio on coborrower transactions is limited to 75 percent of the appraised value of the property.

The only exception to this 75 percent loan-to-value rule would be if the coborrowers were related by blood (parent and child, siblings, aunts, uncles, nieces or nephews, etc.) or for unrelated individuals who can document evidence of a family-type long-standing relationship. Individuals proving these relationships can obtain a maximum loan-to-value loan.

Similar to a coborrower, a cosigner with no ownership interest in the property (who does not take title) will be permitted to become jointly liable for repayment of the obligation. The coborrower's and cosigner's income, assets, liabilities, and credit history will be used for qualifying.

Second Mortgage Simultaneous to a New First FHA Loan

Q. Would the FHA ever allow a borrower to secure a second mortgage simultaneously with a new FHA first mortgage?

Remarkably, the answer is yes. Secondary financing simultaneous with a new FHA first mortgage may be allowed if the combined amounts of the first and second mortgages do not exceed the applicable loan-to-value ratio loan. In addition, the second mortgage must not force a balloon payment before five years, reasonable monthly payments must be made on the second mortgage, and prepayment of the obligation must be allowed at any time.

Borrowers age 60 and older can obtain secondary financing with total loan-to-value ratios of the combined first and second mortgages up to 100 percent of the property's appraised value.

Q. When might a buyer use an initial second mortgage with a new FHA first?

This situation would most likely occur when interest rates on the first mortgage are high and qualifying for an entire loan at that high rate could be difficult, as in the following example:

> FHA interest is 8 percent. Edith Olson can't qualify for a $110,000 loan at that interest rate, so she secures a $20,000 second mortgage from her credit union at 7 percent interest simultaneously with closing a $90,000 FHA first mortgage, less the applicable down payment.

Of course, the FHA lender knows of the second mortgage and qualifies Edith for both sets of debt repayments. The two payments are melded together for the purpose of qualifying, and the lower interest rate of the second mortgage is just enough to leverage Edith into qualifying for both loans.

MORTGAGE INSURANCE PREMIUMS

Q. How is mortgage insurance applied to the loan amount?

There are two kinds of mortgage insurance premiums (MIPs) with FHA loans: initial premiums and renewal premiums. The rates charged are based on the term of the loan, as well as on the amount of the down payment. Figure 8.3 contains the rates charged. For example, on a $100,000 loan, minimum down payment, for 30 years, the up-front premium would be 1.50 percent, for a total of $1,500 (paid in cash at the closing or financed into the loan. Obviously, most borrowers finance it into the loan!). The monthly or recurring premium would be .50 percent, or $41.67 per month (added to the monthly PITI payment).

FIGURE 8.3 *Up-Front and Annual MIP Rates*

Loan Term	Up-Front MIP	95% and Over	90%-95%	Below 90%
30 year	1.50%	.50% – to 78% LTV	.50% – to 78% LTV	.50% – to 78% LTV
15 year	1.50%	.25% – to 78% LTV	.25% – to 78% LTV	None

Q. As with private mortgage insurance premiums on conventional loans, are mortgage insurance premiums tax deductible on FHA loans?

Yes, at least temporarily. The same legislation affecting private mortgage insurance on conventional loans applies to FHA. For FHA mortgages closed from 2007 through 2010, the mortgage insurance premiums paid on both purchases and refinances are deductible on federal income tax returns. Under this legislation, married taxpayers who have an annual income of $100,000 or less ($50,000 for single taxpayers or married taxpayers filing separately) will be entitled to deduct the monthly mortgage insurance premium as well as a portion of the premium they paid up-front at settlement. The tax deductible amount decreases as income increases above $100,000 and terminates entirely if household income is above $110,000.

Q. Does the renewal premium stay on the mortgage for the life of the loan?

No. Effective January 1, 2001, the renewal premium is dropped from the loan payment once equity in the property reaches 22 percent. For most borrowers, this would occur at approximately the 11th year of a 30-year loan.

Q. Can a portion of the MIP be refunded to the borrower?

A borrower may be eligible for a refund of a portion of the insurance premium if the borrower

- originated the loan after September 1, 1983,
- paid an up-front mortgage insurance premium at closing, and
- did not default on the mortgage payments.

Another category of refunds called *distributive share,* however, affects mortgages written before September 1, 1983. To be eligible for these excess earnings from the HUD Mutual Mortgage Insurance fund, a loan must have

- been originated before September 1, 1983,
- shown at least seven years of payments, and
- been paid off before November 5, 1990.

Because the statute of limitations runs for only six years from the date the payoff notification was sent to the mortgagor, the last deadline for applying for these funds was November 5, 1996.

Note this exception: When an FHA loan is assumed, the seller receives no refund.

Borrowers who want to inquire about possible premium refunds can contact HUD at P.O. Box 23699, Washington, DC 20026-3699, or call 800-697-6967 between 8:30 AM and 8:30 PM (ET).

CONCESSIONS

Q. What are sales concessions and why are they limited in an FHA loan?

A sales concession is a cost paid by someone other than the buyer, such as the seller or a third party. It is viewed as an inducement to purchase and limits the buyer's investment in the property. For that reason, HUD requires that sales concessions paid or offered by the seller or a third party are deducted dollar for dollar from the sales price before the maximum mortgage amount is calculated. Sales concessions include prepaid items, personal property items, decorating allowances, moving costs, buyer-broker fees, condominium or homeowners association fees, excess rent credit, or seller payment of borrower's sales commission on present residence.

Q. What's the difference between sales concessions and financing concessions?

Financially, quite a lot. While financing concessions include discount points, interest rate buydowns, mortgage interest payments, or the borrower's up-front mortgage insurance premium paid for the borrower by the seller or a third party, financing concessions are treated differently from sales concessions for qualifying purposes. Financing concessions are not subtracted dollar for dollar from the sales price until they exceed 6 percent of the sales price. Then they are subtracted dollar for dollar before figuring the maximum loan amount.

How does this affect the borrower's position? If possible, it's financially better for a seller or third party to contribute financing concessions rather than sales concessions if the borrower is in need of a maximum-allowable loan. It's best to spell out on the purchase agreement just what the concession is to apply to; otherwise, it would be determined by the lender, possibly not to the buyer's advantage.

ASSUMPTION GUIDELINES

Q. What does the term *simply assumable* mean when referring to FHA loans originated before December 15, 1989?

A simply assumable FHA loan is one that can be assumed by a new borrower without qualifying through the lender. Should the assumptor default on the loan, however, the original borrower could be held responsible for satisfying the debt.

If the initial mortgagor wants to be released of all liability under an FHA loan written prior to December 15, 1989, the assumptor needs to qualify to assume the loan (called a *novation*). This includes providing the lender with information regarding monthly income and debt, as well as credit and employment history, and requesting the novation from the lender. If the borrower meets the lender's criteria, the original borrower may be released from further liability on the loan.

Q. What about loans originated after December 15, 1989?

Borrowers must qualify and meet all FHA guidelines for assumptions. Only owner-occupants, not investors, may assume these loans.

PREPAYMENT PENALTIES

Q. Is there a prepayment penalty on FHA mortgages?

This question has several possible answers. The guidelines state that if an FHA loan was insured prior to August 2, 1985, the borrower must give a 30-day written notice to HUD stating that the loan will be paid in full. This notice can come from a real estate agent or loan officer and carries 30 days of interest. The FHA, however, views this as an interest charge, not as a prepayment penalty.

For loans insured on or after August 2, 1985, the FHA will no longer require a 30-day notice to prepay. Under this guideline, however, the lender can refuse to credit full prepayment without requiring interest to the next due date if the payment is not made on the monthly due date. The solution? Make sure the loan is repaid on the monthly due date!

DISCOUNT POINTS AND BUYDOWNS

Q. Who can pay points on FHA loans?

Anyone can pay points on FHA loans. Because many FHA buyers are short on cash, sellers often assist with points. A third party—such as a relative of the buyer or someone in another real estate transaction who has an interest in seeing this sale close so that his or her home can be purchased—could also pay points. No matter who pays the points, they are tax deductible for the homebuyer.

Q. Could a buyer use discount points and then reduce the interest rate using buydowns in the same transaction?

There's no reason why not. The discount points are charged by the lender to help increase the overall yield and defray the cost of discounting the loan when it's sold to the secondary market. The buydown, on the other hand, uses points (actually prepaid interest) to buy down the note rate either temporarily (like a 3-2-1 buydown) or permanently for the life of the loan (for example, from 8 percent to 7 percent).

REFINANCING

Q. What are the guidelines for refinancing an FHA loan?

If the borrower is taking cash out of the property, the loan-to-value ratio cannot exceed 85 percent of the appraised value, and the borrower must occupy the property.

If the borrower takes no cash out of the property, the maximum loan is based on the lower of the FHA purchase formula or costs and liens on the property.

Q. Is there a streamlined program such as those available with other loan types?

Yes. The FHA streamlined refinance program is designed to lower the monthly principal and interest payments on a current HUD-insured mortgage and involves no cash back to the borrower.

Streamline refinances can be completed with or without an appraisal but must meet the following guidelines:

- Refinances *with* appraisals allow the closing costs and reasonable discount points to be financed. The lender could also charge a higher interest rate on the loan and pay the closing costs on behalf of the borrower. Loan maximums are subject to FHA loan-to-value limits.

* Refinances *without* an appraisal are limited to the unpaid principal balance (but no interest) minus any refund of mortgage insurance premium (MIP) plus the new up-front mortgage insurance premium if it's to be financed in the mortgage. The term of the refinanced mortgage is the lesser of 30 years or the unexpired term of the old mortgage plus 12 years.

Refinancing is considered a payoff of the old loan and releases the original seller on an assumed loan from all liability.

Borrowers could take advantage of this program to lower a 30-year loan into a 15-year term (provided the new payment does not increase by more than $50), or to convert an FHA adjustable-rate mortgage into a fixed-rate loan.

OTHER FHA LOAN OPTIONS

The FHA/VA Tandem Loan

Q. Is there an FHA loan for veterans?

The loan is called FHA/VA 203(v) and it is used to finance only single-family structures: duplexes and other multifamily units are not permitted. The loan is often used by veterans who have used their VA eligibility or who want to preserve their VA certificate for a later time. In other words, the FHA/VA loan does not involve the veteran's entitlement, and there are no limits restricting the amount of times it can be used.

FHA/VA loans are beneficial because the FHA limits some charges typically required with regular 203(b) financing. In addition, some closing costs can be financed into the loan.

The veteran must obtain a Certificate of Veteran Status form from the VA (and a Form DD208 from the commander if the veteran is still in the service). Loan ceiling amounts are the same as with the standard 203(b) program.

The FHA Adjustable-Rate Mortgage

Q. Are FHA ARMs competitive?

The FHA ARM (FHA loan Section 251) is very competitive, combining the down payment guidelines of the standard 203(b) program with the features of an ARM. Here are some of its characteristics:

- Maximum interest-rate increase caps are limited to 1 percent per year and 5 percent over the life of the loan. In addition, the FHA ARM allows no negative amortization.
- The loan is assumable (with borrower qualification) at the loan's current interest rate.
- The index is the one-year Treasury Constant Maturities Index, and the margin is determined by supply and demand for GNMA mortgage-backed securities.
- Qualifying guidelines and maximum loan amounts are the same as those found under the 203(b) program.
- The FHA ARM can be used to refinance any existing HUD loan.

SPECIALIZED FHA MORTGAGE PROGRAMS

Q. Which other FHA programs might be of interest to borrowers?

Although many FHA programs are not widely used, here are some that have sparked interest lately:

FHASecure® Helps Consumers Refinance

Q. With all of the adjustable rate mortgages resetting and people needing refinancing options, does FHA have a loan for this?

Yes, FHA has birthed a new refinancing vehicle called FHASecure®. Designed to assist homeowners whose mortgages are behind due to loan reset and higher payments, or who are likely to fall behind once reset, it's hoped to help nearly a quarter of a million households.

Here's how it works. In order to qualify, borrowers must have

1. a history of on-time mortgage payments before the payment reset;
2. an adjustable rate mortgage that reset between June 2005, and December 2008;
3. a sustained history of employment; and
4. sufficient income to make the new mortgage payment. Qualifying ratios are the FHA standard 31 percent (front end) and 43 percent (back end) respectively.

There are no minimum or maximum months of delinquent payments required to qualify and any type of non-FHA adjustable rate mortgage can be refinanced. All other program guidelines of the standard 203(b) loan apply to this program.

Q. Can I refinance an interest-only mortgage with FHASecure®?

Yes.

Q. What if I have a prepayment penalty and other refinancing costs and there isn't enough equity in my home to refinance?

You could ask your lender to consider a second mortgage to pay the difference or request a short payoff (less than what you owe) from the lender on your existing loan. Either of these options is at the discretion of the lender.

Q. Would FHASecure® assist a borrower who is already in foreclosure?

Possibly. It would depend on many factors including the value of the home, how much is owed, and whether or not the lender is willing to offer a second mortgage to rectify the problem and cure the default. Homeowners facing foreclosure are encouraged to talk to their lender, possibly with the assistance of a HUD-approved housing counseling agency. To find an approved counselor, call 1-800-569-428, or search online for additional FHASecure® information at www.fha.gov/fhasecure.

Q. Which other FHA programs might be of interest to borrowers?

Although many FHA programs are not widely used, here are some that have sparked interest lately:

Disaster Victim Housing Loans

HUD Section 203(h) financing is eligible to anyone whose home has been destroyed or severely damaged in a federally declared disaster area. The loan can be used to rebuild a home or purchase a new one, but the borrower's application for mortgage insurance must be filed with HUD within one year of the president's declaration of the disaster.

Benefits of the 203(h) loan include:

- 100 percent loans can be obtained (including closing costs). Prepaid expenses such as property taxes and insurance can be paid by the borrower, or the lender can premium price the loan (charge more interest) and pay the prepaids for the borrower.

- Limits are set on some fees charged, including appraisals, inspections, and origination fees.

Borrowers under 203(h) must pay FHA mortgage insurance. As with the standard FHA 203(b) program, the up-front fee can be paid in cash at the closing or financed into the loan. The monthly MIP fee is added onto the PITI payment. For more information, check out www.fema.gov/disasters.

Loans to Rehabilitate Properties

Section 203(k), rehabilitation home mortgage insurance, insures loans used to rehabilitate an existing residential dwelling that will be used for residential purposes, or to refinance an outstanding indebtedness plus rehabilitate such a structure. This program also may be used to convert nonresidential buildings to residential use or to change the number of family units in the dwelling.

The 203(k) loan provides the borrower with interim and permanent financing in one loan. The loan amount, which is based on the property's after-renovation value, can't exceed the current FHA maximum mortgage in the borrower's area.

Even though it's called a rehab program, repairs can include almost anything beyond minor or cosmetic adjustments. Replacing floors, tiles, or carpets is considered rehab work, as is new siding, roofing, gutters, plumbing, heating/cooling, and electrical systems.

The 203(k) loan can also be used to finance work performed outside the structure such as major landscaping, patios, or terraces.

While repairs are under way, borrowers don't have to make mortgage payments. Tax or insurance payments, however, may be due. The payment moratorium can last up to six months if time is needed for the repairs and the property is unoccupied.

Manufactured Housing Loans

Q. Does the FHA allow loans on mobile homes?

The FHA calls mobile homes *manufactured homes* and will lend money for their purchase under the FHA Title I program, which is similar to the residential guidelines under the 203(b) program. In fact, a borrower can receive a loan for the purchase of a manufactured home if he or she owns the land on which it will be placed; to fund a combination purchase of home and land; or just for the land, if the borrower already owns the manufactured home.

Because state laws vary regarding manufactured housing as real property, the borrower should check with a local lender to determine program guidelines.

FORECLOSURE ALTERNATIVES WHEN PAYMENTS FALL BEHIND

Q. Does the FHA assist borrowers who fall behind on their mortgage payments?

Yes. Five options are available from HUD to help borrowers sidestep foreclosure: (Note: Since the loan is FHA insured, your lender has to follow FHA servicing guidelines and regulations. First contact the lender's Loss Mitigation Division to seek a workout solution; but if the lender is nonresponsive, you can contact FHA's National Servicing Center (NCS) at 1-888-297-8685).

1. *Special forbearance:* The lender may be able to arrange a repayment plan based on the consumer's current financial situation—including a temporary suspension of payments.
2. *Mortgage modification:* The lender agrees to add the borrower's back payments, interest, and penalties onto the loan and amortize it over the loan term. HUD requires that the new payment must be lower than the present payment. This is accomplished by lowering the interest rate and/or extending the loan term. The rationale is that while the borrower is paying more over time because the loan principal is higher, the lower payment should be easier to keep current.
3. *Partial claim:* The lender may be able to obtain an interest-free loan from HUD to bring the borrower's payments current.
4. *Preforeclosure sale:* Allows the borrower time to sell the property and pay off the mortgage before foreclosure. This encourages the borrower to keep the property in good repair to be able to take equity from the sale.

5. *Deed-in-lieu of foreclosure:* As a last resort, the buyer may decide to voluntarily "give back" the property to the lender. The lender must agree, which means the value of the property must cover the outstanding loan plus costs to market the property. The mortgagor sidesteps foreclosure and avoids attorneys' fees, but receives no equity from a sale.

The bottom line to working out alternatives when a borrower's mortgage payments become delinquent is for the borrower to take a proactive stance, contact the lender as soon as possible, and be prepared to be honest with the lender about the borrower's current financial situation.

9

VA LOAN PROGRAMS

$\mathbf{T}$his chapter offers an overview of VA single-family housing programs. Information in this chapter comes from standard VA guidelines and thus may have different applications, depending on the particular region of the country.

In 1944, Congress passed the Serviceman's Readjustment Act. This legislation, more commonly known as the GI Bill of Rights, was developed to assist veterans in readjusting to civilian life by providing them with medical benefits, bonuses, and low-interest loans. Title III, one of six sections of the bill, guaranteed home loans to eligible veterans. Although loans were to be a type of bonus for those who had served their country, credit standards and underwriting guidelines were strictly enforced so that veterans would not undertake mortgage obligations they could not fulfill.

A local lender makes a loan for up to 100 percent of the appraised value of the property, with the Department of Veterans Affairs indemnifying the lender against loss on a portion of the loan. Unlike FHA loans, with VA loans the veteran does not pay a premium for the loan guarantee (though a funding fee is charged). This factor, plus others discussed in this chapter, helps make VA loans some of the most successful and rate-competitive programs in the mortgage market today.

LEVELS OF VA LOANS

A borrower who talks to someone from a different area of the country about VA loans sometimes finds discrepancies in what he or she thought were firm guidelines or practices. Who is correct? Both probably are. Similar to the FHA, the VA establishes basic guidelines for loan administration. Regional VA offices or local lenders may choose to be more restrictive.

For example, if a military base closing in a local lender's market caused foreclosures to edge up, that lender might choose to be more cautious about risks to help control the problem.

Thus, a borrower should shop not only for the type of VA loan but for the lender who will make it. Lenders who process a high volume of VA loans will be aware of little-known exceptions and underwriting nuances that can help a veteran qualify for one of these loans.

PROS AND CONS OF VA LOANS

Q. What are the advantages of using VA financing?

Advantages to VA financing are:

- There is no down payment requirement unless the purchase price of the property is greater than the VA appraisal called the Certificate of Reasonable Value (CRV) or if, based on the borrower's qualifications, the lender requires a down payment to make the loan.
- There is no VA limitation on the size of the mortgage. However, the lender or the requirements of the secondary mortgage market may set one.
- Loan rates are typically below market rate when compared to conventional fixed-rate loans.
- A seller can assist a buyer in paying closing costs.
- A veteran can own more than one property secured by VA loans.

- Loans originated prior to March 1, 1988, are simply assumable (assumable without qualification of the new purchaser). All VA loans are assumable (even by nonveterans) at the note rate under which they were originated (with the exception of VA ARMs, which are assumed at their current rate of interest).
- The veteran can pay discount points, making VA loans rate-competitive.
- VA loans have no prepayment penalty.
- Because a new VA loan pays off existing encumbrances, the seller receives all his or her equity, less costs of sale.
- Qualifying guidelines are designed to assist the veteran in financing a home; therefore, some guidelines may be more liberal than those found in conventional financing.
- Although the VA doesn't lend money, it acts to guarantee the lender against default on a portion of the loan.
- No mortgage insurance is charged on VA loans (unlike FHA and some conventional mortgages).

Q. What are the disadvantages in financing with a VA loan?

Disadvantages to VA financing are:

- Loans originated on or after March 1, 1988, are no longer assumable under simple assumption guidelines. The VA must approve the new purchase and an assumption fee must be paid.
- For loans originated prior to March 1, 1988, veterans who sell property with assumptions of the mortgage may not be relieved of liability should the subsequent purchaser default.
- In case of default, the veteran may be held liable for repaying the VA any guaranteed amount paid to the lender.
- Sellers and veterans may object to paying discount points or other closing costs.
- Loan-processing time can be longer than for conventional loans.
- Because the seller's costs of sale are higher than those attributable to conventional loans, the seller may accept only his or her full asking price.
- A funding fee based on the amount financed must be paid at the closing.

PROFILE OF A VA BUYER

Q. Who typically buys through VA programs?

Although each buyer's qualifications and profile are unique, following are some typical characteristics. The VA borrower is a veteran who

- has never used his or her entitlement, or has purchased previously with partial entitlement remaining.
- is looking for a zero-down payment loan.
- requests that the seller pay all, or a large portion of the closing costs.
- is looking for a loan that has no mortgage insurance premium.
- wants a loan that can be assumed at the rate originated (with the exception of the VA ARM loan, which would be assumed at the loan's current rate).
- wants a loan that has no prepayment penalty.

ELIGIBILITY

Q. Who is eligible for a VA loan?

The following list gives a breakdown of the amount of days of active duty that must have been served to be eligible for VA home-loan benefits:

	Days of Active Duty
September 16, 1940, to July 25, 1947	90
July 26, 1947, to June 26, 1950	181
June 27, 1950, to January 31, 1955	90
February 1, 1955, to August 4, 1964	181
August 5, 1964, to May 7, 1975	90
May 8, 1975, to September 7, 1980	181
Persian Gulf: August 2, 1990, to present	2 years, or the full period called to active duty (at least 90 days)

In addition, the following guidelines apply:

- Twenty-four months of continuous active service is required for everyone beginning active duty on or after September 7, 1980 (except Persian Gulf/Desert Storm veterans).

- Persons serving in Selective Reserves National Guard are eligible if they have six years of service in the reserves. Service must have been active, that is, one weekend per month and two weeks of annual training each year. Inactive reserve time does not count as qualifying service.
- Veterans who were discharged before they served the minimum amounts of time may be eligible if they were discharged for the convenience of the government, for a service-connected disability, or for hardship. These exceptions do not apply to persons serving in the Selective Reserves/National Guard.
- Spouses of service personnel missing in action or of prisoners of war may be eligible for one VA home loan if the veteran has been missing in action, captured, or interned in the line of duty for more than 90 days.
- Unmarried surviving spouses (widow or widower of a veteran) may claim VA home-loan benefits if the veteran's death was caused by a service-connected injury or ailment. The surviving spouse cannot have eligibility by virtue of his or her own military service. Any VA eligibility previously used by the veteran will not be subtracted from the full guarantee allowed the surviving spouse.
- Any U.S. citizen who served in the armed forces of a country allied with the United States in World War II is eligible.
- A veteran who meets the qualification guidelines is eligible for VA home-loan benefits even if he or she is hospitalized pending final discharge.

Q. How does one show proof of eligibility?

The certificate of eligibility (COE) must be submitted at the time of the loan application. This certificate is VA form 26-8320 and contains the following information: veteran's name, Social Security number, service serial number, entitlement code, branch of service, date of birth, date the certificate was issued, signature of an authorized agent, and the issuing office. On the reverse side of the form is the amount of entitlement or guaranty used, as well as the amount of any guaranty available for real estate loans.

Q. How does a veteran obtain a Certificate of Eligibility?

The applicant must complete VA form 26-1880, Request for Determination of Eligibility and Available Loan Guaranty Entitlement.

This request must be accompanied either by a form DD214 (a synopsis of the applicant's military record and the veteran's physical characteristics) issued to service personnel discharged after January 1, 1950; a form WDAGO, Notice of Separation (for veterans discharged before this date); or a computer-generated certificate of eligibility, which was issued to veterans who served for one period of service after approximately 1970.

Mortgage lenders who originate VA loans usually will have the necessary filing forms on hand and will assist in procuring the certificate. In fact, some lenders allow you to apply for your certificate of eligibility directly from their secure server (SSL) website under a system called automated certificate of eligibility (ACE).

Q. What happens if the applicant has lost his or her form DD214, WDAGO, or other evidence of military service?

The applicant could substitute GSA form 6954, Certification of Military Service, which is available from the applicable service department.

If the veteran has lost the DD214, a duplicate may be obtained from the War Records Department; county records; a civil service agency employing the veteran; the local draft board, if the veteran was drafted; or the branch of service from which the veteran was discharged.

Q. What does an applicant currently on active duty use for eligibility documents?

Form DD13, Statement of Service, is acceptable; or the applicant can submit a statement in letter form on military letterhead from his or her personnel officer or commanding officer. Included in this statement should be the applicant's name, service serial number, active duty dates, previous periods of service (if any), character of service, and notation of any lost time.

Q. Does the veteran have to be present for the loan application or the closing?

No. The veteran's spouse or another member of his or her immediate family can apply on the veteran's behalf. In regard to signing papers, a power of attorney can be used; however, the VA has several guidelines that must be met. If a loan will be closed in the veteran's absence, the borrower should consult the lender for current VA requirements.

Q. If a veteran served in more than one conflict, would it be possible to apply for and receive two VA loans?

When the first property is purchased (for example, using World War II eligibility), the dual eligibility would have no impact. If the home was later sold and the loan payments were not delinquent, however, the veteran could apply for a second VA loan pertaining to benefits from a second conflict period (for example, the Korean War) regardless of the release from the first loan or the amount of the outstanding guaranty. The VA has set specific time limits within which to apply for the second loan.

Q. How long does a veteran have to use his or her eligibility?

There are no specific time frames, other than the requirement for dual eligibility just discussed. Eligibility is good until used.

CALCULATING THE GUARANTY AMOUNT

Q. What are the VA guaranty and veteran's entitlement and eligibility?

The difference in the terms guaranty, entitlement, and eligibility when referring to VA loans is more semantic than actual. *Guaranty* in VA loans refers to the amount of the loan the VA will indemnify or guarantee for repayment to the lender should the borrower default. The terms *entitlement* and *eligibility* are used more when referring to the VA's relationship with the veteran.

In 1944, the original maximum entitlement available for home-loan purposes was $2,000. But as you'll see in the guidelines that follow, entitlement has been updated and fine-tuned over the years to keep pace with the increased cost of home prices.

Guaranty Guidelines

The maximum guaranty on a VA loan is the lesser of the veteran's available entitlement or

1. 50 percent of the loan for loans up to $45,000.
2. $22,500 for loans of more than $45,000 and not more than $56,250.

3. 40 percent of the loan with a maximum guaranty of $36,000 for loans of more than $56,250 and not more than $144,000.
4. the calculation method is different for loans of more than $144,000 made for the purchase or construction of a home, or to purchase a residential unit in a condominium, or to refinance an existing VA guaranteed loan for interest-rate reduction.

To keep pace and be loan competitive in a rising price market, Veterans' Benefits Act of 2004 changed the maximum guaranty amount available on loans in excess of $144,000 to 25 percent of the Federal Home Loan Mortgage Corporation (Freddie Mac/FHLMC) conforming loan limit was $417,000, making the VA guaranty $104,250 (25% of $417,000). In the higher-cost housing areas of Hawaii, Guam, and the Virgin Islands, the guaranty is 50% higher. (Note figure 9.1, "Amount of Guaranty").

FIGURE 9.1 *Guaranty*

Amount of Guaranty:
The maximum guaranty on a VA Loan is the lesser of
- the veteran's available entitlement indicated on the certificate of eligibility (COE) or
- the maximum potential guaranty amount from the following table:

LOAN AMOUNT	LOAN TYPES	MAXIMUM POTENTIAL GUARANTY	SPECIAL PROVISIONS
Up to $45,000	All	50% of the loan amount	Minimum guaranty of 25% on IRRRLs
$45,001 to $56,250	All	$22,500	Minimum guaranty of 25% on IRRRLs
$56,251 to $144,000	All	40% of the loan amount, with a Maximum of $36,000	Minimum guaranty of 25% on IRRRLs
Greater than $144,000	Must be for: • Purchase or construction of a home, OR • Purchase of a condominium unit, OR • Refinancing with an IRRRL	25% of the loan amount, with a Maximum of $104,250 for 2008.	• Cash-out refinances have a Maximum guaranty of $36,000. • Minimum guaranty of 25% on IRRRLs

Note: The basic $36,000 entitlement is increased for home purchase, construction, and condominium loans in excess of $144,000 to provide 25% guaranty for loans up to the Freddie Mac) FHLMC conforming conventional annually-adjusted loan limit ($417,000 in 2008).

Q. Will that guaranty amount buy much of a home in today's real estate market?

Don't confuse the guaranty amount with the loan amount. As a rule of thumb, most lenders will loan four times the amount of the guaranty with no down payment required. In other words, if the VA will guaranty the lender repayment on 25 percent of the loan, the lender making the loan will take the risk.

Q. Is there a VA loan maximum?

No, there isn't. However, some lenders don't make VA loans that exceed the GNMA/FNMA/FHLMC maximum allowable conforming loan limits because most VA loans are sold in the secondary market.

Q. Could someone use a VA loan to purchase a house and finance more than the amount of the conforming loan limit? If so, how would that work?

As mentioned previously, there would be no down payment required on the amount up to the conforming loan cap (i.e. $417,000) since the lender is guaranteed 25 percent against loss. But to obtain a loan exceeding that amount, the borrower would need to make a down payment of 25 percent on the additional amount borrowed. For example, a loan of $690,000 exceeds the $417,000 conforming loan cap by $273,000. To obtain a loan of that size, the borrower would need to make a down payment of 25 percent on the difference, or $68,250 in order to obtain a VA mortgage.

Q. Does the government set the interest rates allowed for VA loans?

No. Interest rates for VA loans are negotiated between the lender and the borrower. In essence, this means that if more discount points are paid, the borrower can receive a lower interest rate. These points must be paid in cash at the time of the closing and cannot be financed into the loan.

Q. If just a portion of the loan is guaranteed, what actually happens if there's a default?

First, because the lender becomes the owner of the defaulted property after foreclosure, the VA could accept the property from the lender by reimbursing the amount of the outstanding loan balance plus foreclosure expenses. Second, the VA could instruct the lender to keep title to the foreclosed property and accept a check equal to the remaining balance times the guaranty percentage originally issued when the loan was originated. Typical risk to the lender in the case of default is minimal. Even with a mere 25 percent guarantee from the VA, the lender will generally recoup 100 percent of the outstanding balance.

Q. When could a veteran have more than one VA loan at a time?

While the veteran must agree, and sign papers to the effect that he or she will live on the property when purchased, the veteran could have more than one outstanding VA loan at a time. For example, the veteran could purchase another home using VA eligibility and rent the current home. Obviously, he or she would have to have adequate eligibility, and any payments on outstanding loans must be current.

Q. If someone can use his or her remaining VA eligibility for subsequent purchases, how does one calculate the amount of the guaranty available?

This is a little tricky, but here's an example:

Joan Koch previously used $12,500 entitlement not restored (paid off). The VA imposes a cap for calculating remaining eligibility at $36,000 for loans up to $144,000. So to finance her new $120,000 home, she has $23,500 additional entitlement available to her ($36,000 – $12,500 = $23,500).

Q. How large a loan could a veteran with a remaining entitlement of $23,500 receive?

Remember the rule of four times the amount of the guaranty. If the veteran could qualify, the lender would probably make a loan of $94,000 with no down payment. She could finance the difference by making a 25 percent down payment.

Q. Although the veteran must reside on the property after the initial purchase, does the property have to be a single-family residence?

No, the veteran could purchase up to a four-unit building as his or her residence; however, no additional guaranty is available just because the number of units in the purchase increase.

QUALIFICATION GUIDELINES

Q. What are the buyer's qualifications for new VA loans?

Following is an overview of how a veteran qualifies based on income, residuals, and long-term debt.

The VA loan uses a debt-to-income ratio for loan qualification. It is calculated by taking the sum of PITI, any special assessments (such as condominium fees or local improvement district levies), and long-term obligations (those with repayment in excess of ten months). Divide that amount by the total income, which includes gross salary and other compensation. The resulting percent or ratio cannot exceed 41 percent. If it does, it is fairly unlikely that the application will be approved without some pretty convincing compensating factors entering the picture. Residual income remains a secondary VA qualifier along with the ratio. Residual income is determined by subtracting PITI, heat, maintenance, and utilities from the net effective income (income after taxes, long-term monthly debts, child care, child support, or alimony).

Think of residual income as leftover income. According to figure 9.2, for example, a family of four in the West must have a residual income of $1,117 per month when applying for an $80,000 mortgage.

While each case will be decided on its own merits, these are fairly firm guidelines that most local lenders will use in accepting or rejecting a loan.

Q. Can a borrower exceed the 41 percent ratio rule and still be acceptable?

The borrower can exceed the 41 percent ratio rule if the residuals are 20 percent or more than the residual income amount required based on the number of family members, the veteran's geographical area, and the loan amount requested.

COMPENSATING FACTORS

Q. What compensating factors could a veteran use to get VA loan approval, even with marginal qualifications?

As with other loans, the VA has its own set of compensating factors:

- Excellent credit history
- Conservative use of consumer credit
- Minimal consumer debt
- Long-term employment
- Significant liquid assets
- Down payment or the existence of equity in refinancing loans
- Little or no increase in shelter expense
- High residual income
- Tax credits for child care
- Tax benefits of home ownership

Note: Compensating factors CANNOT be used to offset unsatisfactory credit.

Q. Do in-service veterans and retired service persons get any concessions in qualifying for a VA loan?

They certainly do. They can qualify with 5 percent less residual income than other applicants. The only criterion is that they must prove that their military benefits will be continuous.

FIGURE 9.2 *VA Table of Residual Incomes by Region*

Loan Amounts of $79,999 and Below

Family Size	Northeast	Midwest	South	West
1	$390	$382	$382	$ 425
2	654	641	641	713
3	788	772	772	641
4	888	868	868	967
5	921	902	902	1,004
over 5	Add $75 for each additional member up to 7.			

Loan Amounts of $80,000 and Above

Family Size	Northeast	Midwest	South	West
1	$ 450	$ 441	$ 441	$ 491
2	755	738	738	823
3	909	889	889	990
4	1,025	1,003	1,003	1,117
5	1,062	1,039	1,039	1,158
over 5	Add $80 for each additional member up to 7.			

Geographic Regions

Northeast Connecticut, Maine, Massachusetts, New Hampshire, New Jersey, New York, Pennsylvania, Rhode Island, and Vermont

Midwest Illinois, Indiana, Iowa, Kansas, Michigan, Minnesota, Missouri, Nebraska, North Dakota, Ohio, South Dakota, and Wisconsin

South Alabama, Arkansas, Delaware, District of Columbia, Florida, Georgia, Kentucky, Louisiana, Maryland, Mississippi, North Carolina, Oklahoma, Puerto Rico, South Carolina, Tennessee, Texas, Virginia, and West Virginia

West Alaska, Arizona, California, Colorado, Hawaii, Idaho, Montana, Nevada, New Mexico, Oregon, Utah, Washington, and Wyoming

Q. Even though long-term debts are considered debts that can't be paid off within ten months, what about substantial short-term payments?

The lender must consider the impact of any substantial monthly payment, even though it is scheduled to last less than ten months.

A VA qualifying form can be found at figure 9.3.

FIGURE 9.3 *VA Qualifying Form*

Loan Amount $ _____

Gross Income Per Month (Veteran or Spouse) (Including pension compensation or other net income)	$ _____	(A)

Less: Federal Income Tax $ _____
State Income Tax _____

Social Security Tax _____
Other _____

Net Take-Home Pay $ _____ (B)

Housing Expense:
House Payment $ _____
(Principal and Interest)
Taxes + _____

Insurance + _____
HOA/Assessments + _____

Subtotal $ _____ (C)

Utilities $ _____

Other (pool, air-conditioning, etc.) + _____
Maintenance + _____

Total Housing Expense $ _____ (D)

Fixed Obligations:
Total of all monthly debt payments
that will last six months or longer
including "job-related expenses." $ _____ (E)

Balance Remaining for Family Support (B less D and E) $ _____

Family Support
Number of Family Members _____ Balance Required $ _____ %*
(round down to two digits)

*A statement that lists all compensating factors that justify approval must be provided if ratio exceeds 41 percent unless the residual income exceeds the required amount by at least 20 percent.

Employment History

Q. Do VA loan applicants need a two-year employment history as required with other loans?

Yes. Two years of employment history must be verified. In addition, the borrower is asked to supply an original pay stub from his or her current employment.

Q. What about active-duty applicants? What do they have to verify?

Active-duty military must provide the lender with a current (not more than 120 days old) Leave and Earnings Statement.

Service members within 12 months of release from active duty will require additional information. The veteran will need to provide reenlistment documentation, verification of civilian employment following release, or a statement from the service member that he or she intends to reenlist or extend the period of active duty. The latter alternative would need to be supported by a letter from the service member's commanding officer confirming that the veteran is eligible for reenlistment.

Other offsetting factors that would weigh heavily in favor of the veteran getting the loan would be a down payment of at least 10 percent or significant cash reserves at the closing, or both.

Recently Discharged Veterans

Q. What about recently discharged veterans who are currently employed but haven't held a civilian job for two years? Would they be able to qualify for a loan?

Perhaps. Veterans who are recently discharged (including veterans who have retired after 20 years of active military duty) may be able to secure a loan without the two-year employment history. Consideration is made on a case-by-case basis, weighing how similar the current line of work is to the veteran's military duties.

For example, a veteran who was formerly an airplane mechanic in military service and is currently successfully employed as a machinist would provide the lender with a good indication that the work could be performed and the employment steady. But a former airplane mechanic who is now selling insurance may not give the lender a strong indication of employment stability in the early stages of the new job.

INCOME GUIDELINES: OVERTIME AND PART-TIME INCOME

Q. Could overtime and part-time income count for VA qualifying?

Again, the guidelines are pretty much the same as with other loans. Unless there is a two-year work history and the income is likely to continue, this income might be used as a compensating factor, but not as true qualifying income.

Q. Can educational-loan benefits be included in income qualification for a VA loan?

No, just on-the-job training benefits and VA retirement or disability income can be included for qualifying.

Q. If the veteran can't qualify on his or her own, could a coborrower be considered?

Yes, the VA will consider the income and credit of a comortgagor who resides on the property. The VA will guarantee only the portion for which the veteran has qualified. This may pose a problem from the lender's standpoint for a partial guaranty is usually unacceptable to the lender.

One solution might be to use two veterans as joint mortgagors, thus allowing an extended guaranty amount. Any loan in coborrower situations must be processed directly by the VA, not through automatic approval by direct endorsement lenders. (These are lenders who have met approval guidelines of the VA and can approve loans in-house, without first submitting them to their respective regional VA offices.)

Borrowers with Bankruptcies

Q. Would a veteran who has declared bankruptcy ever be able to get a VA loan?

Obviously, each situation is evaluated on its own merits, and because there are several chapter filings of bankruptcy, each may be handled differently.

In general, the VA will want to see that the bankruptcy has been discharged for at least 24 months and that credit has been satisfactorily reestablished. However, bankruptcies discharged less than two years may be considered if credit has been reestablished and the bankruptcy was beyond the control of the consumer (such as medical bills, prolonged strikes, etc.).

LEVERAGE

Q. To what extent can a seller financially help a buyer purchase his or her home under VA guidelines?

Possibly to a great degree. If the buyer has adequate eligibility, the lender can lend 100 percent of the CRV (VA appraisal), and the seller is allowed to pay all closing costs, including prepaid items (such as insurance impounds and property-tax impounds). This is sometimes referred to as *zero down, zero closing.*

Q. Regarding VA loans, what's a seller concession?

A seller concession on a VA loan is a negotiated contribution to help the borrower qualify and must not exceed 4 percent of the appraised value of the property. However, seller payment of normal discount points and/ or the buyer's closing costs is not counted in the 4 percent cap.

Q. Could the veteran borrow the down payment for a loan?

It depends. It would be acceptable if the borrowed funds were used to pay the closing costs, or the down payment, provided the total of the down payment and the loan do not exceed the CRV. Loan terms would have to be included in the application, and therefore the repayment amounts would be included in the qualifying ratio.

This is one of the areas where a borrower may have to shop for a lender who will take on this type of increased risk.

Q. Can a borrower have a second mortgage simultaneously with originating a new VA loan?

It is possible to use secondary financing simultaneously with the origination of a VA first mortgage within certain boundaries:

- The CRV must exceed the amount of the first mortgage. In this way, the second mortgage could be used to secure the monetary difference between the appraised value and the first mortgage.

- The lender will want to know the repayment terms on the second mortgage and will add the debt service payment into the veteran's debt ratios.
- The lender may ask that the interest rate on the second mortgage not exceed the rate of the first mortgage, and that any second mortgage be assumable. The idea is to avoid putting undue stress on the borrower and to keep both loans from defaulting.

Even though second mortgages initiated simultaneously with first mortgages are approved by the VA, many lenders shun the practice, for they feel it creates too much leverage and possible stress on the veteran, which may strain the loan and cause default. The key here is to shop for local lenders who won't be afraid to take the risk with an otherwise qualified buyer.

Q. When might someone use an initial second mortgage simultaneously with a new VA first mortgage?

A veteran might consider initiating a second mortgage simultaneously with a first not only for a down payment but for qualifying as well, as in the following example:

The lender's VA interest rate has just jumped to 8 percent, making it impossible for Joe Smith to financially qualify for a $200,000 loan. However, if his credit union would carry a second mortgage of $20,000 at 6 percent with the balance of $80,000 at the lender's 9 percent first-mortgage rate, he could qualify. The melding of the two rates for qualifying was enough to make the difference between no loan and owning his dream home.

CLOSING COSTS

Q. Could someone other than the seller pay for the veteran's costs of sale?

Yes. In addition to those charges enumerated previously that could be paid by the seller, a third party might pay part of the closing costs— e.g., attorneys' fees, title company fees, and escrow closing agent fees. In fact, it would not be considered an illegal kickback for a lender to pay any or all of the costs mentioned, particularly if the loan was made to a buyer who was short on closing costs.

Q. What closing costs can the borrower pay?

Although allowable charges to the veteran vary by VA regional office, here is a list of some of the more typical allowable costs for the borrower:

- Credit report charge
- Appraisal fee
- Recording and tax fees
- Proration of taxes or assessments
- Survey charges
- Hazard insurance
- Title fees
- Funding fee charged by the VA
- Any allowable discount points

Additionally, the lender has the option of charging a flat 1 percent origination fee, or charging actual costs for the items listed below, as long as the total does not exceed 1 percent of the loan amount:

- Assignment fees
- Notary fees
- Warehousing fees
- Commitment fees
- Underwriting fees
- Photo charges
- Amortization fees
- Application fees
- Tax service fees
- Builder's 10-year home warranty
- Closing or settlement fees
- Document preparation fees
- Attorney fees

Note: Termite reports and courier fees are allowable charges to veterans only on refinances.

Q. Does each regional office tell the veteran exactly what costs he or she can pay?

Somewhat; however, the offices phrase it as "costs the veteran is *not allowed* to pay." Remember that closing costs (except the ones specified for payment by a certain party) are negotiable between the buyer and seller. The VA loan is the most restrictive type of loan when it comes to mandating which party can pay which cost.

FIGURE 9.4 *2004 VA Funding Fees*

VA Funding Fee Schedule

Loan Type	Required Down Payment	Active Duty Personnel and Veterans	National Guard and Reservists
First Time Use of VA Loan Guaranty Benefits			
Purchase/Construction	0% down	2.15%	2.40%
	5% down	1.50%	1.75%
	10% down	1.25%	1.50%
Regular Cash Out Refinance		2.15%	2.40%
Second or subsequent use of VA Loan Guaranty Benefits			
Purchase/Construction	0%	3.30%	3.30%
	5%	1.50%	1.75%
	10%	1.25%	1.50%
Regular Cash Out Refinance		3.30%	3.30%

Note: The funding fee may be financed into the loan amount (over and above the appraised value of the property).

Q. Does the buyer have to pay the funding fee charged by the VA?

No. In fact, anyone can pay the funding fee—the buyer, the seller, or a third party; or the fee can be financed into the loan. Also, the funding fee does not have to be paid by veterans receiving VA compensation for service-connected disabilities, or veterans who, if they had not received retirement pay, would have been entitled to receive compensation for service-connected disabilities. The funding fee is also waived for surviving spouses of veterans who died in service or from service-connected disabilities.

Q. Are funding fees different based on whether a veteran was active-duty military, Reservist, or National Guard status?

Yes. Figure 9.4 compares funding fees, including a category for veterans who are making a subsequent (repeat) purchase using a VA loan.

DISCOUNT POINTS

Q. What are discount points and how do they work with VA loans?

Lenders use discount points to increase the yield of a loan. Because VA and FHA loans are usually made below conventional-loan market rates, what lender in his or her right mind would be excited about making a guaranteed or insured loan at a lesser rate of interest? They wouldn't. That's why points can help bridge the gap between what they could lend conventional money for compared to what they can receive on government programs.

By definition, a point is equal to 1 percent of the amount financed. Depending on the value of the dollar, it takes from four to six points to increase the interest rate by 1 percent over a 10-year period. Knowing this, the lender is now ready to evaluate where conventional rates are today, how many discount points need to be charged to equalize the two rates, how much of a discount secondary market investors will charge, and what competing lenders are charging for points.

Therefore, if conventional money is typically going for 7 percent, while VA/FHA funds are at 6.5 percent, the lender would probably be looking at several points to equalize the rates.

Q. Do lenders ever negotiate points?

It depends on the lender. Many times, in an effort to be competitive, a lender will negotiate or even waive part or all of the potential points to make the loan. This might occur if someone has been a good customer of a lending institution or has the potential to be a good customer. Lenders will sometimes loosen up on points when there's a glut of money in the marketplace and demand is down, or if they're in an expansion mode, vying for a heftier share of loans in the marketplace.

Q. Who can pay points on a VA loan?

Anyone! Points are negotiated between the parties in the purchase agreement. VA loans are getting more competitive; allowing veterans to pay points makes the VA loans even more so.

Q. Are there times when the veteran is most likely to pay VA points?

Yes, when he or she is building a home on his or her own property, refinancing an existing loan, or purchasing a property from a legal entity that cannot or will not pay points, such as the executor of an estate, a trustee, or a sheriff at a sheriff's sale.

VA APPRAISALS

Q. Could the veteran ever pay more for the property than the value shown on the Certificate of Reasonable Value?

Yes, if the difference was paid in cash and did not come from a borrowed source. Note the amendatory language clause (see figure 9.5) that must accompany each VA purchase and sales agreement.

Q. Would it be wise for a seller who would consider selling a home with VA financing to get a CRV before putting it on the market?

It depends. Although the CRV does give a reasonable estimate of value, it may sometimes lean toward the more conservative end of the price range. This is particularly true when a VA appraisal is ordered prior to having an offer on the property. More strain is put on the appraiser to determine valuation when there is no offer setting the stage for what someone is ready, willing, and able to pay for a property. And if the appraisal is low, the damage has been done because it is very difficult to massage the price up to where it should or could be. Unless a particular buyer demands a VA appraisal prior to making an offer, the borrower should use a well-prepared comparative market analysis by a real estate agent to estimate value.

An appropriate time to secure a CRV prior to placing a property on the market could be with a specialty property, where the approximate market value might be difficult to determine.

Q. For what period is a CRV good?

A CRV is generally good for six months on existing construction and up to one year on proposed new construction.

Q. Are there any other facts one should know regarding CRVs?

Here are several additional tips for dealing with VA appraisals:

- The VA accepts FHA appraisals.
- Proposed construction should be preapproved by submission of plans and specifications to the VA so that it can then make periodic inspections. Exceptions to this rule might include any dwelling with previous approval by the FHA, a new dwelling that has been substantially completed for more than 12 months, or a house located in a rural area, making routine inspections impossible.

FIGURE 9.5 *VA Amendatory Language Clause*

The purchase agreement entered into _____ , between the
(date)
undersigned seller and purchaser, is hereby amended to include the following statement:

"It is expressly agreed that, notwithstanding any other provision of this contract, the purchaser shall not incur any penalty by forfeiture or earnest money or otherwise be obligated to complete the purchase of the property described herein, if the contract purchase price or cost exceeds the reasonable value of the property established by the Department of Veterans Affairs. The purchaser shall, however, have the privilege and option of proceeding with the consummation of this contract without regard to the amount of reasonable value established by the Department of Veterans Affairs."

_____   _____
(Date)   (Seller)

_____
(Seller)

_____
(Purchaser)

_____
(Purchaser)

- A veteran cannot be charged for a CRV unless the appraisal is ordered in his or her name.
- The VA uses only VA-designated fee appraisers. Some private individuals who have met certain VA criteria are authorized to make VA appraisals.
- A particular VA regional office may change or adjust the value or conditions specified by a particular VA appraiser.

LOAN TYPES

Q. What types of VA guaranteed loans are there?

There are far more varieties of VA loans than we tend to think of! Even though VA loans must have a fixed rate of interest, payment amounts can vary according to the needs of the veteran. If, for example, a young couple wants to begin with a moderate payment to suit their budget and then increase the amount paid monthly at the end of five years, they have several VA alternatives from which to choose, as described in this chapter.

VA Graduated Payment Mortgage (GPM)

Q. What is the VA GPM?

The VA GPM is a great loan for using a minimal down payment while "graduating" the payment, typically over the first five years, by approximately 7.5 percent. The starting interest rate for the loan is usually 2 to 3 percent below the standard VA rate.

VA Growing Equity Mortgage

Q. Does VA have a GEM?

The VA permits a growing equity mortgage (GEM). Basically, the GEM grows equity more rapidly because, based on a 30-year amortized amount, payments increase 3 percent, 5 percent, or 7.5 percent per year (based on the plan), with the additional monthly payment being applied directly to the principal. Under this program, loan payoffs usually occur in a little less than 17 years.

As mentioned previously, not all lenders may be interested in working with "creative" VA programs, which differ in underwriting guidelines from the regular VA programs. Borrowers may need to shop for the right lender just as fervently as they shop for the right program.

UNDERWRITING GUIDELINES

Q. Is it possible for a VA loan to have a late charge?

A late charge may be levied if any installment is more than 15 days late. The amount charged cannot exceed 4 percent of the installment due.

Q. Does the VA insist that all tax and insurance payments be collected monthly along with the regular principal and interest payment?

Interestingly enough, the VA does not mandate that impounds be held. However, the VA feels that it is a sound practice and therefore allows individual investors to hold escrow accounts if they so desire. In other words, this is a lender request and criterion rather than a VA requirement. The buyer may be able to use this as a bargaining point when applying for a VA loan. For example, the veteran may be willing to hold taxes and insurance fees in escrow monthly with the lender in return for lower points.

Q. Does the VA require fire insurance as well as title insurance?

The VA does require fire insurance to protect its collateral; however, the policy coverage could exclude the value of the land.

Q. Is there a prepayment penalty on a VA loan?

VA loans can be paid at any time without penalty. Lenders may require that partial payments may not be less than one monthly installment or $100, whichever is less. And, unlike FHA loans that need at least one month's notice before prepaying (otherwise there will be a payment penalty), VA loans can be paid in full without notice.

Q. What is a certificate of commitment?

That's what this chapter has been about—getting the loan! The certificate of commitment, or loan approval, is valid for six months for existing and proposed dwellings. Although it cannot be extended for an existing dwelling, there is an extension period of six months if a proposed dwelling is involved.

ASSUMPTION GUIDELINES

Q. What about selling a home encumbered by a VA loan? Would the loan have to be assumed by another veteran?

A veteran or nonveteran can assume an existing VA loan. Loans written prior to March 1, 1988, can be simply assumed, meaning that there is no mandatory qualification process by anyone assuming an existing VA loan unless the veteran wanted either a total release of liability or a substitution of certificate. A total release of liability means that the veteran would not be held liable for any delinquencies or deficiency judgments should the loan default. Substitution of certificate goes one step further and releases the veteran from all liability on the loan, plus reinstates that amount on his or her certificate of eligibility. The latter can be accomplished only if the assumptor is a veteran who substitutes his or her certificate of eligibility for that of the selling veteran.

Q. What are the assumption rules governing loans written on or after March 1, 1988?

All VA loans originated after March 1, 1988, require prior approval by the loan holder (as trustee for the VA) before transfer of the property. Mandated by Public Law 100–198, the mortgage or deed of trust must clearly state the following in large letters on its first page: "This loan is not assumable without the approval of the Veterans Administration or its authorized agent." If the veteran fails to notify the lender before transferring the property or if the property is transferred to a buyer who has failed the creditworthiness test, the lender could accelerate the loan, with the outstanding balance becoming immediately due and payable. The selling veteran has 30 days to appeal to the VA if a lender determines that a buyer is not creditworthy. If the VA overrides the lender's determination, the lender would then approve the assumption.

The assumption clause, which should be placed in all purchase and sales agreements of VA loan properties, is shown in figure 9.6.

The inclusion of the assumption clause will not, of course, ensure that a release from the VA can be obtained. This will depend on the deed being recorded, the loan being current, and the purchaser's income and credit being acceptable.

Such inclusion will, however, permit releases in many cases that could not otherwise be approved. Also, the inclusion of the assumption clause will afford the veteran a right of action against the transferee and thus give the veteran some measure of protection even though the VA may decline to release the veteran because the loan is in default or the transferee's income and credit are not acceptable.

Q. Will there be a charge for this assumption policy?

An assumption fee equal to half of 1 percent of the loan balance as of the date of transfer shall be payable to the VA at the time of transfer. If the assumptor fails to pay this fee, it will constitute an additional debt and will be added to the principal amount of the mortgage. In addition, the loan holder may charge a processing fee to determine the assumer's creditworthiness.

Q. If the selling veteran wanted to be free of liability plus have his or her eligibility reinstated from a particular loan, would the new buyer either have to pay off the loan or be a veteran willing to substitute his or her certificate of eligibility?

FIGURE 9.6 *VA Assumption Clause*

Subject to a mortgage dated _____ , 20_____ , in favor
of _____ , which mortgage grantee hereby
assumes and agrees to pay according to its terms and also hereby assumes the
obligation of _____ , under the terms
(Name of Veteran Mortgagor)
of the instruments creating the loan to indemnify the VA to the extent of any
claim payment arising from the guaranty or insurance of the indebtedness above
mentioned, and consents to his release from his obligations under the loan
instruments.

That's correct. Although it may seem to be a minor point, it's easy to
see the possible conundrum created after the veteran sells the property
and wants to use his or her entire VA eligibility to buy a new property
with a VA loan, only to find that part of his or her eligibility is still tied
up (for years to come!) on the property just sold.

Q. If the veteran who initiates a mortgage under the old guidelines
sells without obtaining a release of liability, could he or she ever obtain
a release?

Yes, if a subsequent purchaser down the line applied to the VA for
the release of liability. The following conditions must be met to qualify:

- The loan must be current.
- The income and credit of the purchaser must be acceptable to
  the VA.
- The purchaser must assume the loan and the indemnity obligation
  (owner occupancy is not required).

Remember, too, that unless that subsequent purchaser was also a
veteran and substituted his or her certificate of eligibility, the original
purchaser's certificate of eligibility (pertaining to that property) would
not be released.

Q. Is there any way the veteran could avoid liability from the VA when
the property is sold without a release of liability?

No, but the veteran can keep apprised of the condition of the existing
loan. The veteran can write the lender using certified mail, with return
receipt requested, asking that the veteran be notified of any pending

default on the loan. Better yet, have the new buyer agree to and execute a small second mortgage (e.g., for $100) recording it at the court house for public record. That way, should any potential default occur, you'd be notified by the lender and could potentially protect your liability position.

Q. But doesn't the lender have to notify the veteran of any possible default?

No VA regulation or law requires that the initial mortgagor be notified. This has become a misconception by the public because sometimes the lender searches out the veteran to step back in and take over payments in lieu of foreclosure (especially given the high cost of foreclosure to the lender). The VA generally attempts to contact the original veteran borrower because courts in some states have ruled that the VA may not collect an indebtedness from a veteran who did not receive notice of the foreclosure proceedings.

Nevertheless, should the loan default, the original obligor would still be secondarily liable. And remember, that original veteran was the one who pledged that he or she would repay the obligation, along with his or her VA eligibility entitlement.

The *VA Home Loan Guaranty Informational Issue* looks at foreclosure in this manner:

> Under the governing law, a veteran who obtains a loan from a private lender that is guaranteed or insured by the VA is legally obligated to indemnify the U.S. government for the net amount of any guaranty or insurance claim the VA may hereafter be required to pay to the holder of the loan. This right of indemnity has been upheld by the Supreme Court of the United States, notwithstanding that a deficiency judgment was not obtained or was not obtainable by the mortgage holder under local state law. (*U.S. v. Shimer,* 367 U.S. 374, 1961)

Q. In a default, could the original veteran purchaser ever be responsible for paying the guaranty amount back to the VA?

Yes. The VA is entitled to receive indemnification from the veteran, which can be enforced by judicial action within our court system. Through this channel, the VA could attach the veteran's pension or Social Security income, and also withhold any subsequent VA benefits until the defaulted guaranty amount is paid in full.

REFINANCING

Q. Can a veteran refinance an existing loan with a new VA loan?

Yes. Up to 91 percent loan-to-value of the appraisal amount could be refinanced using a VA loan if equity is being pulled out. (This is 90 percent loan-to-value plus the 1 percent funding fee.)

The VA encourages using an interest rate reduction refinancing loan (IRRRL). The loan must be a VA loan and the new rate must be lower than the previous rate. No appraisal or credit check is required and the veteran does not have to currently occupy the property.

The refinanced loan amount may include the outstanding balance on the existing loan, allowable fees, and closing costs, including discount points and funding fees. In addition, up to $6,000 in energy-efficiency improvements may be financed.

The lender may agree to pay all closing costs for the borrower and set an interest rate high enough to recover the advance of costs (but the final rate must be lower than the loan being refinanced).

Q. Is the certificate of eligibility automatically released to the veteran if the home is refinanced outside of the VA program?

Home loan entitlement may be restored one time only, if the veteran has repaid the prior VA loan in full, but has not disposed of the property securing the loan. After such, any future restoration will require the veteran to dispose of all property financed with a VA loan, including the property not disposed of under the "one time only" exception.

Q. Does an owner have to live in a property to refinance it with a VA loan?

No, the property does not have to be owner-occupied. This is good to know if the original VA residence was purchased with a high interest rate and is currently being used as a rental. Refinancing may be a chance to bring the rate down, lower the monthly payment, and increase the rental cash flow.

FORECLOSURE ALTERNATIVES: WORKOUT PROGRAMS

Q. It sounds as though the VA really wants to work with veterans to secure home loans. Does it ever help borrowers if they get behind in their payments, rather than forcing foreclosure?

The VA understands that base closures, layoffs, and similar situations not only have adverse affects on borrowers but can add incredible costs to guaranteeing VA loans in general. That's why the VA introduced a preforeclosure, or "compromise" program to eliminate formal foreclosure and work out loans in trouble.

Here's how it works: A veteran behind in payments contacts the lender. As discussed earlier, any borrower should not hesitate to contact the lender once he or she has trouble making any monthly payment. The lender will evaluate the situation, and if it appears that time, effort, and money can be saved with a workout program, the regional VA office will be contacted. If the regional office agrees and is willing to front any shortfall, the workout is accomplished.

If the veteran's property has $100,000 worth of liens against it and the fair market value of the property is only $95,000, that's a $5,000 shortfall. The workout program would allow the real estate agent to bring in (and receive a commission for) a new buyer to step into the $95,000 loan, the $5,000 shortfall would be advanced to the lender from the regional VA office, and the seller (veteran) would be responsible for repaying the shortfall over time. Guidelines require that the veteran start repaying the shortage within 12 months of closing, plus a nominal rate of interest between 7 and 9 percent.

While the veteran's loan eligibility is frozen until the shortfall is repaid in full, at least formal foreclosure has been sidestepped and the veteran may be able to qualify for another loan in the future. In fact, the lien that the veteran pays back is no longer secured by the property, merely by a promissory note to the VA regional office. Should the veteran fail to repay the note, however, the VA would be able to take action to enforce payment, including attachment of the veteran's assets. The VA and lender both win because they have a new, stronger buyer in the property and have not spent the time or expense in a formal foreclosure action. The veteran can then get back on track to use his or her VA eligibility on another home loan in the future. To learn more about preforeclosure and view properties currently for sale by the VA, visit http://www.homeloans.va.gov/pmoffices.htm.

It's encouraging to see that the VA and lenders are agreeing that foreclosure is not always the only way to satisfy a potential loan default, and that they are willing to work with borrowers to find alternative remedies. You can find additional information about mortgage forbearance options in chapter 14.

10

LOAN PROGRAMS
WITH LEVERAGE

As the saying goes, money talks. But for many real estate purchasers today, there is barely enough in their pockets to whisper. That's why many loan programs employ the concept of leverage. By definition, real estate leverage is using a small amount of an asset to purchase a larger asset (something like robbing Peter to pay Paul). Just like anything else, leverage is an excellent tool when used in moderation. When taken to the extreme, robbing Peter to pay Paul makes Peter a "Paul-bearer."

Lenders offer special programs—usually identified with acronyms such as GEM, RAM, and GPM—tailor-made to assist a targeted market segment of mortgage buyers. Many of the programs discussed in this chapter are based on leveraging concepts introduced in earlier chapters.

GROWING EQUITY MORTGAGES

Q. What is the GEM and how does it work?

The growing equity mortgage, or GEM, is a fixed-rate, 20-year or 30-year amortizing loan, with annual payment increases of 3 percent, 5 percent, or 7.5 percent, depending on the lender's individual plan. These characteristics alone may not sound unique; the difference, however, is that the monthly payment increases are applied directly to reduce the principal. Thus, most 30-year loans will be paid in full between years 13 and 15.

Most lenders will qualify GEM borrowers at the initial payment amount and ask for a minimum of 10 percent down. A bonus GEM program even allows the borrower to qualify at a discounted introductory rate, sometimes as low as 2 to 3 percent below the standard rate, by using an up-front temporary buydown of the interest rate.

It's clear to see what type of buyer can benefit from the GEM—one who needs up-front leverage today, but who will be able to meet the payment increases of the future: young professionals, M&Ms (married and mortgaged), and first-time buyers who need help qualifying.

Q. How about buyers making a final home purchase? Is the GEM good for them?

It certainly is. As stated previously, depending on the GEM plan chosen, the loan will be retired between 13 and 15 years. This is great for a final home purchase for people in their early 50s, because they are usually building into their highest income years. Many middle-aged buyers have trimmed their family expenses because their children are grown, and they want their new loan to retire by the time they do.

Q. Are there special types of GEM programs?

The VA allows GEM mortgages.

REVERSE ANNUITY MORTGAGES

Q. What are reverse annuity mortgages and how do they differ from other types of mortgages?

As the name denotes, reverse annuity mortgages (RAMs) allow persons over the age of 62 to release equity in their primary residences without having to sell and move from their homes. Instead of making payments immediately after taking out the mortgage, the flow of payments is reversed to the borrower in flat sum amounts, a credit line account, monthly cash advance, or any combination of these. The RAM was designed to help house-rich and cash-poor seniors tap equity from their homes without having to move or repay mortgages while they live in their homes.

The mortgagors must occupy the home as a principal residence (where they spend the majority of the year). All programs lend on single-family, one-unit dwellings, and some programs also include two- to four-unit owner-occupied dwellings, condominiums, and manufactured homes.

Q. How do RAMs work?

Because the borrower makes no monthly payment, the loan amount grows larger over time (thus the equity decreases). But federal guidelines on reverse annuity mortgages will not permit the loan value to ever exceed the value of the home at the time the loan is repaid.

Q. What size loan could a borrower obtain?

The loan size depends on several factors, including the borrower's age, the value of the home, its location, and the cost of the loan (many of the fees can be financed into the loan to limit the out-of-pocket cash required). The maximum-size loan also depends on the loan program chosen. The most well known in the marketplace are the FHA-insured program Home Equity Conversion Mortgage online at www.hud.gov (HUD) and Fannie Mae's HomeKeeper mortgage. You can find information at www.efanniemae.com.

Additionally, you can obtain a personalized quote about the size RAM you could qualify for at the website of the National Center for Home Equity Conversion at www.reverse.org.

Q. When does a borrower have to repay the loan?

The loan doesn't have to be paid back as long as the borrower lives in the home. But it must be repaid in full (including all interest and any other charges) when the last living borrower dies, sells the home, or permanently moves away.

Q. What kind of interest is charged for a reverse annuity mortgage?

Most are ARMs that adjust monthly and have maximum lifetime caps (e.g., loans that can't increase more than X percent over their lifetime). The lender is at risk because the total amount of interest accrued would be capped (should the borrower outlive the estimated life of the loan), so rates are considerably higher than with standard ARM programs.

Q. Where can potential borrowers obtain more information?

From a variety of sources, including:

AARP Home Equity Information Center
601 E Street, NW
Washington, DC 20049
Phone: 202-434-6042
www.aarp.org/money/revmort

Fannie Mae Consumer Resource Center at 1-800-7-FANNIE
(ask for its HomeKeeper Guide, *Money from Home*)

And if you'd like a list of preferred counselors who abide by a code of conduct and ethical principles that provide additional safeguards for consumers, send $1 (for postage and handling) in a self-addressed stamped business-size envelope to the nonprofit National Center for Home Equity Conversion:

NCHEC
7373 147th Street West, Suite 115
Apple Valley, MN 55124
www.reverse.org

GRADUATED PAYMENT MORTGAGES

Q. What are graduated payment mortgages?

A graduated payment mortgage (GPM) is a loan where the payment graduates (increases) annually for a predetermined period (e.g., five or ten years) and then becomes fixed for the duration of the loan. During times of high-rate interest, borrowers use them as leverage to be able to more readily qualify (because the initial payment was less). But the downside is that even though the initial payment is less, the interest owed is not—and the payment shortfall in the early years is added back onto the loan, which can result in negative amortization.

Q. What kind of borrowers would be well suited for this type of loan?

GPMs can be good for borrowers if

- they have predictable income increases.
- the property value is expected to rise or at least keep pace with the payment increase.
- ownership of the property is not short term (requiring that they sell quickly, especially if negative amortization has caused the loan to exceed the home's value).
- they have the ability to refinance eventually into another type of loan.
- they require jumbo loans (those over the secondary market limit). For example, initial payments on a $450,000 mortgage with increased payments for the first five years would be more than $560 per month less using a graduated payment mortgage.

Q. Does the FHA insure GPMs?

Yes. In fact, the FHA offers plans that vary in annual payment increases and number of years over which the payments can increase. The greater the rate of increase or the longer the period of increase, the lower the mortgage payments are in the early years. After a period of five or ten years, depending on which plan is selected, the mortgage payments level off and stay at that level for the remainder of the loan.

BIWEEKLY MORTGAGES

Q. Can a borrower save money by paying one-half of the regular monthly mortgage payment every two weeks?

Yes. In fact, considerable interest can be saved over the life of a 30-year loan with payments via the biweekly mortgage.

Instead of making 12 monthly payments per year, the borrower makes 26 half-payments (52 weeks in the year divided by 2), which converts to one additional monthly payment each year. By attacking the principal balance with a reduction every two weeks, the borrower saves substantially on interest and the loan's payoff period is reduced by approximately 12 or more years, depending on the rate of interest.

A 30-year $100,000 fixed-rate loan with interest at 8 percent pays off approximately seven years faster with biweekly payments than it does with monthly payments—and costs nearly $55,000 less! When the biweekly payment mortgage is paid off, there would still be more than $47,000 worth of principal remaining on the monthly payment loan!

Q. What are the drawbacks to having a biweekly mortgage?

For a loan cast as a biweekly mortgage, a buyer who misses just one payment in a two-week period would potentially be in default. Also, most lenders require that payments be automatically withdrawn from the borrower's checking account (and often charge a fee for doing so). This means that the borrower loses the use and the float of the money with less likelihood of it generating interest for him or her.

Q. Can borrowers convert their existing loans into biweekly payment plans?

Yes, depending on the lender. In fact, many mortgage lenders and servicers are blanketing borrowers with flyers touting "Cut thousands of dollars off your mortgage by converting your monthly payment loan into a biweekly plan." But there's a catch. To do so, borrowers must pay a conversion fee (often hundreds of dollars). Financially this makes no sense. Borrowers would be better off structuring their own prepayment program by making additional principal payments monthly or annually and pitching these flyers in the circular file! Be sure to check for any prepayment penalty on the loan before proceeding.

BRIDGE LOANS

Q. What is a bridge loan?

A bridge loan is really an equity loan or line of credit used for a specific purpose—usually to bridge the cash-flow gap from selling one property to purchasing another, as shown in the following example:

> Nalda Negri has $20,000 worth of equity in her home and wants to purchase and close a loan on another property because it's such a great buy. Small problem: Her first home has not yet sold. A lender might loan a percentage of the current equity in the home to bridge the transactions (usually not more than 75 to 80 percent, which would be between $15,000 and $16,000 in this case).

Q. Is using a bridge loan a good idea?

The bridge loan can be an effective acquisition tool, but the borrower needs to answer the following questions:

- *What are the terms of repayment for the bridge loan?* Many lenders may accept "interest only," or waive any monthly payment, with balloon payments within 6 to 12 months or longer
- *What would happen if the first property does not sell within the estimated period of time?* Can you afford additional mortgage payments?
- *What are the costs of borrowing bridge loan funds? Do they counter any anticipated savings on the second property?*
- *How will the bridge loan affect the financing possibilities on the sale of the first property?* (This is particularly important to consider if there's an underlying assumable first mortgage at a low interest rate.)

Q. Where would I find a lender to make an equity loan?

The local retail bank you do business with is a good start. As always, be sure to shop for both interest rate and fees.

11

LEVERAGE FROM
THE SELLER

Few purchasers of real property to-
day have the financial capability to pay cash for their purchases. In reality,
anytime someone finances all or part of a property purchase, he or she
is using leverage. A 5 percent down payment may be considered a highly
leveraged purchase when using seller financing, while that amount of
down payment may be the norm for a conventional loan from an insti-
tutional lender.

This chapter will show the positive and negative effects of leverage
and the ways it can be used to purchase real estate. The focus will be
on seller financing, including its use with conventional programs. Two
other techniques involving the seller will be discussed—lease purchases
and loan assumptions. Seller financing is often an option in a buyer's
market. Depending on the circumstances of the seller, this can work
well for everyone no matter what the market conditions are.

THE POWER OF LEVERAGE

Following is a simple example to show the power of real estate leverage:

> The Patels have $50,000 to use as a down payment. They can use it in a variety of ways. They can put the entire sum down on the $100,000 property A; or they can put $10,000 down on each of five separate $100,000 properties, B, C, D, E, and F. If appreciation were estimated at 10 percent per annum, should the Patels decide to sell in one year, they will make $10,000 on property A. But look at the increase in property value with properties B through F—a whopping $50,000! By using leverage, the Patels will be able to double their investment in one year.

The previous example shows how leverage can be positive. When does it become negative? Possibly when any combination of the following is present in extreme amounts: low equity, low appreciation, or low inflation.

The following example shows how these three items may interact to create a leverage nightmare:

> The Carpenters have purchased their first home, using a land sales contract/seller finance agreement. They felt that this was the best way to purchase the property because they had less than the typical 5 percent down payment required by local lenders in their area, and were marginally qualified for the $1,150 per month principal and interest payment. Their offer to the seller contained a provision that they would refinance the property at the end of their fifth year of ownership. This was agreeable to the seller, for she would soon be retiring and would need her equity out of the property at that time to supplement her Social Security.
>
> The Carpenters closed the sale and all appeared fine—until the balloon payment due date neared. A preliminary loan qualification appointment with the lender revealed that not only were the Carpenters not qualified to receive a loan the size of the one needed, but the property would not appraise for anywhere near the amount of the balloon promised to the seller. What could be done? The seller needed her equity to retire and the Carpenters' financial hands were tied, not to mention

that they felt that they had purchased a property that might be capable of wagging its tail and barking! The alternative, to not fulfill the balloon payment, could mean foreclosure, with the Carpenters forfeiting their down payment and any potential equity in the property, plus blemishing their credit rating.

But luck was with the Carpenters. The seller was willing to extend the period on the balloon, which not only helped the Carpenters build equity, but gave inflation a chance to bring up the appraisal price.

Q. Is seller financing negative because it creates too much leverage?

Absolutely not. Seller financing can serve as one of the most beneficial ways to finance a property, not to mention one of the best sources of higher return on seller investment. To create a win-win situation, however, reality, desires, and the financial capabilities of the parties must be addressed.

PROS AND CONS OF SELLER FINANCING

Q. What are the advantages to the buyer by having the seller finance all or part of a real estate purchase?

Depending on the circumstances, there can be quite a few. Here are some common positive points the buyer should consider:

- Unlike with lender financing programs, there are no constraints on what the seller can and cannot pay to assist the buyer.
- The buyer could negotiate the interest rate and the repayment schedule, and might even request that payments be made twice a month to save interest during the life of the loan. The buyer could also negotiate a partial amortization of the loan. For example, a $100,000 obligation might have monthly payments on only $50,000 for the first five years. The remaining $50,000 would sit idle, waiting to be amortized at a predetermined date. Balloon payments could also be used to satisfy the balance.
- The buyer could request special conditions of purchase, such as having a portion of the property released free and clear on the repayment of a certain sum of the principal.

- The buyer could include personal property in the purchase, such as household appliances or vehicles.

- The buyer can save on closing costs because loan-processing fees and points are eliminated and can therefore make a larger down payment or buy a more expensive home.

- The buyer would only have to pass the scrutiny of the seller and not a loan underwriter as with traditional lender programs. In addition, he or she could purchase a more expensive property than customarily could be afforded if qualifying through conventional mortgage lenders.

- The buyer could sidestep the cost of PMI by using seller financing.

- The buyer could purchase a property that does not meet appraisal guidelines required by most lenders. The property might vary from the norm in condition, age, and amount of land included.

- The buyer can purchase the property without the constraints of an appraisal. Sometimes buyers may want to offer a price at the top of market value to compensate the seller for carrying the financing.

- The buyer could help determine what type of security document is used to secure the sale, such as a mortgage, deed of trust, or land sales contract. For example, if the buyer desired that the title not transfer until the obligation was paid in full, an unrecorded land sales contract might be used (depending on the statutes of the state). On the other hand, if the buyer were making a large down payment and desired that the title pass at closing, a mortgage or deed of trust might be more appropriate. Obviously, the seller and his or her attorney would have an equal, if not greater, amount of input here.

Q. What are the negative factors of seller financing for the buyer?

Although the negative factors will vary based on the situation, here are a few of the more common problems. It's interesting to note that the advantages can also become disadvantages, depending on the circumstances.

- The buyer could pay the loan in full and still not receive title to the property. Although uncommon, this could occur when a land sales contract is used and the title does not pass until the obligation is paid in full. In rare cases, the seller may not have title vested in his or her name, or the buyer or seller was unaware of any liens or other encumbrances against the property. The buyer might have to sue the seller to gain title. This is one reason why no matter what type of financing is used, buyers should always seek title insurance for their purchases.

- The purchaser could make payments to the seller, but the seller might not make payments on senior loans that could result in property foreclosure. Placing the documents with, and making the payments through, a third-party escrow holder is advisable for buyer and seller.

- The buyer might be paying too much for the property, because properties are not always appraised in seller-financed transactions.

- Because technical property inspections or appraisals generally are not part of seller-financed transactions, a buyer might buy a property with severe physical deficiencies that go uncovered.

- The buyer may be using only a small down payment and may not be strongly committed to the purchase in case of tough financial times.

- The buyer might get in over his or her head as far as the size of the monthly payment is concerned. If creative terms such as interest only are used, payments will not be decreasing the principal balance. This could be dangerous, particularly if appreciation is low and the property will be held only for a short period.

- The buyer could finance personal property into the loan, causing depreciated property to cost the buyer many times its value.

- The buyer would have no mortgage insurance to protect any loss he or she might incur. Depending on state statutes, a deficiency judgment could attach to all property owned by the buyer, real and personal, if the property were foreclosed.

- The buyer would not necessarily have the property in his or her name until the loan was paid in full (depending on the type of security document used). Therefore, additional loans secured by the equity in the property could not be made to the buyer until the property loan was paid in full.

Q. How does the seller benefit by carrying financing for a buyer?

Following are several of the more common advantages to the seller who carries financing for the buyer:

- The seller could increase his or her yield on investment in the property because of the return of equity plus interest. For example, a $30,000 seller-carried 15-year second mortgage with interest at 9 percent per annum would give the seller $24,774 in additional proceeds on the sale. This is an 83 percent increase over what would have been received without seller financing.
- The seller could possibly negotiate a higher interest rate than could be received on many other types of investments. (Rates are typically on a par with those of commercial real estate funds.)
- The seller could ask for full price because he or she is assisting the buyer with financing.
- The seller could negotiate the terms and conditions of the sale, including remedies for default, maintenance of property conditions, and the repayment schedule (biweekly, etc.).
- The seller could open up the property to a larger field of buyers by offering seller financing.
- The seller could trim closing costs, especially the payment of points and other fees, typical to mortgage lenders.
- The seller could sell the property "as is" without costly repairs required by conventional lending institutions.
- The seller could screen the buyer for creditworthiness, ability to pay, and verification of employment.
- The seller could ask the buyer to provide a PMI policy to protect the seller against default on the financing.
- The seller could choose (with legal counsel) which security document is best to secure his or her interest until the loan is paid in full.
- The seller could defer payment of tax on gain because tax only would be paid as proceeds are received.

Q. What is the downside of seller financing for the seller?

Obviously, many buyer advantages, reversed, could become seller disadvantages. Here's how they stack up:

- The seller could accommodate the buyer by taking a small down payment or paying closing costs, then have the buyer walk away from the property because his or her investment was minimal.
- The seller may not have gotten the true credit picture of the buyer, or the financial strength of the buyer may have changed after the sale was closed. Because no loan officer qualifies the buyer based on ratios or debts, the buyer may also have taken on too much of a payment obligation.
- The seller may have to foreclose to regain ownership of the property. Depending on the type of security document used, as well as where the property is located, this could take from 30 days to more than a year.
- The seller may find the foreclosed property in a different condition than when it was sold; repairs may be needed to restore it to proper condition.
- The owner could sell personal property with the real estate, only to find it destroyed or missing should default occur.
- The seller could use creative terms in the loan, such as interest-only or balloon payments, then find that the property value has not increased because of insufficient appreciation, making any subsequent buyer refinancing impossible.
- The seller might use a security document that transfers title to the borrower, such as a mortgage or deed of trust, only to find that the buyer secured a junior lien against the property to pull out equity, and then abandoned the property.
- Judgments or liens may attach to the property, clouding the title and making it impossible to transfer it free and clear to the buyer, even though the loan has been satisfied.
- Tax liens for unpaid taxes may attach to the property, causing it to be sold at a tax sale.
- The seller might not use a competent real estate attorney to prepare a land sales contract; therefore, the seller's interests may be ill-protected in a weak, loophole-laden agreement, which is indefensible in court.

Q. Although seller financing seems to have many strong points, what are some steps both the buyer and the seller could take to protect their respective interests?

A seller-financed sale won't be good for either party unless it's good for both parties. In addition to having a meeting of the minds between the buyer and the seller, the following questions need to be answered thoroughly and satisfactorily:

- *Is the seller aware of the buyer's credit status? Has the buyer's employment been verified? What assets does the buyer have in addition to the property?* Remember, the seller is serving the same capacity as a mortgage lender and should ask many of the same qualifying questions.
- Is the payment structure feasible and plausible for the buyer?
- *Is the down payment coming from a borrowed source?* (Repayment of the down payment may create extra leverage, causing financial strain on the buyer.)
- *If creative terms or a balloon payment is part of the transaction, how much stress does this place on the sale?* It's amazing how time flies when a balloon payment is due in five years.
- *Are both parties' interests addressed in the contract drafted between the parties?* Even though one party's attorney may be drawing the document, it's wise for the second party's attorney to review the paperwork before closing.
- *Will a third-party escrow holder keep the documents in safekeeping for the parties, as well as receive and disburse payments between the parties?*
- *Is the remedy feasible for curing a default should it occur? Is the time frame for doing so standard, based on the security document and applicable legal statutes?*
- *What are the provisions for insurance coverage? Will the seller continue to carry any coverage?* This is particularly important if there are senior lien holders. *Will funds be impounded monthly for payment of taxes and insurance, or will the seller merely require that the buyer deposit paid receipts annually with the escrow holder?*

As with any type of real estate transaction, the sale should be an equitable, positive experience. This is particularly important with seller financing, however, because the business relationship between the parties extends until the loan is paid in full. In this way, the success or demise of the transaction is directly proportionate to the terms and conditions negotiated between the parties.

USING SELLER FINANCING

Q. In what ways could seller financing be used to put sales together?

As Second Mortgages

Seller financing typically has been used as a method of bridging the difference for the buyer between an existing loan and the down payment he or she has available, as illustrated in the following example:

> The purchase price of the Carlsons' house is $120,000. The Carlsons have an assumable loan of $95,000. Therefore, it would take $25,000 for the Buxtons to cash out all the Carlsons' equity. But if the Carlsons would take the Buxtons' $10,000 down payment and agree to carry the remaining $15,000 in seller financing, the sale could be made.

Q. With so many mortgage loans today containing the due-on-sale clause, isn't it difficult to assume an underlying loan and use a seller-carried second loan without disturbing the terms of the first mortgage?

Yes. Since the alienation, or due-on-sale, clause began receiving renewed interest in the early 1980s, it has been more difficult to simply assume existing mortgage loans without lenders altering interest rates, charging assumption fees, and/or qualifying new buyers. In fact, most lenders will not allow loans with due-on-sale clauses to be assumed at all. Seller financing, it should be stressed, is not a method to sidestep the due-on-sale clause in loans. The potential downstream effects of trying to hide a sale from a lender are not worth the benefits a seller or buyer might glean from making the sale.

As Wraparound Financing

Q. I've heard of people trying to sidestep the due-on-sale clause by using wraparound seller financing. Is this a good idea?

No, it isn't. Wraparound financing, whether financed by a seller or an institution, is exactly what its name implies—it's new financing that wraps around existing financing. The best way to explain it is to contrast it with the previous example:

> The Carlsons had an existing $95,000 mortgage, at an interest rate of 7 percent, on their $120,000 house. Because the Buxtons had only a $10,000 down payment ($15,000 short of cashing out all the Carlsons' equity), the Carlsons agreed to carry the $15,000 on a second mortgage for 15 years, including interest at 9 percent per annum. The monthly payment on the second mortgage will be $152.14, plus, of course, the payment on the first mortgage that was assumed by the Buxtons. This situation would be an assumption, with a seller carryback.

The configuration of the wraparound is different from that of the assumption and second mortgage. With the wraparound, the sales price minus the down payment gives a new principal balance to amortize, as in the following example:

> Going back to the Carlsons and the Buxtons, if the Buxtons' $10,000 down payment is subtracted from the $120,000 purchase price, it creates a new loan to amortize of $110,000, including interest at 9 percent, payable at $1,116.50 per month for 15 years. These terms could be anything negotiated between the parties, but should at least match the term of years remaining on the first mortgage. This is so title on the underlying loan could be released on satisfaction of the obligation.
>
> The Buxtons would ideally make their monthly payment to an impartial third-party escrow holder, who would subtract the payment on the underlying first mortgage, mail it to that lender, and send the balance to the seller, or to any other depository the seller designates. This system has some definite benefits for both the buyer and the seller.

Court cases came hard and fast during the early 1980s, ruling in favor of the lender in virtually all cases (except in California). According to the lender viewpoint, because the lender had loaned money to one party who was approved of and trusted, and only to that party, any subsequent transfer or assignment of interest in that property could only be accomplished under the lender's approval and scrutiny.

Even though it was presumed that the lender wouldn't discover the wraparound sale, because no documents were recorded at the courthouse, the lender did know. Most of the time the sale was discovered when the lender received an insurance rider amendment, showing a new party as the policy holder. The lender could then legally force the first borrower to pay off the initial loan.

Q. If a first mortgage didn't have a due-on-sale clause, and could be assumed, why would the buyer and the seller choose to use a wraparound mortgage to secure a secondary loan?

Wraparound financing might be attractive to both the buyer and the seller for several reasons:

- Higher yield on the seller's investment
- Careful accounting of all payments because they are best made through an escrow holder
- Knowledge that the payment on the underlying mortgage is being made in a timely fashion (best to have the escrow holder disburse it)
- Costs saved by the new buyer in not having to pay new loan fees
- Seller does not have costs customary to lending institution loans
- Loan documents held in safekeeping by the escrow holder

Seller Financing in First Mortgages

Q. Can seller financing also be used for first mortgages?

Absolutely. In fact, in many rural areas in the United States, seller financing has been and continues to be a primary source of real estate financing. This is partly because of qualifying guidelines coupled with the fact that much of the real property contains large parcels of bare land that are not traditionally financed by mortgage lenders.

Seller financing is also considered by many to be the wave of the future. The graying of America finds more than 50 percent of those over the age of 65 owning property that is free and clear of debt. If these citizens have saved well and have funds available for living expenses, this is a golden opportunity for them to sell their real estate through installment sales, thus creating a retirement annuity.

Q. Carrying seller financing sounds like a good financial move for the seller, right?

That's correct. A strong major advantage to the seller carrying financing is that many times he or she can receive a higher return on investment than with other investment vehicles. The seller, however, must be doubly sure that several vital points of the sale are covered:

- Sufficient down payment from the buyer
- Creditworthiness of the buyer
- Strong security document written by a competent real estate attorney
- Capacity of the buyer to repay the debt in a timely fashion

Q. What techniques could be used to negotiate seller financing?

Following could be major negotiating points between the buyer and seller:

- Interest rate
- Term of the loan
- Balloon payments allowed or disallowed
- Type of security document used (contract for deed, deed of trust, or mortgage)
- Prepayment privileges or penalties
- Time allowed for curing defaults
- Payment of taxes inside or outside of the monthly payment
- Allowing a quitclaim deed (that quits all interest the buyer has or may have in the property) to be placed with the escrow holder to be recorded in case the buyer defaults
- Personal property financed with the real estate
- Collateral in addition to the property secured in the case of default and foreclosure
- The right of the seller to assign or sell the contract to another party (the buyer might be considered a potential purchaser of the contract—maybe even with a discount on the principal balance)

CREATIVE DOWN PAYMENTS

Using Personal Property and Services as Down Payments

Q. I heard that someone once used a pickup truck as a part of her down payment on a seller-financed property. Could she?

That's being creative, and there's certainly nothing wrong with that. One of the advantages of using seller financing is that whatever the buyer and seller agree on (within the law, of course) can create a sale. The buyer might offer a combination of cash, personal property, collectibles (such as coins, guns, and antiques), or even services in trade as a down payment. (As a real estate broker, I once took three head of cattle as earnest money and down payment on a piece of property. Unfortunately, they were still eating and nearly broke us in hay costs until the sale closed! We negotiated with the seller—at his request—that the cattle become part of our commission.)

The premise is that anything of value can potentially serve as a sales incentive. One word of caution: Be sure there is a definite value placed on the item being offered. It's best to get an outside opinion or appraisal of value (especially if the buyer and seller can't agree or when the item has fluctuating value). Examples would include gold, jewelry, coin collections, vehicles, even beef! In the latter case, heaven forbid the collateral should die before closing! For a checklist exploring financing options between seller and buyer, see figure 11.1.

Q. How are services used as a down payment?

This is really not as difficult as it sounds. Suppose a husband and wife are just shy of having enough down payment to satisfy the seller, but because the wife provides professional child care, the buyer and the seller strike a bargain. The buyers' attorney drafts a personal service contract as part of the down payment, stating that within a specific period the buyers will provide X dollars' worth of service in child care to the sellers. Obviously, if the buyers do not fulfill their obligation, the sellers would have no other recourse than to sue them. But in most cases the services are rendered, and all are happy.

A second area of down payment negotiation in seller financing can occur in the area of sweat equity. If the seller agrees to repair certain aspects of the property, but doesn't have the time or money, why not let the buyer do physical labor as part of the down payment? The seller might retain the right to inspect the improvements and probably set

FIGURE 11.1 *Seller Financing Checklist*

Exploring Financing Options with the Seller

	YES	NO
1. Carry seller financing?	____	____
If so, at what interest rate?	____%	____
For what term? / What LTV?	____ yrs. /	____ LTV
Are balloons acceptable?	____	____
In how many years?	____ yrs.	____
2. Participate in seller financing on a partnership basis (low buyer down payment and seller share in equity)?	____	____
3. In lieu of a seller buydown, give the buyer a cash rebate (or seller price discount) that would assist in securing institutional financing?	____	____
4. Consider a lease option?	____	____
5. Consider a lease purchase, with a portion of the monthly lease payment applied to closing costs or to reduce the purchase price?	____	____
6. Purchase a buydown mortgage for buyer (for all or part of the purchase price)?	____	____
7. Consider borrower if strengthened by a coborrower?	____	____
8. Consider liening buyer's other real estate or personal property for collateral? Or take lien positions in same until the property is liquidated?	____	____
9. Have buyer purchase term life insurance with seller as beneficiary?	____	____
10. Seller take out second mortgage, and buyer assume same?	____	____
11. Allow buyer to assume seller's personal debts (using an "assignment of debt" contract)?	____	____
12. Consider a property exchange?	____	____
13. Accept chattel (personal property) as all or part of down payment?	____	____
14. Accept notes held by buyer as partial down payment?	____	____
15. If rental property, take a portion of rents in addition to monthly payments for a period of time?	____	____

a specific time frame for completing the work. The concept of sweat equity is also acceptable (with guidelines, of course) on conventional loans as well as FHA and VA financing.

Using Seller Debits as Down Payment

Q. Is it possible to transfer a property with outstanding debts against it when selling with seller financing?

Yes, it is. Although this method is sometimes overlooked, it can be one of the best methods of leverage, working positively for both the buyer and the seller.

Following is a real-life example of a property I purchased in the early 1980s using this technique:

I was the principal broker and owner of a northwestern real estate company. One of my salespeople had listed a six-unit building with a market value at that time of approximately $50,000. (Yes, it's true—it was in pretty sad shape, even for studio apartments.) The agent had decided to follow his wife to the Seattle area because she had "a real job," so I took over the listing. Times were tough, the property had not sold, and one evening the owner called me to say, "I'm two months behind on my contract payments to the seller, one year behind on my taxes, and I want to give the property to you!" At first I thought it was a bad connection, but she assured me that my hearing was not impaired and that she couldn't go on mismanaging the apartment building any longer.

It's easy to see a potential conflict of interest here—I was the broker, the listing agent, and could potentially be the buyer. To separate myself from the negotiations, I had her contact her attorney to bargain for her. In addition, I insisted that an appraisal be secured before we proceeded.

I was buying a new home for myself at the time, so I had very little money to put into a purchase. The only offer I could make to the seller was that I take over her debits (including back payments and delinquent taxes) and use them as my down payment. In real estate, debits are items that have been used up or are owing; credits, on the other hand, are items that are paid in advance.

The debits totaled $8,000 (including a $4,000 commission charge for I had, in essence, sold the property); credits totaled $220 (see figure 11.2). The debits minus the credits left a balance of $7,780, which I used as my down payment. Obviously, this down payment was merely on paper because I was assuming the obligation to pay these amounts in the future.

The title insurance, attorneys' fees, recordation, and water, sewer, and garbage charges totaled $445. This was the only cash I brought to the closing table. So for less than $500 cash, I had leveraged into a $50,000 asset!

I assumed a land sales contract at 7.5 percent interest and gave the seller a second contract for her equity, including interest at 9 percent (as shown in figure 11.2).

But what about the delinquent amounts I assumed? I went to the holder of the first contract (with credit report and letters of reference in hand) and asked him if I could pay the delinquent $520 owing him at $100 per month over the next six months. He was most happy to not have to foreclose and signed an agreement to the fact that he would give me the extra time requested to retire the delinquent debt.

In addition, over the next six months I paid the delinquent taxes. (Even though penalty and interest charges were accruing, it made sense to catch up the taxes gradually as the cash flow from the property improved.)

What had been the problem with the property? It appeared to be a classic case of mismanagement. The owner was spending the gross rents as fast as they were paid to her, not enforcing timely payment from the tenants, and ignoring maintenance. An on-site manager remedied most of the problems, and giving the tenants a rent reduction for rents paid for the semester in advance helped, too, because the building is across the street from a college. I even sold my old washer and dryer to the building, converting them to coin-op and therefore creating a new source of revenue (and depreciation).

The moral of this example is that many debits owed by the seller in seller-financed property transactions do not necessarily have to be paid in cash at closing. Letters of debt assumption can be written by attorneys, with negotiations between sellers and buyers setting the stage.

The seller was happy because she protected her credit rating while being able to receive her equity, plus interest, over a period of time. I was pleased because I had been able to turn a negative situation into a positive one.

FIGURE 11.2 *Example of Using Seller's Debits as Buyer's Credits*

Leverage with Expenses, Costs, and Prorations

Items	Debit	Credit
	Closing November 1	
	Purchase Price $50,000	
Seller's Expenses		
Current Year's Taxes at $100/Month	$1,000	
Prior Year's Delinquent Taxes	600	
Utilities		
Water, Sewer, Garbage	50	
(LIDs) Local Improvement District		
Current Month's Rent Due		200
Delinquent Rents	500	
Transfer of Rental Deposits	500	
Personal Property (plus coin ops, etc.)		20
Title Insurance Costs	225	
Attorneys' Fees and Recording	170	
Discount Fees		
Commissions at 8%	4,000	
Interest on Current Loan(s)	175	
Current Month's Loan Payment	260	
Delinquent Loan Payments	520	
Other: _____		
Totals	−8,000	+220

Buyer's Costs ("Hard" Costs to Pay)
    Title Insurance, Attorney, Recording (W,S,G) = $445

Debit	Credit	
−8,000	+220	$−7,780

Costs Assumed by Buyer (Total Down Payment)	$7,780
Cash to Close	**445**

Payment Calculations
    $50,000
    <u>− 7,780</u> Down
    $42,220
    <u>−18,000</u> Assume 7½ % Contract
    $24,220 at 9% = Second Contract

OPTIONS FOR SELLERS HOLDING FINANCING

Q. When a seller takes a second mortgage on a property, isn't he or she saddled with it until it is paid off?

It's true that many times the seller thinks in terms of collecting the principal (and of course, the interest) over the life of the second mortgage. And it's generally thought that should that seller want to convert that second mortgage to cash, he or she will have to deeply discount the face of the mortgage to provide a good yield to an investor purchasing it.

Here's a solution to both concerns—the "half now, half later" play. Why not find an investor to purchase all or part of the payment cash flow in lieu of selling the second mortgage outright? Here's how it works. This example is illustrated in figure 11.3:

> Charlene Morgan is willing to sell her home at the $120,000 sales price with the buyer, the Schmidts, assuming the first mortgage of $64,000. In addition, Morgan will take a $44,000 second mortgage at 8 percent ("interest only," with a balloon in seven years). The only problem is that the Schmidts' $12,000 down payment will leave only $2,500 remaining after the costs of sale, which is not enough for Morgan to relocate.
>
> Here's the solution. Simultaneously with closing the sale, an investor is secured to give Morgan one-half of the $44,000 second mortgage, or $22,000. (Investors may be bank officers, relatives, retirees, even the real estate agent.) This, less approximately $2,500 to cover attorneys' fees and extra title insurance (plus 10 percent for fees if a mortgage broker secures the investor) leaves $19,500—plus $2,500 net from the sale—for a total of $22,000. This is much more palatable to Morgan than merely netting $2,500 from the sale.
>
> What do the Schmidts get for the $22,000? They get the assignment of the interest-only proceeds from the $44,000. And, based on the fact that only $22,000 has been advanced, $3,520 interest per year equals a 16 percent yield!
>
> But it's not over yet. Morgan still has $22,000 principal due at the payment of the balloon; or she could buy the note back at any time for the $22,000 advanced her (depending on

FIGURE 11.3 *Converting a Second Mortgage to Cash without Discounting*

**Cash for Second Mortgages with No Discount
"Half Now, Half Later" Plan**

$120,000	Sales Price
− 64,000	First Mortgage Assumed by Buyer
− 12,000	Down Payment from Buyer
	Second Mortgage to Seller At 8% Interest-Only
− 44,000	with a Balloonin Seven Years
$ 12,000	Down Payment
9,500	Less Costs of Sale
$ 2,500	Net to Seller Not Enough Cash to Relocate

SOLUTION:

Investor Gives Seller Half   (half now)
of the Second Mortgage

	$22,000
Less Costs	2,500
	$19,500
Plus Net Sale Proceeds	+ 2,500
	$22,000 to Seller

Seller still has $22,000 due at payment of the balloon (half later), or can buy the note back at any time for the $22,000 advanced her.

---

the minimum amount of time the investor wants to stay in the picture). Thus, the term, "half now, half later."

While the seller is actually sacrificing valuable interest on the principal, the face of the note is not being discounted. This can work well when the seller needs cash for a short period of time and can later step back into the position of receiving interest on the loan.

Seller Financing and 80/10/10 Mortgages

Q. Can seller financing be used in addition to a new conventional loan?

Yes. The secondary market will allow a buyer to originate a new conventional loan with a loan-to-value ratio not to exceed 80 percent of the appraised value to be placed with a seller-carried second mortgage. Of course, if the lender's conventional loan is not going to be sold into the

FIGURE 11.4 *80/10/10 Flexible Conventional Financing*

Sales Price	$150,000
80% Lender First Mortgage	– 120,000
10% Down Payment	15,000
10% Seller Financing in Second Mortgage	$ 15,000

Advantages:

- The seller receives some cash.
- The buyer may secure a good rate of interest on the second mortgage.
- No origination fee is due on the second mortgage.
- No private mortgage insurance is required.

Note: The lender will count the debt service for both mortgages for the purpose of loan qualifying.

secondary market, the loan-to-value ratio allowed would be determined by the individual lender. This loan is often described as 80/10/10 or a piggyback loan—80 percent conventional loan, 10 percent down payment, 10 percent seller-carried second mortgage (see figure 11.4).

When qualifying for this type of financing, the lender will include the repayment of the second mortgage in the qualifying ratios for the first mortgage loan. But the advantages to both parties are great. The seller receives some cash (from the proceeds of the first mortgage, less costs of sale) plus interest on the second mortgage. The buyer sidesteps any origination fee on the second mortgage because it's financed by the seller. In addition, the buyer may negotiate a good interest rate and good terms on the second mortgage, as well as avoid paying PMI, because the first mortgage is 80 percent loan-to-value.

What circumstances might be best for using the 80/10/10 approach? The 80/10/10 loan might appeal to a borrower who wants the lower costs and interest rate of an 80 percent loan and who will have cash coming in several years to pay off the second mortgage.

Or a borrower might use this approach to avoid the higher rates of a jumbo mortgage (a loan amount exceeding the traditional secondary market guidelines). The borrower would secure a first mortgage that is less than a jumbo loan and make a 10 percent down payment, and the seller would carry the balance.

The 80/10/10 option could also be used by a relocating buyer who can only afford a 10 percent down payment now, but who has the monthly cash flow to qualify for both payments and could later use proceeds from another home to pay off the second mortgage. The possibilities (and flexibilities) are endless.

One caution: As a condition of making that loan, the lender of the first mortgage may require a copy of the second mortgage's terms and conditions to approve them. The rationale is that the lender's first mortgage, although superior to a second mortgage, could be at greater risk if the second mortgage has highly leveraged terms (for example, with a large balloon in two years). Some lenders will require that balloons not occur before five years, that regular monthly payments be made on the second mortgage, and that the terms exceed interest-only payments to the seller.

Q. Can a second mortgage be used with an existing FHA loan?

Yes. If the first FHA loan was written prior to December 1, 1986, and the property is being sold on a simple assumption (without qualification), there would be no lender requirement to review and approve (or disapprove) of the terms of the second mortgage.

Q. Can a second mortgage be originated simultaneously with that of an FHA first mortgage?

It's a rare occurrence since the borrower's down payment can be a mere 3 percent (creating high leverage) and the amount borrowed cannot exceed the area statutory limit for the sales price/mortgage amount. Additionally, a second would not remove the requirement for total mortgage insurance coverage. One exception to a second mortgage being originated with a first is with certain bond financing (home affordability) programs.

Q. Is it possible to place a second mortgage behind an existing VA first mortgage?

It's possible, but there are several downsides. First, the new buyer must qualify with the lender for both loans and pay an assumption fee of $500. Second, the seller will not be released of liability or VA eligibility on the first mortgage and will have the added risk associated with carrying a second mortgage for the buyer.

Q. Can a second mortgage be originated with a new VA first mortgage?

Yes, under certain guidelines. VA national underwriting guidelines state that second mortgages can originate simultaneously with VA first mortgages under the following circumstances:

- The loans do not exceed the CRV on the property.
- The mortgagee is not a party to the transaction (e.g., seller or real estate agent).
- The second mortgage must be a minimum of five years.

DISCOUNT POINTS AND BUYDOWNS

Q. Is it true that borrowers who use discount points and interest-rate buydowns and pay extra to lock in an interest rate are using leverage to help them purchase?

That's correct. All those techniques are forms of leverage, no matter who pays them. (For more information about points, buydowns, and lockins, review Chapter 4.)

Discounting the Purchase Price

Q. Is it better to have the seller discount the purchase price than to pay a buydown?

It depends. Figure 11.5 shows a comparison of buydown and discount situations, and is based on the following example:

Ed Frye is a builder who prefers to pay $3,600 to a buyer in either a buydown or price discount arrangement rather than pay another month's worth of interest on his construction loan.

If Frye pays the $3,600 in increments of $100 per month for three years toward the buyer's payment (temporary buydown), his total cost is $3,600. If, however, the buyer decides she would prefer to have the up-front price of the home discounted by the $3,600, the numbers change. Not only will the buyer's 20 percent down payment be figured on a lesser purchase price, but so will the other costs of borrowing, including origination fees, title insurance, and PMI (if applicable). In fact, should the buyer hold the loan for the entire term, the $3,600 savings will increase to more than $4,000 plus closing cost savings using the discounted sales price.

What about builder Frye? Are there any additional benefits for him in using the price discount? The most obvious drawback is that he may not want to discount the price of the home for fear that it will impact future comparable sales. (Many times not wanting to discount a price is more of a mental roadblock than a financial one.) Nevertheless, if he does discount the price, he also discounts the price of those closing costs based on the sales price, including title insurance, loan origination fees, loan closing fees, and real estate commissions. Discounting can be an advantageous sales technique in a buyers' market.

FIGURE 11.5 *Buydown Compared with Price Discount*

A builder will contribute $3,600 to pay for a buyer's temporary (three-year) interest-rate buydown or will discount the purchase price by the same amount. Here's the comparison:

	Buydown	**Discount Sales Price**
Sales price	$200,000	$196,400
Loan size (20% down)	$160,000	$157,120
Monthly buydown	$100	NA
Buyer's monthly payments		
Years 1 – 3	$964	$1,045
Years 4 – 30	$1,064	$1,045
Projected interest cost	$223,214	$219,197
Projected buyer savings	$3,600	$4,017*
Qualifying income (for PITI)	$4,480	$4,399

*Plus reduced loan and closing costs based on the lower sales price and loan amount.

In comparing buydowns to price discounts, buydowns usually work best with short-term ownership; price discounts work best with long-term ownership. As with most types of creative financing techniques, unless both parties realize some advantage, they may not want to make the concessions it takes to put the sale together.

Q. What are blended rates and how do they work?

Blended rates are exactly that—two or more rates blended together to yield a more preferential rate to the borrower. They usually make the most sense when the gap between the old and the new interest rates is great, and new mortgage money rates are high. The following example shows how blended rates work:

> The Martins have a home worth approximately $120,000, with an outstanding $80,000 mortgage at 7 percent. They want to pull an additional $20,000 out of the property to add on a family room, but are not excited about refinancing with new first mortgage money because rates are at 9 percent. The other option of second mortgage money at 10 percent is also not enticing, so they make a proposal to the holder of their mortgage. Knowing that the lender would like to move the 8 percent loan off the books, the Martins ask that the lender make them a new first mortgage, based on a blended rate of the 8 percent old money and the 9 percent new money. The new loan will be $100,000 for 30 years, at a rate of 9 percent. This moves the 8 percent loan off the books, while giving the Martins a much more attractive overall rate of interest.

Obviously, the lender has to win, too, so it may require some new origination and processing fees.

Also, as with most types of lending, if the borrower has other borrowing options, the pressure on the lender to make these concessions will be greater. In other words, the borrower who doesn't need the money can probably get it! For example, if the existing loan can be assumed, that's in the borrower's negotiating favor. If the interest rate on the underlying loan is at a rate much lower than current market interest, that's a plus for the borrower, too. And if the borrower has cash on hand, letters of credit from other banks, or second-mortgage alternatives with competing lenders, this is all in the borrower's favor.

Q. Could a new purchaser use a blended-rate loan rather than using a second mortgage or a wraparound?

Yes, by working with the right mix of circumstances. It's a little more difficult to convince a lender to use a blended rate with a new purchaser, however, because recycling funds is a primary base of profit for the lender, through charging origination fees, exercising the due-on-sale clause, etc. But remember, if you don't ask, you don't get!

Q. When a buyer uses a second mortgage simultaneously with a first, isn't that similar to blending the rates?

Effectively, yes. Even though the rates may differ on the two separate loans, overall, the rates are blended. The effect of this blended rate could be seen if a lender were qualifying the buyer on ratios from the standpoint of the two interest rates and the loans' repayments. The lender would use the debt service on both loans to determine whether the buyer could qualify to pay both obligations.

LEASE-PURCHASE

Q. Is there a difference between lease-option and lease-purchase?

Most definitely, yes. A lease-option is a lease with an option to buy, which the optionee is not obligated to exercise. Only if he or she exercises the option to purchase is a sales contract created.

A lease-purchase is already a purchase. It is drafted on a purchase and sales agreement and is merely awaiting the fulfillment of a term or condition before it culminates in a closing (the date of which is predetermined). Here's an example:

> Joan Cohn, who is short of the total down payment to purchase, might ask that the seller, Walter Jones, enter into a lease-purchase arrangement. The terms of the contract would set a future closing date, as well as spell out the balance of the terms, such as financial arrangements and payment of closing costs. The buyer usually takes possession of the property, and the terms and conditions of the occupancy are spelled out.
>
> In addition, Joan might ask that a portion of her monthly lease payment apply to reducing either the purchase price or the closing costs. Note the difference here: If on a $1,000-per-month lease payment $100 per month will be attributed to her closing costs when the sale closes in six months, $100 should be impounded monthly for a total of $600 actual cash available to her at closing. On the other hand, it would not be quite so important to impound the $100 monthly if the total amount were merely to be subtracted from the sales price (unless Walter had virtually no net proceeds coming from the sale).

Most lenders will only allow a credit to the buyer if the credit exceeds the fair-market rent paid. In the previous example of the $1,000-per-month lease payment, the monthly credit would have to exceed the fair-market rent to be counted. So if $1,000 was truly fair-market rent, usually as determined by an appraiser or other market expert, the buyer would have to pay $1,100 to receive a $100-per-month credit toward the purchase price or closing costs.

The Seller's Advantage

Q. When could a lease-purchase be an advantage for a seller?

A lease-purchase could make sense for a seller if the real estate market is slow and the property hasn't sold, or if the seller needed to move quickly. In addition, the seller might feel that a prospective buyer of the property would take better care of it than a renter would, and might add improvements.

The Buyer's Advantage

Q. When could a lease-purchase be an advantage for a buyer?

A lease-purchase could allow a buyer time to accumulate the balance of a down payment, establish a two-year work history, or meet some other lending requirement, such as paying off debts.

Q. It sounds as though a lease-purchase could be quite tricky to put together. What questions can be asked to make it a positive choice?

It's true that lease-purchases, particularly if engineered incorrectly, can result in nightmare situations. That's why they should be utilized only for the right reasons.

The buyer needs to be a strong buyer, merely needing extra time to fulfill his or her obligation because of special circumstances. For example, the buyer's prior home may be in the final closing process, the balance of the down payment may be coming from a verifiable estate, or the buyer may be waiting until his or her CDs mature to avoid penalty for early withdrawal. It's sometimes difficult to tell how legitimate the lease-purchase buyer is, but here are some questions to pose:

- *Is the down payment source valid, timely, and logical?*
- *Is there sufficient safe earnest money?* Depending on the area and property price, minimums may range from $1,000 to 5 percent of the sales price. *Also, what happens to the earnest money should the sale fail? Is it returned to the buyer or defaulted according to the language in the purchase and sales agreement?* Most contracts go with the latter.
- *Has the buyer had a preliminary financing prequalification for the type of loan he or she is seeking? Also, what will be the seller's costs, if any, for the buyer to secure this financing?*

Q. What are the lease-purchase guidelines?

Either in the purchase and sales agreement, or as a lease-purchase addendum to the sales agreement, the following questions should be answered:

- *Who pays what and when in regard to the lease?* (For example, when are utilities prorated? When are deposits transferred?)
- *Are improvements allowed on the property prior to closing?* (This is one area the seller should consider carefully because mechanics' liens for unpaid materials or labor could attach to the property and become the seller's debt.)
- *Who has insurance coverage?* (It's usually a good idea if the seller keeps his or her existing coverage until the closing, with the buyer adding any additional liability insurance deemed necessary.)
- *What are the provisions and the remedies for default?* (Usually, they are the same provisions for default as under the purchase and sales agreement.)
- *What monthly lease amount credit will apply (if applicable) to the closing costs or to reducing the purchase price?*

Additionally, it may be wise to have a preliminary title report drawn prior to the buyer taking occupancy. This will list any possible defects on the title, liens against the property, and judgments against the seller.

By using these guidelines, there should be less havoc should the buyer and seller choose to take this course of sale.

ASSUMPTIONS

Q. Is loan assumption a form of leverage?

Yes it is, because it means that the borrower has less of a loan to arrange or needs to bring less cash to the closing. When the borrower assumes a seller's debt, that amount is subtracted from the purchase price. For example, a buyer assuming a $40,000 loan as part of a $90,000 purchase price would only have to make up a $50,000 difference, either in cash or in another type of financing.

Q. Why don't borrowers hear more about loan assumption if it's a form of leverage?

Many of the previously assumable types of loans have gone the way of the dinosaur! Lenders realized that buyers assuming loans were not always as good a risk as first borrowers, not to mention that lenders wanted to make new loans with new fees and possibly higher interest rates.

While some loan types (such as FHA and VA) originated today are assumable with a qualified borrower, most others are not. And a majority of the simply assumable (without qualifying) loans are those originated before the mid-1980s, many of which bore high interest rates and were either refinanced or paid off.

Q. If a borrower did get a loan that allows an assumption, would he or she automatically be off the hook for the loan if someone assumed it?

Not necessarily. There are three different types (or levels) of assumptions, each with different sets of obligations and liabilities attached to them. They are *assignment, subject to,* and *novation.*

Q. What is an assignment of mortgage?

An *assignment* of mortgage is the first level of loan assumption. Assignment transfers the responsibility to pay an obligation from one party to the other. In essence, the assumptor actually steps into the shoes of the first mortgagor, assuming the repayment of the debt. Should the second party default, however, the first party is secondarily liable for paying the remaining balance on the note. (In other words, a costuckee!) Note that the first borrower is responsible only for repaying the note balance should the assumptor default—for example, there could be no deficiency judgments against the first borrower for other liens if the property did not sell for enough to satisfy the debts.

This is a less common type of assumption than the "subject to" assumption.

Q. What is assuming a "subject to" mortgage?

A *"subject to"* mortgage assumption is subject to the terms and conditions of the existing loan. This rather dangerous type of assumability is very much like the assignment for it transfers the obligation to pay the debt from one party to another. But the "subject to" assumption goes one step further. In addition to being secondarily liable for repayment of the debt should the second borrower default, the original borrower is also responsible for any deficiency (shortfall at foreclosure sale) against the property. This excess of debt can attach to the first mortgagor in the form of a judgment against him or her, depending on the state and the type of security document used, for example, a mortgage or deed of trust.

In other words, on a sale subject to the loan, the assumptor of the loan is liable only for the loss of his or her equity in the property should default occur. Following is an example:

> An assumptor of a "subject to" loan hires a contractor to build a carport on the property. The owner does not pay for the improvements, and mechanics' liens subsequently attach to the property. Simultaneously, the property falls into default, causing the lender to foreclose. Should the property not bring enough at sale to satisfy both the outstanding mortgage plus the mechanics' liens, the original obligor could be held responsible for satisfying the deficiency to the lender! Not only would the original borrower be stuck with the mortgage obligation, but he or she could be faced with other debts secured by the property as well.

Because each state's statutes vary regarding deficiency judgments, the consumer should check with local lenders, title company representatives, or legal counsel before taking on this kind of assumption.

If a loan written today is assumable, it typically contains either assignment or "subject to" language.

Q. What is it called when a seller is relieved of both the mortgage payment and the liability when he or she sells on an assumption?

That's called a *novation,* coming from the root word *nova,* meaning new. A novation is an entirely new obligation, releasing the original obligor from all further liability on the loan. The buyer steps into the loan and the seller steps out.

One of the reasons that many sellers erroneously believe that they are receiving novations when they sell is because the lenders ask the new buyers "to qualify to assume" the existing mortgages. This process includes employment verification, a credit check, and research to ensure that the qualifying ratios are within standard guidelines. The sellers, however, may not be receiving novations but are merely transferring ownership; lenders go through nearly the same qualifying process for all types of assumptions.

Depending on the loan type, additional paperwork and assumption charges may be involved with the novation, but in most cases the biggest difference comes in asking. Many lenders will not grant or process a novation unless one is requested. The rationale is that the lender has made the loan to one borrower based on that party's qualifying strength, and until the second borrower can provide the information needed to prove that he or she is equally strong, the lender will not relieve the original mortgagor of secondary liability.

Q. What can happen when a lender is asked for a novation?

Responses can vary. First, it will depend on the type of loan being assumed. Most conventional mortgages originated today are not assumable. Period. With FHA and VA loans (see Chapters 8 and 9), some cannot be assumed without qualification (depending on the date of origination). A payoff notice is used to request loan payoff information from the lender, including whether the loan is assumable and under what conditions.

Q. If the seller can't get a novation, doesn't the lender have to notify the seller in case of any pending default by the assumptor?

No. Realistically, most lenders notify the original obligors so that financial arrangements might be worked out prior to foreclosure proceedings, but lenders are not required by law to do so. Typically, original obligors are notified in times of low appreciation, when property values have actually decreased, and when selling properties at a loss only compounds the situations. Because foreclosure is expensive for the lender, avoiding it saves time and money.

If the original mortgagor had carried back seller financing, and notice of it was recorded, he or she would be formally notified prior to sale of the property.

The prudent thing for the original mortgagor to do, however, is to send a written request by certified mail to the lender, asking that he or she be notified of any potential default on the outstanding loan. In addition, this notice should be recorded at the county courthouse. Even though it creates no lien or other encumbrance on the property, the notice is on record. If these steps are taken when the sale to the assumptor occurs, a lender would later find it difficult to claim that the lender was not aware that the original mortgagor wanted notification in advance of any pending default.

In addition, a seller could even request that the buyer purchasing with an assumption give the seller a small second mortgage (for example, $100), payable at some time in the future (the year 2030) with no payment due until that time. Once this mortgage is recorded, the seller is a lien holder of record and he or she would be notified in the case of any default by the second owner. The seller would have to release the lien before the second buyer could sell with a clean title.

Q. When is the best time to ask the lender about assumption options?

The time to inquire about assumption policies regarding a specific loan is before the loan is originated, not when the property is put up for resale. If the initial borrower asks questions concerning the assumption guidelines of a particular loan prior to the loan closing, he or she may be able to negotiate to change the loan language and assumption guidelines (depending on the lender and the loan type). The borrower may even ask the lender to hold the loan in portfolio to allow for a novation later.

It may not always be possible to get a definite answer from the lender. The lender may state that it depends on how well the borrower repays and to whom the loan is sold, as well as the policies of the institution's board of directors at the time of the assumption. What the borrower can do, however, is to ask what the current assumption procedures are for that specific loan. Assumption policies rarely get easier, so if the borrower can live with the current guidelines, chances are they will set the stage for future policies. The downstream effect of this action may more than compensate for the time and effort it takes the borrower to clarify the situation.

12

AFTER THE CLOSE
Managing the Mortgage and Your Equity

The buyers and sellers have made it through the closing, albeit with some sweaty palms. The buyers don't need to be reminded that the mortgage is a significant financial obligation. But it's also a financial opportunity, and buyers should give it attention as they plan their families' financial futures.

This chapter answers some common questions borrowers have after the mortgage is closed: when it makes sense to prepay the mortgage and how to do so successfully (thus building equity faster); what are the pros and cons of tapping equity to purchase investment real estate; plus how to effectively correspond with the lender to troubleshoot questions and concerns with a mortgage. Equity management is a critical issue today, especially because it represents many a family's largest asset. These tips will give you the leg up you need to preserve and grow your equity nest egg!

Q. After buying a house, we've been inundated with calls from telemarketers wanting to sell us something. How can we stop this?

Recording a mortgage or a deed in public records alerts the world that you either bought a house and need to buy stuff for that house, or you freed up equity in a refinance and now have money to spend or invest. Either way, you're a prime target for telemarketers.

But there's potential help in the form of the National Do-Not-Call list. Enforced by both the Federal Communications Commissions (FCC) and the Federal Trade Commission (FTC), you can place your home phone number or numbers, including wireless numbers, on the national Do-Not-Call list and callers will be prohibited from making telephone solicitations to you. While you may be able to register a business number, your registration will not make telephone solicitations to that number unlawful. To register online, go to www.donotcall.gov or sign up by phone at 1-888-382-1222 24 hours a day. You will be registering for all members of your household and the listing will be effective for five years unless you remove it from the list or your phone number is disconnected. Note, however, if you didn't register on the list prior to August 31, 2003, telemarketers have 90 days from the time you register before they're actually in violation of the law for calling you. Exempt from the law are calls or messages placed with your express prior permission, or by or on behalf of a tax-exempt nonprofit organization, or from a person or organization with which you have established a business relationship.

If you decide not to register on the National Do-Not-Call list, you can still instruct the telemarketer to place you on its company-specific do-not-call list in order to stop calls from that company. For your own reference, make a note of the date and time you asked to be put on this list in case they do contact you again and you wish to file a complaint with the FCC.

Q. What about the plethora of junk mail we receive as homeowners? Can anything be done about that?

Yes. Through the Mail Preference Service of the Direct Marketing Association (DMA), you can remove your name from mailing lists including those that involve prescreening your credit. DMA represents more than 3,600 companies worldwide and takes your request directly to those companies. Online registration at www.DMAchoice.org is immediate and free of charge, or you can register by snail mail after printing out and completing a form from the site and remitting a $1 processing fee. You can change your preferences at any time and your renewable registration is good for a three-year period.

ESCROW/IMPOUND ACCOUNTS

Q. Is there a limit on how many months of cushion the lender may require in an escrow account for taxes and insurance?

Federal law allows the lender to impound no more than one-sixth of the anticipated annual charges as a cushion. The rule of thumb used by lenders is that at least once each year, the balance should fall to a level no greater than the two-month cushion immediately after paying taxes and insurance. Any overage must be automatically returned to the mortgagor/consumer.

Nonpayment of Property Taxes Changes Terms of Mortgage

Q. The lender sent me a letter stating that unless I pay my property taxes within ten days, the lender will pay them, charge me interest, and also force me to pay them monthly in my mortgage payment. Can the lender force these changes to my loan agreement?

Absolutely. By not paying your property taxes, you are in default of the mortgage agreement. Technically, much like the penalty for not making mortgage payments, the lender could "call the loan," requiring you to pay off the entire outstanding loan amount. In other words, the remedy could be much tougher than merely catching up the delinquent property taxes.

Most lenders give borrowers the privilege of paying taxes outside of the monthly payment if the mortgage has a down payment of at least 20 percent. But this privilege only applies as long as the borrower keeps his or her promise and pays the taxes in a timely fashion. The lender does not want to lose the investment (the mortgage) to the county for nonpayment of property taxes. That's why the documents the borrower signed at the closing allow the lender to pay the taxes, ask the borrower for reimbursement plus interest, and then require the borrower to pay $\frac{1}{12}$th of the annual taxes monthly into an escrow impound account for the duration of the mortgage.

The lender may offer the borrower approximately 60 days from the date of the initial letter to get taxes current. The lender also provides a telephone number, often a toll-free one, to call to explain the situation and possibly work out an alternative solution. If the lender is contacted in a timely manner, the borrower might be able to preserve his or her annual tax payment status provided the delinquent taxes are paid in the lender's required time frame.

Q. Our homeowner's insurance rates are through the roof. We found a new insurer with lower rates that said they'd write us if we'd agree to pay $200 to have our home reinspected. What's this about?

The insurance company is hedging their bets by making sure that your home is in good shape and, hopefully, a sound risk. The increased number of events by Mother Nature coupled with insurance losses in vacant foreclosure properties has wreaked havoc on the industry. That's why requiring four-point inspections for reinsurance have become the new norm in many parts of the country.

The home inspector will check the roof, heating/cooling system, electrical system, and plumbing for condition, operation, and any code violations. His written report is then sent to the insurance company for review.

Even though the inspection will cost you $200, it hopefully should save you multiples of that in annual homeowner's premiums.

WHEN THE MORTGAGE IS SOLD

Q. Sometimes a borrower obtains a loan through one lender but is advised after closing to send payments to a different company in a different state. Why?

The loans or their servicing (payment collection) have been purchased by another company. The terms and conditions of the original loan stay the same; just the company and the location to which payments are sent change.

By law, the original lender must send the borrower a "good-bye letter" at least 15 days before the date of the next payment. This letter should state the name of the new company, its location, and the name and telephone number of a contact person or department in case the borrower has questions.

Under the same time guidelines, the new company is also required to send the borrower a "welcome letter" that outlines the same information.

It is very important that the borrower receive both letters, and that they are on both companies' letterheads. If a letter is received only from the supposed new servicer, the borrower should call the original lender to verify that the loan was sold. Several bogus operations have recently attempted to intercept mortgage checks by claiming to be new servicing companies.

If the borrower's monthly payment is made through automatic checking withdrawal or electronic transfers, the borrower must cancel the present arrangement and fill out new forms. Often there is a time lag, so the borrower may need to send a check directly to the new company before the new servicer receives the withdrawal. The welcome letter (or a call to the new company) can help determine this.

If during the loan transition a payment is sent on time but to the wrong company, late fees will be waived for up to 60 days after the loan transfer.

A free booklet entitled *When Your Loan Is Transferred to Another Lender* is available from the Mortgage Bankers Association of America. It can be requested by writing to the association at 1125 Fifteenth Street, NW, Washington, DC 20005, or online at www.mbaa.org.

UNDERSTAND HOW MORTGAGE PAYMENTS APPLY

Q. The loan balance on my mortgage hasn't decreased much after paying on my loan for three years. Is this normal?

Yes. During the first several years of a mortgage, there is very little principal reduction because a large amount of the monthly payment applies first to interest. If you think of your mortgage as a mathematical system (called amortization), it will help you understand what you're paying every month and how it's being applied.

A mortgage is a loan where the majority of interest is paid early on in the payment schedule. This prevents the principal from being whittled down early on, which is offset somewhat by providing a substantial annual tax deduction.

Let's take a look at a $100,000 loan amortized for 30 years with interest at 7.5 percent. If you made all 360 payments, you'd pay $151,721 plus the $100,000 you borrowed for a total of $252,721. That means that for every dollar lent you, you'd return $2.50 to the lender ($1.50 of which represents interest). Fortunately, the $1.50 in interest is a federal income tax deduction. That's why some borrowers prefer to roll their mortgages over annually into the lowest fee/lowest cost adjustable-rate mortgages they can find.

Using this information, let's answer your question. How much principal reduction will there be in the first years of the loan? Out of your first year's total payments of $8,391, a whopping $7,469 would go to pay interest, leaving only $922 attributable to the principal. That means that after 12 months, you've reduced your mortgage balance by 0.92 percent, or less than 1 percent. Interestingly, because amortization is based on a formula, whether your mortgage amount is larger or smaller, the approximate percentages hold true. The actual numbers may change but the percentages do not.

After five years of payments, you will have reduced the principal by a little more than 5 percent. After ten years of payments, you begin to make a bit more headway with approximately 13 percent of the loan whittled down; there's a 25 percent principal reduction around year 15, but it's not until year 23 that you hit the magic halfway point in repaying your 7.5 percent $100,000 loan. During the last five years of the loan, the majority of what you pay is applied to principal.

If you understand how mortgage payments are applied, you can evaluate the pros and cons of prepaying your mortgage, refinancing, and/or working toward owning the property free and clear.

PREPAYING A MORTGAGE

Benefits of Prepaying

Q. What benefits does a borrower receive for prepaying a mortgage?

Prepaying a loan offers a borrower many advantages:

- *Saving thousands of dollars in interest.* For example, a $100,000 30-year loan with interest at 7 percent would cost the borrower $139,509 in interest if the loan ran to maturity. But the same loan amount paid in just 15 years would cost the borrower only $61,789, or $77,720 less, almost 50 percent less interest. Even though mortgage interest is tax deductible, the savings are real!
- *Owning a home free and clear can be a liberating feeling.* If monthly cash flow were to shrink, owners would not be plagued with worry over making monthly mortgage payments and potentially losing their homes. And their equity could always be a potential source of cash through refinancing or equity lines of credit.

Detriments to Prepaying a Mortgage

Q. Are there any detriments to prepaying a mortgage?

Every positive can have a negative. You need to weigh the following:

- *You'll be parting with cash that could deplete your financial liquidity.*
- *You'll be using funds that could otherwise be used to make other financial investments* (with perhaps higher yields).
- *Paying less interest may impact your tax picture* (although paying more interest is never a valid reason for carrying a mortgage).
- *It doesn't make financial sense to prepay a mortgage before you retire high-interest, nondeductible-interest consumer debts.*
- *The lower the interest rate, the less you'll save when prepaying.* Prepayments you made when your loan was at 9 percent won't have the same impact if you've refinanced into a 6 percent loan.
- *Make sure you monitor your mortgage to guarantee that prepayments are being properly applied to reduce the principal balance.*

Questions to Ask before Prepaying a Mortgage

Q. What questions should a borrower ask before choosing a mortgage prepayment plan?

Here are a few potential questions a borrower should explore:

- *Is the current mortgage payment a burden? Have some payments been late or even missed?* If you receive a windfall of cash, paying off the mortgage may make sense, because erratic payments may jeopardize the loan and damage your credit.
- *What impact will the lack of interest deductibility have on your overall tax picture?* Consulting a tax advisor for preplanning is always a wise move.
- *What are your long-term cash needs? Are your current savings sufficient to meet them?* If savings are minimal or nonexistent (a six-month minimum of living expenses is suggested), it may be financially premature to use extra funds to prepay a mortgage.
- *Is a change pending in your financial future that would make it prudent to save more money instead of using cash to pay off the loan?* Financing a child through college or aiding an elderly parent might be better

paid in cash, rather than borrowing through a nondeductible consumer interest loan.

- *How long do you plan on keeping the property and the loan?* Retiring the loan may not be a wise financial move if you are going to sell quickly or replace the loan with another one soon.

The Best Time to Start Prepaying a Mortgage

Q. Should a loan be prepaid when it has just a few more years to run?

While there's never a bad time in a loan's history to make prepayments, a look at a loan amortization schedule (see figure 12.1) can help answer this question. Considering how much of the monthly payment goes to principal and interest, it's easy to see that a larger portion goes to interest in the early years of the loan. The best time to make extra principal reductions, then, is in the early stages of the loan where prepaying has a bigger impact.

A Structured Prepayment System

Q. What logical, systematic plan should a borrower follow to reduce the loan balance without going bankrupt?

Before the borrower begins any prepayment program, structured or not, he or she should make sure the loan has no prepayment penalties, even if it means contacting the lender or loan servicer to find out. This is important, since many lenders offer newer loans that include prepayment penalties and thus lower interest rates to consumers.

If the borrower receives prepayment information from the lender over the telephone, he or she should ask the lender to put this information in writing and send it to the borrower. At the very least, the borrower should document on the mortgage payment book the date he or she called and the name of the person who gave the prepayment information. Putting the lender on notice of the intention to make loan prepayments also alerts the lender to make sure advance payments are posted correctly.

The following program is a favorite of many savvy real estate purchasers because it's simple to calculate, methodical, and won't financially break the borrower. Be sure to mark on both your check and your loan payment coupon that this payment should be applied to the principal.

1. The borrower should obtain an amortization schedule of the loan, showing each payment's principal and interest distribution for the life of the loan. A computer printout can be secured from the lender (or any financial institution), real estate professional, or financial advisor. Additionally, many online sites, such as www.interest.com or www.hsh.com, can be accessed to calculate the principal and interest.
2. The borrower should look at the next payment, for instance, January. When the January payment is made, the borrower should make an additional payment to include February's principal reduction (see figure 12.1).

The borrower, in essence, eliminates one full payment from the 30-year loan schedule because the loan balance after that payment would correspond to the loan balance shown at the end of February.

In February, the borrower should send in March's principal reduction payment in addition to the February payment, and so on, every month thereafter.

FIGURE 12.1 *Loan Amortization Chart and Prepayment Schedule ($100,000 loan, 30-year term, 8 percent interest)*

Month of Loan	Payment	Interest Portion	Principal Portion	Balance
January	733.77	666.67	67.10	99,932.90
February	733.77	666.22	67.55	99,865.36
March	733.77	665.77	68.00	99,797.36
April	733.77	665.32	68.45	99,728.91
May	733.77	664.86	68.91	99,660.00
June	733.77	664.40	69.37	99,590.63
July	733.77	663.93	69.84	99,520.79
August	733.77	663.47	70.30	99,450.49

Note how the portion of the monthly payment that is interest payment goes down as the principal is reduced. By making extra payments applied to the principal only, the interest portion will be reduced even faster.

If this procedure is followed religiously every month, a 30-year loan will be paid off in a little more than 17 years. How's that for savings?

Remember, however, that just because a principal prepayment has been made, the borrower cannot skip a payment! Missing payments would put the loan in default because prepayments have no bearing on scheduled payments.

Documenting Prepayments Is Vital

Imagine the myriad terror stories from borrowers who thought they had made prepayments, only to later discover that the amounts had been erroneously applied to late fees, advanced interest, insurance premiums, or taxes.

Following are some precautions borrowers can take:

- If using payment coupons, be sure to mark "principal prepayment" and the amount on the face of the coupon.
- Make the prepayment with a separate check so it can be tracked and shown as evidence if prepayments are later disputed.
- Borrowers should be sure to mark the loan number and the words "principal prepayment" on the face of each check.
- If paying online, print out a copy of the payment screen before sending and request that a receipt be emailed to you.
- If possible, the borrower should request an annual accounting of payments. While many lenders don't do this normally, many will accommodate a borrower who requests it. The borrower can compare the lender's balance with canceled checks to make sure the prepayments were applied correctly. If you have online access to your mortgage information, you can check your payments at any time.

Being afforded prepayment options with a loan can add incredible payment and financial flexibility to the borrower's situation, while not saddling him or her with the higher payments of shorter-term loans.

Prepaying a Lower-Interest-Rate Mortgage

Q. I made prepayments for two years on my previous 8 percent interest-rate mortgage of $185,000. But now that my interest rate is 6 percent, will it make as much financial sense to prepay?

While there will be less savings in prepaying a lower-interest-rate loan, you will still save.

For example, prepayments of $75 per month on your old 8 percent loan would save you more than $60,000 in interest over the life of the loan. But the same monthly prepayment on a 6 percent loan would reduce that savings to less than $40,000.

Does this mean that prepaying is less valuable? Not really, because what you're saving is not taxable so your yield is actually greater than 6 percent, somewhere closer to 8 percent.

Be sure to ask yourself questions similar to those found in the prepayment questions earlier in this chapter. To be financially effective, prepaying your mortgage should make long-term as well as short-term sense.

TAPPING EQUITY TO PURCHASE INVESTMENT REAL ESTATE

Q. What are the pros and cons of taking out an equity line of credit against your home to purchase rental property?

Consumers should make their home's equity work for them. Strong real estate appreciation in this decade has many owners borrowing against their equity to make down payments on rental or investment property. That said, it's got to make both financial and psychological sense for the long term before you take the leap.

Here are a few of the questions you need to answer before proceeding:

- *How long will you stay in your home and what is the amount of annual appreciation anticipated during that time?* If you take out a substantial equity line of credit loan on your home but will sell in a short period of time, you'd need strong appreciation to provide enough equity to cover the costs of the sale.
- *How much equity will you need to tap and will you be comfortable having a debt that size against your home?* (Remember, should you default on line-of-credit repayments, your home could be foreclosed on.)
- *What is the interest rate of the equity loan and does it provide for increased interest and/or a balloon payment over time?* This could have an impact on how long you hold the investment property.
- *What is your strategy for purchasing/holding/selling the investment property? Will it be short or long term? What are the anticipated expenses, including the ability to cover the debt service, property taxes, property management costs, and soon? What is the return on investment anticipated, including any tax consequences?*

Tapping into your home's equity is much more than merely taking out a loan. It puts your home on the line and should be undertaken only after receiving answers from financial counsel, including your tax advisor or a certified public accountant.

COMMUNICATING WITH THE LENDER

Q. Is there a law that requires the lender to respond to inquiries about a mortgage loan?

Yes. The Real Estate Settlement Procedures Act (RESPA) requires that the lender respond within 20 business days after receiving a borrower's *qualified written request*. This is any written correspondence other than a note on the premium notice or payment coupon. Within 60 days after receiving the request, the lender must correct any errors found on the account and/or send the borrower written clarification regarding the dispute.

13

REFINANCING

Refinancing makes great financial sense if it lowers a borrower's interest rate and trims his or her monthly payments, not to mention saving tens of thousands of dollars over the life of the mortgage. But used improperly and for the wrong reasons, refinancing can be a financial coffin nail, decimating precious equity, causing a borrower to bring a check to the closing table to pay off debt when selling—or even potential foreclosure should the borrower overleverage with multiple mortgages he or she can't pay. That's why it's important to keep in mind that even when mortgage interest and corresponding payments are both low, it's still debt! It's still money that the borrower owes, and must repay the lender.

WHEN DOES IT MAKE SENSE TO REFINANCE?

Q. When does it make sense to refinance?

The answer lies in what it can achieve for the borrower. Depending on the borrower's circumstances, good reasons could include lowering the interest rate, lowering the monthly payments, refinancing out of an adjustable rate loan, or reducing the term of the loan (e.g., from 30 to 15 years). It might even make sense to pull out cash to pay off high, non-tax-deductible debt (provided that you cut up the credit cards!)

The bottom line is to look at the total picture of refinancing. How can this be done? The borrower can ask the lender to prepare an analysis to evaluate the options. The homeowner should also answer the following eight questions before refinancing:

1. *How long will the homeowner keep the property?* (If this period is not long enough to recoup the costs of refinancing, the homeowner should not refinance.)
2. *What types of situations are anticipated in the homeowner's personal and economic future?* (Will equity be needed in three years to send a child to college or pay possible expenses for personal health care or nursing home care for an elderly relative?)
3. *Will cash pulled out now be used for a sound reason that makes economic sense* (such as adding a second bath in lieu of moving to a more expensive home)?
4. *What are the benefits in keeping the existing loan on the property* (such as easy loan assumability or flexibility by adding seller financing if the property is sold)? *Do they outweigh the tradeoffs?*
5. *Would a new loan require additional costs of PMI or impound accounts for taxes and insurance that weren't previously required?*
6. *How does the proposed loan compare to others based on interest rate, points, closing costs, and fluff or garbage fees* (unregulated extra fees for services such as tax checking, courier service, and so on)?
7. *How would a lower interest rate affect the homeowner's tax picture?*
8. *If the homeowner wants cash out, which is better for his or her situation: a new refinanced loan or a home equity line of credit (HELOC)?*

The reality is that a home and its equity are, for most people, their largest personal asset and savings account. The homeowner should make changes with the right loan and the right lender, and for the right reasons.

USING YOUR HOME AS A PIGGY BANK? THINK AGAIN

Q. We have a lot of credit card debt and still owe money on a car loan. After pulling out the money we need, we'd have just enough equity for a 10 percent down payment and closing costs on a new conventional loan. This will be our second refinance in the past three years to pay off debt.

You're describing what I term the pre-2006, "consumer debt reduction approach"—borrowing against your home's equity to pay off high interest rate consumer debt. With home appreciation in the double digits and prices skyrocketing, it was tough back then to make a misstep in using equity to pay off consumer debt. Your home equity would magically replenish itself and you'd once again be on even ground financially. Tapping into home equity was like raiding the piggy bank.

In many cases today, the piggy bank has lost its jingle. Home appreciation has slipped. A glut of homes on the market and the mortgage meltdown is putting downward pressure on prices for both listed and unlisted properties. And the strategy for tapping equity that was a saving grace previously could put homeowners like you in damaging, irreversible positions.

Here's why. It's true that you'd be paying off high interest rate non-tax-deductible consumer debt. But at what price? Unless you cut up your credit cards and vow to never use them again, this won't be the last time you'll need to visit the financial well. And since you last refinanced, there's a world of difference in the mortgage community.

First, appraisals have tightened which means that you might not be able to receive the amount of cash you need.

Second, the mortgage mess has lenders taking a tougher look at underwriting mortgages in general, especially those with very little equity. And with the 10 percent down that you mentioned, you'll be required to add private mortgage insurance (PMI) which will increase your monthly payment. Unlike loans with down payments of 20 percent or more, you'll also be required to pay your property taxes and homeowner's insurance monthly, impounded into the lender's escrow account. And since both taxes and insurance are on the rise nationwide, these monthly amounts are likely to increase your payment annually. Last, but certainly not least. when you refinance a higher mortgage amount is recorded and your property becomes a prime target for a new property valuation from the county, resulting in a higher assessed value for property tax purposes.

Perhaps the greatest concern is that, should you need to sell in the short term (i.e. in less than two years); leveraging the property in this way could put you on the verge of being upside down in your equity when you close with a buyer. With only 10 percent equity or less at the time of refinance (especially if you finance some of your closing costs) you might have to bring a check to pay for sales costs, loan prepayment penalties, and so on.

Before you make a step, meet with a mortgage advisor to crunch the numbers, check out various loan programs, and then take time privately to mull over the pros and cons involved before eroding precious equity.

Q. How can a homeowner crunch the numbers to see if it makes financial sense to refinance?

In most cases, it financially pays to refinance your mortgage if you can lower your interest rate and/or lessen your loan amortization period and you'll keep the property (and the loan) long enough to recoup the costs of refinancing. The refinancing formula in figure 13.1 can help you make more exact calculations, or you can use an online calculator like the one found at www.interest.com, or www.mtgprofessor.com.

FIGURE 13.1 *Refinancing Worksheet*

A general rule of thumb is that if a borrower can cut the interest rate and/or trim the loan term and will hold the property (and loan) long enough to recoup the cost of refinancing, it may pay to refinance. Use the following worksheet to analyze each individual situation.

Refinance Worksheet

Present Monthly Payments	$	
*Number of Months to Pay	$	
Total Payments	$	A
Payments at the Lower Rate	$	
*Number of Months to Pay	$	
Total Payments	$	B
Difference in Total Payments (A – B)	$	C

Refinancing Costs

Prepayment Penalty (if applicable)	$	D
Closing Costs for New Mortgage, Including Points	$	E
Added Income Taxes Over Loan Term Due to Reduced Deduction from Lower Interest	$	F
Total (D + E + F)	$	G
Net Savings Over Life of Mortgage (C – G)	$	

*Be sure that the number of months to pay is for the period the borrower expects to own the property, not the number of months remaining on the loan.

Basically, you would tally up the total amount of payments you would make for the remaining time you would own the property, subtract the lower payments you would make under the lesser interest rate, then add back the costs of refinancing, plus any additional income taxes you would pay because of the reduced interest deductions. You would then take what you saved in payments and deduct what you paid in refinancing and taxes to figure your net gain or loss.

Selling Soon? Crunch the Numbers before Refinancing

Q. Does it make sense to refinance from a 30-year loan to a 15-year loan to save $100 per month if I plan on selling in two years or less? The loan fees would be $2,000.

What you're considering doesn't make financial sense on several fronts. In fact, doing what you describe could end up costing, not saving, you money.

First, it's unlikely that you'll break even based on the costs you'll pay to obtain the new loan and the length of time you'll hold the property. To determine your breakeven point, divide the closing costs of $2,000 by the $100 per month payment savings. It would take 20 months to break even. If you sold prior to that time, you'd lose money refinancing under these terms.

Since you've been paying on your current mortgage for nearly five years, the amortized payment is picking up speed to whittle down the principal amount quicker. Even though the refinancing would place you in a 15-year loan, it's unlikely that you'd gain any real ground on reducing the principal because all loans are interest-heavy in the early years.

Third, even though perhaps a lesser concern, a lower-interest-rate loan will generate fewer income tax deductions come tax time.

Before you give up, try one or all of the following: (1) If your current mortgage has not been sold to another company/servicer, ask if it can be recast into a 15-year loan. Depending on the lender, this may be a quick, low-cost solution to obtain the shorter-term loan you're looking for. (2) Check with a lender about using an adjustable-rate mortgage (ARM) for the refinance. Because ARM interest rates are lower than fixed, you should be able to recoup your closing costs quicker to make refinancing cost-effective. (3) Shop for a mortgage with lower or no closing costs.

Refinancing If You're Seasonally Employed

Q. We need to refinance a balloon mortgage that's coming up but I'm seasonally employed (just made partner with more money) and looking at a longer layoff later this year because of the economy. My wife has obtained a better-paying job in the same line of work she's been in for five years. How should we time the refinance?

Explore refinancing as soon as possible, especially because you anticipate your seasonal layoff to be lengthier than usual. Lenders are big on employment history and seeing income increase for borrowers. By becoming a partner with stronger income for both you and your wife, you're sitting well in that department. The downside could be that if you wait until the lengthy layoff to apply, the lender could term this as a negative (higher risk). The penalty could be a less competitive interest rate and/or less of a loan than you're seeking.

WHEN NOT TO REFINANCE

Q. Could refinancing cost more money than it saves?

Yes. The following example shows how refinancing can be an imprudent choice:

The Johnsons own a home worth approximately $200,000. They wish to refinance to reduce their mortage to 6 percent, and they won't be taking any cash out.

The lender informs them that it will loan up to a maximum of 85 percent loan-to-appraised value (LTV) or $170,000 (including points and closing costs). With out-of-pocket expenses (such as title work, etc.) plus two discount points to obtain the lowest possible rate, the Johnsons finance these costs into their loan. At the time of the closing, the Johnsons' new loan total is $169,500.

One year after refinancing, the Johnsons decide they need a larger home. The market has shown little appreciation in real estate values, so the Johnsons list their home for $200,000 (the previous appraisal figure). After six months of marketing the property, a buyer, Jim Judge, offers them $190,000 contingent on his obtaining a 100 percent VA loan.

Judge asks the Johnsons to pay the two discount points needed to get the loan ($3,800). With the other costs the Johnsons need to pay—$15,400 for the real estate commission and miscellaneous closing costs (plus paying off the remaining loan, reduced now to $169,100), how much the Johnsons will net from the sale? A whopping $2,070. That's not even enough to pay the first and last month's rent, let alone make another purchase.

If they accept the sale, they will have used $20,000 worth of their equity in one year's time on refinancing and sales costs, and will still be unable to achieve their goal of buying a larger home.

What should the Johnsons have done? They should have thought ahead to their future housing needs and purchased a new home instead of refinancing their old one. Their mistake was using precious equity to buy a lower interest rate in the refinance while forgetting how long it would take to recoup the cost of refinancing (based on their monthly payment savings). Come April 15, they may find that they actually owe income tax because they now have less mortgage interest to deduct.

As with the Johnsons, refinancing could cause a low-equity or no-equity position should the homeowner sell in a short period of time. In fact, good lenders counsel and caution homeowners to carefully evaluate refinancing if they do not plan to own the property for a minimum of three to five additional years. (Lenders will be glad to provide breakeven projections based on a homeowner's individual circumstances.)

One way the Johnsons could have radically improved their equity position was to shop for lower refinancing costs in the first place. Fees and points can vary widely from lender to lender. Taking the time to check out what's available from several lenders may make the difference between preserving equity or losing money.

Q. Does the loan you're paying off have an impact on whether or not you should refinance?

While somewhat rare, an assumable low-interest-rate loan may be more enticing when you sell than one that is not assumable. And remember, too, that if you obtain a new loan of greater than 80 percent of the appraised value, you may be faced with PMI. This could add approximately $35 more per month to an $80,000 loan.

Later in this chapter, we'll discuss one of the most equity-draining costs when you refinance, the prepayment penalty.

REFINANCING ROADBLOCKS

Why Credit Errors Return When Refinancing

Q. If I corrected my credit report the last time I refinanced, why is the error showing up again?

You may have corrected the error at the local credit-reporting bureau and it verified the correction with the lender. Unfortunately, the update didn't get processed into all three of the nationwide credit-reporting repositories the mortgage lender uses to access your merged credit report.

Here's how to remedy the problem. First, look through your old mortgage/closing papers for a copy of the letter that resolved the error. In fact, you might find a copy of what you need in the papers provided you at the last closing.

If a hard copy can't be located, contact the credit bureau you worked with. You'll need to provide it with the approximate date of the error, the name of the creditor, as well as when the error was corrected. Be sure to let the credit-reporting bureau know you have a refinance pending and that it's important to quickly resolve this issue.

Once you find the documentation, be sure to correct the error with all three of the national credit repositories. Otherwise, this error may haunt you again in the future.

Other Common Refinancing Roadblocks

Q. Besides credit report errors, are there any other common roadblocks that can impede the refinancing process?

Unfortunately, yes. While underwriting guidelines vary depending on your financial picture and the loan type, here are some of the more common errors/roadblocks that get in the way of speedy refinancing:

- *All the pages, please.* If your lender requests that you submit your bank statements for verification, make sure that you include all the pages. This applies even if page seven of seven is merely an advertisement for life insurance or car leasing. Otherwise, the loan processor may assume that something derogatory about your finances was on the missing page and you subsequently decided to leave it out of what you provided them.

- *Hazy W2s/1099s.* The lender must be able to easily read the income documents you provide. If you can't make a readable photocopy, please ask your employer's payroll department for a duplicate.
- *Don't take "no cost" loans literally.* Be prepared to write a check even if this is a "no cost" loan. In general, you need to prepay some interest and possibly property taxes. Make sure that you work out these details with your loan officer so you won't be blindsided at the closing.
- *Keep the settlement statements from a previous loan.* If you're refinancing, be sure to keep a copy of the final settlement statements from the previous loan for at least two reasons: It shows whether or not you took cash out, which the lender will need to know, and it shows who was paid off. This is particularly valuable if that lender failed to issue a deed of reconveyance in a timely manner showing that the lien was paid in full. In fact, when you are re-financing, make sure that the lender who is getting paid off records the reconveyance with the county recorder's office. If you receive an unrecorded reconveyance, it is your responsibility to have it recorded to show that the debt has been satisfied. You can also verify this with your County Recorder's office.
- *Special steps for Home Equity Lines of Credit (HELOC).* (1) If you have a HELOC second mortgage, make sure to keep the promissory note handy (which is your agreement to repay), tell your loan officer about it, and provide a copy to him or her. (2) If you have a HELOC second mortgage and are going to pay it off, check the agreement to see if it has an "early closure fee." In general, if you paid nothing to get the HELOC and have had it for less than one or two years, a financial penalty could apply. (3) If you have a HELOC and are going to subordinate it to a new first mortgage, you'll need to send a complete copy of the HELOC agreement or note to your loan officer. The new lender needs to see the details, including what your maximum financial liability is if you draw the entire line in order to factor it into your qualifying ratios.

FHASecure® May Assist Rate-Ravaged Borrowers

Q. The interest rate on my adjustable rate mortgage has risen so high that I've been late making the last two payments. Is there any way that a lender will make me a fixed-rate loan?

In the wake of rising foreclosures caused in part by adjustable rate products and subprime loans, the Federal Housing Administration (FHA) released a new refinancing vehicle called FHASecure®. Designed to assist homeowners whose mortgages are behind due to loan reset and higher payments, it's hoped to help nearly a quarter of a million American households.

Here's how it works. In order to qualify, borrowers must have:

1. A history of on-time mortgage payments before the payment reset
2. Interest rates that reset between June 2005, and December 2008
3. Three percent equity in the home (Note: At the time of this writing, the "FHA Modernization Act" is pending passage on Capitol Hill. If passed under its current guidelines, the down payment requirement would be eliminated and the 3 percent equity rule would no longer apply).
4. A sustained history of employment
5. Sufficient income to make the new mortgage payment

There are no minimum or maximum months of delinquent payments required to qualify and any type of mortgage can be refinanced. All other program guidelines of the standard 203(b) loan apply to this program.

Effective January 1, 2008, FHA programs (including FHASecure®) moved from flat fees for mortgage insurance premiums to risk-based fees on new loan originations. Done in part to ensure that FHA remains solvent, riskier borrowers will pay higher mortgage insurance premiums as has been the case on conventional mortgages for decades.

You can learn more about the FHASecure® program online at www.hud.gov.

TIPS AND TRAPS WHEN REFINANCING

Use Cash-Outs Prudently

Q. Many people don't seem to use the cash they receive from refinancing responsibly. Isn't this important?

Absolutely. Because lenders estimate that more than 50 percent of borrowers take cash out of their properties when they refinance, prudent use of this cash is important. To use the cash to add a hot tub, pool, or other improvement to the real estate that may not add dollar-for-dollar resale value to the property is not a prudent decision. Paying off nondeductible high-interest consumer loans is good. Using equity to pay cash for a lessening value asset such as a car or new refrigerator may not be prudent based on the individual's financial circumstances.

Should a Borrower Pay Points When Refinancing?

Q. Is it a good idea to pay higher points to get a lower interest rate?

Paying higher points to secure a lower rate of interest depends on several things. First, how long will the borrower keep the loan on the property? Obviously, paying hefty points up front to secure an interest-rate loan that's lower than market rate won't be as valuable if the loan and the property will be held for only a short time. This is illustrated in the following example:

> A lender gives Gus Wellington a choice of a $225,000 loan at 6 percent with two points ($4,500 paid at closing) or at 7 percent with no points. Which is better?

It depends on what Gus wants to accomplish. While the difference between the rates is just $148 per month principal and interest, it would take more than 30 months to retrieve the $4,500 ($4,500 divided by the monthly payment savings of $148). So paying points only makes sense if Gus is planning to hold the property for at least 30 months.

Paying points at the settlement also means the borrower has lost the use of that money, plus any possible interest or investment potential.

Q. Is there a rule of thumb about when you should pay higher closing costs to get a lower interest rate when you refinance?

In general, keep loan costs low if you'll hold the mortgage for only a short time. Once you part with cash or equity at the closing table, it's gone forever. The reverse is true if you are holding the property for a longer term. It's wise to pay more closing costs to drop the interest rate and the subsequent payment.

Refinancing into Shorter-Term Loans

Q. What are the pros and cons of going to a shorter-term loan when refinancing?

It may be helpful to review the basic differences of payment terms in chapter 4.

The following example shows some of the benefits and problems of short-term loans:

> Mr. and Mrs. Russell are in their late 40s and are thinking of refinancing their 8 percent 15-year mortgage, which is paid down to $51,000 after five years. Their choice is between a 7 percent loan for another 15 years or higher payments for a 10-year term.
>
> After crunching the numbers, they find that it would be a financial misstep to take another 15-year loan. While their monthly payments on the 10-year loan would be $592 per month compared to the 15-year monthly loan payments of $458 (a difference of $134), the 15-year loan would add another 5 years of payments for a net increase in cost of more than $10,000!
>
> Because the Russells have paid 5 years on their existing loan, they've whittled down a fair amount of interest. That's why the new 10-year loan makes the most economic sense.

Remember, when making this decision, the borrower should consider the time he or she wishes to keep the home and the amount of monthly payment he or she can afford to make.

Q. My friend just refinanced into a lower-interest-rate zero-closing-cost mortgage. Is he saving anything since he's already paid on a 30-year loan for 4 years?

Yes, the trick is in not only getting the lower-interest-rate loan but not having closing costs involved. For example, let's say he refinanced his old loan of $150,000 at 7 percent interest with a new no-closing-cost loan at 6.5 percent. While the monthly payment difference is only $49 less, the impact of the lower interest rate creates $3,300 more in principal reduction during the next five years of payments!

Closing Costs

Q. When would a borrower find out exactly what the closing costs would be if he or she were refinancing?

Lenders disclose the costs for a refinance as they would for a new purchase loan. Lenders make certain disclosures to a borrower at application or within three days after application, describing the settlement costs of the loan, the effective interest rate, and the possibility that the lender will transfer the servicing rights.

Because many lenders take refinance applications over the telephone and via the Internet, disclosure may be verbally minimized. Broad quotes on costs and discount points may change drastically by the time the closing rolls around.

If the refinanced loan were for an ARM, the lender should disclose a worst-case scenario on the loan at the time of application or before any nonrefundable loan fees are paid.

If a borrower feels he or she can't close on a refinance loan that was misrepresented, the borrower can apply the federal three-day right of rescission law that allows a borrower to cancel a loan if he or she does so in writing within three business days of the loan settlement.

Because there are no maximum ceilings on costs of refinancing, the term *standard costs,* used by some lenders, means little. A lender not willing to update cost estimates for the borrower may have something to hide and may not be worth the borrower's time and effort. Avoiding these lenders is the consumer's best protection.

Q. How can I calculate the amount of net proceeds I'd receive if I refinanced?

Calculating proceeds from refinancing can be a bit tricky and can depend on the type of loan you have, the new one you'll obtain, the lender's policies/costs, and whether or not you'll pay your taxes and insurance monthly in your mortgage payment. Obviously, the best time to clarify all costs you'll be responsible for is at the time you apply for the loan. Both you and the lender originating your loan are best served by no surprises and a smooth path to closing.

Here are the most typical categories of things you'll have to pay when refinancing:

1. *Your old loan balance and any early prepayment fees per your mortgage documents.* These are particularly prevalent in "no cost" home equity lines of credit (HELOC) loans if you're paying one off prior to holding it for

three years. If your loan does contain a prepayment penalty and you're refinancing with the same lender, it may be waived as a repeat customer courtesy, but you'll have to make this request from the lender and it's suggested that you get it in writing since the person originating the loan may not be the same one closing it.

2. *Per diem (daily) interest on your old loan.* Mortgage interest is paid in arrears. That means that your February payment is for the use of the money/outstanding loan amount in January. The lender will prorate the amount of interest due plus typically two days extra in order to give the old lender time to receive the payoff.

3. *Prepaid per diem interest required on the new loan.* The prepaid interest is the interest that you are paying at closing for the remaining days in the month on the new loan. For example, if your new loan closed on March 8th, you'd pay interest for that day through March 31st, have no April payment, making your first payment due in May.

4. *Nonrecurring (one-time) closing costs like title insurance, document preparation fees, recording fees, origination fees to the lender, credit report, and appraisal.* If you're getting a "no cost" loan, the lender will be covering these.

5. *Recurring closing costs like property taxes and homeowner's insurance.* If you have delinquent property taxes or any other type of lien against the property (i.e. mechanic's lien for unpaid materials or labor), those will need to be paid at closing.

6. *Funds for an impound account if you're going to pay property tax and home owner's insurance payments monthly in your mortgage payment.* Many lenders will let the borrower pay for them outside of the payment if a 20 percent or larger down payment is made on the new loan.

Other glitches in the refinancing process can cause you to part with more money/equity than you need to. Make sure that you do not make a payment on your old loan at the beginning of the month that does not have time to be credited by the day of closing. Your loan originator can help you decide what to pay and when, based on the anticipated closing date. Second, double-check to make sure that you don't need ready cash or "seed money" for impounds. Being short on funds to close can cause you to lose a rate lock or pay a "redraw fee" to draft new closing documents.

While the initial good faith estimate quoted at loan application will provide you with estimates of closing costs, it's good to ask the lender to explain, in detail, the disbursement sheet used for closing when you first apply for the loan. It will help you visualize the expenses you'll incur and the credits you'll receive and will give you the best vehicle for calculating your net proceeds.

Q. Can I deduct the points I pay in refinancing?

Yes, but not in the same way you deducted the points paid when you purchased. Discount points paid in refinancing must be amortized over the years of the loan for the purpose of tax deductions. For example, $2,000 paid to refinance a 20-year loan would provide an annual deduction of $100.

Ways to Sidestep Prepayment Penalty

Q. The quote for paying off my old loan was several thousand dollars higher because of a prepayment penalty. Is there any way I can get out of paying it to refinance especially because I don't remember seeing it in the documents?

Prepayment penalties have become popular with lenders because the shelf life of a mortgage from refinancing mimics that of a fruit fly. Most prepayment penalties apply if the loan is retired in the first three to five years. Because the bulk of a lender's profit traditionally comes not from originating the loan but from later activities such as selling and servicing it, prepayment penalties beef up profit margins and bottom lines.

Unfortunately, it's no defense that you don't remember the prepayment penalty being in the mortgage documents. Verbiage for it can be found either in the promissory note you signed at the closing and/or as a rider to it. If you failed to read the documents in detail, you could have missed it. Worse yet, some lenders assume that you'd prefer a mortgage with a prepayment penalty if you could secure a lower interest rate on the loan. In fact, sometimes the lender might switch you to a prepayment penalty-type loan midstream in the mortgage process to help you qualify more easily using the lower interest rate.

The good news is that the lender holding the mortgage can waive this penalty, which most often occurs if you agree to refinance with that lender. The lender hopes to make up its financial loss of retiring the first loan by keeping you as a borrower for another.

Contact the lender and ask under what circumstances the penalty can be waived and who in the company would make that decision, and then have that person write out the conditions for you (or at least keep good notes of the findings). If the lender doesn't budge on your request, threaten to take your business to another lender, one who might choose to be competitive enough with points and fees to help offset what you'll lose by paying the prepayment penalty.

Duplicate Interest May Apply When Refinancing

Q. The last time I refinanced, I was charged interest for several of the same days on both the old and the new loan. Why did this happen?

Double-interest payments happen more often than not when refinancing. Mortgage interest is paid in arrears, which means that at the closing you'll owe interest for each of the days since your last payment. This is termed per diem (daily) interest. Simply stated, your September payment is for the use of the money loaned you during the month of August.

Suppose that your new loan is going to fund on September 8 and that you have not yet made your September payment. You'll be required to pay interest on your old loan from August 1 (the date of your last payment) until the day the lender receives the payoff for the old loan. The current lender will inform the closing company of the per diem interest as well as the amount of the outstanding loan balance.

Unfortunately, there is a lag time between funding the loan and the lender receiving the payoff. This typically takes approximately two days. In this example, that would be September 10. That's why many closing companies/lenders charge the borrower interest on both the old loan and the new loan for those days, or what is called duplicate interest. In this example, you'd pay interest on the old loan for 41 days—August 1 to September 10. This is calculated by multiplying the loan balance on August 1 by the interest rate (as a decimal) divided by 365 days. Because interest is paid on both loans until the payoff is received, you may not want the new loan to fund on Friday. Doing so might require four days of duplicate interest instead of two.

At first blush, duplicate interest may seem unfair; but remember, the lender making the first loan doesn't care that you're being charged interest from the new lender. The first lender wants and deserves every day's worth of interest on the outstanding loan until it's paid in full.

Depending on when you close, you may be asked to prepay interest on the new loan as well, to cover the remaining days in the month. In the example this would be interest from September 8 to September 30. Because interest is paid in arrears, this covers the period up to October 1, making your first loan payment due November 1.

The first time to ask about interest proration amounts is when the lender gives you the good faith estimate for the new loan. Because the lender may not have the facts and figures on paying off the old loan at that time, ask for a net sheet for the old loan as soon as the lender receives the payoff information. Check this information with the final figures on the closing statement for any differences or discrepancies.

REFINANCING VIA THE INTERNET

Q. Can you really save time and money refinancing via the Internet?

As with any system, there pros and cons. Handled carefully and prudently, online refinancing may save time and even money. In fact, many lenders offer interest-rate and closing-cost discounts because online applications limit the amount of personal contact (and therefore lender overhead) required to effect mortgages.

There are various ways you can use online resources for refinancing. You can shop online for competitive rates and closing costs, submit your application via the Internet, or merely request that an employee contact you to take your application over the telephone, then fax documents to the lender. The possibilities are endless.

If you'd prefer to work with a lender face-to-face, the Web is a great initial place to glean information regarding competitive rates, fees, and programs to use as ammunition with the lender you do choose.

But with the positives come the negatives. Many online mortgage platforms are great at dispensing information, but fall short when it comes to customer service and responding to borrower questions in a timely manner. Therefore, communications may fall apart causing delays or worse yet, no closed loan. Failed communications can also cause a lot of "assuming" to go on between the parties. For example, a lender might assume that his client would want a lower interest rate even though the mortgage contained a prepayment penalty. At the long-distance closing, the client refused to sign the documents and they had to be redrawn and reovernighted (at the lender's expense, of course). Then there's the potential problem of not understanding what you're signing. In fact, some lenders don't use closing agents or title companies to close their online originated loans. They pay a notary in your state to show up at your door with the documents! Good luck if you have trouble deciphering the closing statement or need questions answered.

Last, while there is concern that a borrower's personal information will fall into the wrong hands, this can be equally true when dealing in person with a lender who's less than scrupulous. No matter how you initially contact a lender, it's wise to take the time to check out a lender, using resources such as business references and the better business bureau. Don't let the ease and convenience of online refinancing take the place of good common sense when it comes to security.

HOME EQUITY LOANS

Q. How do equity loans differ from refinancing?

Equity loans (or home equity lines of credit—HELOCs) don't disturb the existing first mortgage and have in the past not required the strongest of personal financial profiles because these loans are underwritten primarily based on the value of the property. Equity loans don't have to be sold to the secondary market so lenders may more likely accept higher-risk borrowers (although high foreclosure rates and the subprime shakeout are shedding new light on this topic). There are some negatives, however:

- Some lenders may make equity line of credit loans (up to 125 percent loan-to-value for conventional loans) solely on a "drive-by" appraisal. This could result in overleveraging, especially if the owner needs to sell in a short period of time.
- Equity lines of credit can bear higher-than-market interest rates and/or adjustable rates and can overleverage borrowers who make "interest only" repayments. Deeply discounted initial interest rates may be used to lure a borrower into a financially unfavorable loan.
- While borrowers access only the amount needed (up to a predetermined ceiling) and interest accrues only on the amount borrowed, the loan may include balloon payments or other negatives. If these obligations are not met, the borrower could risk losing the property.
- If the borrower tries to refinance a first mortgage and not disturb the equity line, the equity line holder probably won't allow it. Thus, a new refinance loan would have to pay off both loans, causing a higher payment on the combined loans.

Q. When does it make sense to roll a home equity line of credit into a refinanced first mortgage?

While it depends on the loan terms and the conditions of the loans in question, a general rule of thumb is that if you have no contingency plan for paying off the equity line in the next four years, you should probably roll it into a new competitive interest-rate first mortgage now. This is especially true if the HELOC rate will change/adjust after an initial period of time (e.g., five years).

125 PERCENT MORTGAGES

Q. What are 125 percent mortgages?

They are first and second mortgages that total up to 125 percent of a property's market value. Lenders have made them in times of strong property appreciation and hope that the homeowners won't need to sell until the debts are paid down. Due to the mortgage morass, these loans should go the way of dinosaur. Lenders typically require that borrowers have great credit, which helps limit the lender's risk.

Potential borrowers under this approach should be incredibly cautious. The high-leverage approach of the 125 percent loan can be the kiss of death for many borrowers, especially if they have trouble managing debt in general. You should *not* consider taking on one of these loans if you:

- Have unstable income and/or have ever had trouble making mortgage payments
- Use this type of leverage to pay off credit cards or other types of consumer debt but are unwilling to permanently eliminate those cards/accounts and control spending habits
- Are planning to sell the house in five years or less. With low annualized appreciation, you probably will be required to bring a check to the closing to pay off the outstanding debt

As with any type of mortgage debt, if you don't have a clear-cut idea of what you want to accomplish and are fairly assured of the outcome, don't risk your house on the line with the 125 percent leverage route.

Q. When would the 125 percent mortgage approach make sense?

A 125-percent mortgage may make sense if the borrower:

- Owns a home with above-average appreciation in a stable neighborhood
- Is realistic about what the future holds for the local economy (a single-employer town could convert to a ghost town, with no real estate selling, virtually overnight)
- Anticipates keeping the house long enough to whittle down the debt

- Is willing to shop diligently to obtain the lowest interest rates and costs because this type of financing can easily run 2 to 3 percent over first-mortgage rates

Be cautioned that the IRS only allows homeowners to deduct interest up to 100 percent of the market value of their property—and yes, the IRS will be watching for 125 percent mortgages!

Q. Is it a good financial idea to keep pulling equity out of your house, keeping it highly mortgaged, so the money can work in other ways?

Some financial planners would like you to believe so. But just as there's no one stock market investment panacea, handling your home equity is a very individual decision.

Having a large mortgage is a better alternative than paying loads of nondeductible consumer debt. And it's great to have equity to use for financial events such as sending a child to college. But it's up to each homeowner to decide how much mortgage debt is enough, based on the levels of both financial and psychological risk.

14

WHEN THE BORROWER
FALLS BEHIND
IN PAYMENTS

You love your house, but the payments are getting tougher to handle. You rework your budget, but it doesn't make a dent. One late payment becomes two and before you know it, late notices from the lender have piled up.

The recent mortgage morass and subprime fallout show homeowners the importance of protecting hard-earned equity from loss. This chapter addresses how to best interface with the lender to explore payment options and enumerates your rights as a borrower under the federal Fair Debt Collection Act.

WHY ARE FORECLOSURES
THROUGH THE ROOF?

Q. How can mortgage foreclosures be at record highs when interest rates have been so low?

While it's easy to point a finger at the subprime market as the primary cause of current mortgage foreclosures, there are many other challenges that fuel late payments and subsequent foreclosures:

- *Not everyone took advantage of refinancing.* While some people played the "how low can I go" limbo game, refinancing two or more times within as many years, some borrowers chose not to refinance and/or were unable to meet the financial criteria required. Reasons range from loss of employment, underemployment, and/or inadequate qualifying income, high debt, and/or a personal situation such as the divorce or death of a coborrower. In some cases, high refinancing costs and/or prepayment penalties would strip out any equity in the property, making refinancing unfavorable, especially for a short-term owner.

- *Many who refinanced didn't cut up their credit cards.* While it made financial sense to lower your monthly payment by refinancing, the gain was offset by heavy credit use for short-term disposable items such as vacations, or new furniture—at high rates of nondeductible interest! Some homeowners refinanced into 125 percent mortgages. The lender who makes you a loan for 125 percent of the value of your property may not be doing you any favor. This is especially true if you need to sell quickly before new equity has a chance to grow. The end result could be bringing a check to closing to sell the house, or, worse yet, mailing in the keys to the lender in what's called a *friendly foreclosure*, a.k.a. a *deed in lieu of foreclosure.*

- *Costs of home ownership have increased.* It's not merely buying the house, but maintaining it for the long run. Cost increases for insurance, property taxes, repairs, and utilities have outpaced inflation and wage increases and are likely to continue to rise.

- *Heavy financial leverage is available through creative loan programs.* Previous changes in underwriting guidelines coupled with little or no down payments on mortgages have consumers qualifying for more houses than ever before. But just because a lender qualifies you, doesn't mean that you'll be comfortable making the payment for 30 years. Once the honeymoon period cools (usually within the first 18 months), late payments become more prevalent. While more liberal lending practices have helped boost U.S. home ownership to more than 67 percent, foreclosures have risen at an even faster speed.

- *Unemployment or underemployment has become widespread.* One of the strongest reasons behind rising foreclosures is unemployment and/or underemployment that impacts a large percentage of American households. Until the economy becomes more buoyant and workers are provided a living wage instead of meager hourly compensation, foreclosures are likely to remain high.
- *To some consumers, less interest is synonymous with less debt.* It may be tough to imagine, but some homeowners erroneously believe that having a low rate of interest is synonymous with having less debt. While I was on a radio show recently, more than one caller remarked that they couldn't be upside down in their equity because their interest rate was "incredibly low." Debt is debt, no matter how low the interest rate.
- *The stock market has been erratic.* An explanation on foreclosures wouldn't be complete without blaming the fluctuating stock market. Shrinking portfolio values have caused net worth to drop and dividends to shrivel. Especially impacted are those living on income generated by their stock portfolios, including the retired and senior citizens.

THE KEY: CONTACT
THE LENDER IMMEDIATELY

Q. If a borrower's financial position changes after getting the loan, and he or she falls behind in the payments, what can be done?

Contrary to popular belief, lenders really do want to work with delinquent and potentially defaulting borrowers. The cost of foreclosure for the lender can be as high as 20 percent of the remaining principal balance. And a delinquent loan on the books as a nonperforming asset continues to cost the lender money. That's why most lenders see foreclosure as a last, and many times unattractive, resort.

The borrower who is behind on payments should not take a wait-and-see approach. Being proactive and immediately contacting the lender to discuss the situation is imperative. Some of the most attractive alternatives are those exercised in the early stages of default.

The lender will want to know what caused the borrower to let payments fall behind, whether that cause has been remedied, and how the situation can be reversed. For example, a borrower with delinquent payments caused by a temporary job loss, who is once again employed, may need just a few additional months to catch up payments. Conversely, a borrower with a severe long-term illness might need other options.

Q. I've hesitated returning the lender's call about my delinquent payments because my friend said that the lender has to wait at least 90 days before foreclosing. Is this correct?

No. Run, don't walk to the nearest telephone and return that call! Your friend is dead wrong. While it's true that most lenders will wait to file a foreclosure until more than one payment is late, technically the mortgage is in default when your payment is not in the lender's hands by the close of business on the payment due date. Attempting to sidestep the savings and loan debacle of the past decade, many lenders are calling earlier in the default period to work out payment arrangements.

When you call the lender, don't make repayment promises you know you can't keep for this will further erode the business relationship and the lender's faith in you. Be sure to ask for the name of the person you're speaking to (for documentation) and ask that any agreement you make on the telephone be confirmed in writing and sent to you. Documenting what's said and the promises made is important should you later have to prove that the discussion occurred. If discussion with the lender goes well (and you're feeling brave), you might ask that all or part of the late fees be waived, that the lender not report your late-payment history to the credit-reporting bureau, and so on (but don't count on it because you're the one that's caused the problem!).

Because the person assigned to collections often has a personality to match the job, avoid the temptation to lose your temper. Keep in mind that the representative is only doing his or her job, and that as soon as the payments are caught up, this person will be out of your life—hopefully, forever.

NATIONAL PROGRAMS TO THE RESCUE

Q. With the growing numbers of foreclosures, have there been any federal or industrywide efforts to assist delinquent borrowers?

Yes. Beginning in 2007, a handful of federal solutions were ramped up to assist those behind in payments and yet other programs for consumers to sidestep mortgage delinquencies. At the time of this writing, four major housing bills are pending on Capitol Hill, designed to increase consumer protection in the mortgage process.

Passed in December of 2007, the Mortgage Forgiveness Debt Act creates a three-year window during which a consumer can receive mortgage debt forgiveness from a lender without it being taxed as ordinary income (as previously was the case). The act also increases incentives for borrowers and lenders to work together to refinance loans in order to secure lower mortgage payments.

The FHASecure® Initiative of 2007 allows delinquent borrowers to refinance adjustable rate mortgages that did reset, or are scheduled to reset, into fixed-rate FHA products. (For more information, check out chapter 13 on Refinancing and chapter 8, Federal Housing Administration loans.)

Another initiative, "Hope Now" is a combination of a federal program coupled with private-sector players, investors, and mortgage counselors. It's designed to freeze the teaser rate on adjustable rate mortgages for a period of up to five years, allowing consumers to keep payments low while accumulating equity in their homes. For more information, check out www.hopenow.com, or call 1-(888) 995-HOPE (4673).

Congress, investors, and the mortgage industry have received the wake-up call that nothing positive happens when borrowers default on home loans. The impact creates a downward economic spiral felt nationally and internationally.

FORECLOSURE ALTERNATIVES

Q. A person from the loss-mitigation department of my mortgage lender called to discuss forbearance on my late payments. What does this mean?

That's lender lingo for the lender would like to explore a way to keep your mortgage out of foreclosure! Most lenders and loan-servicing companies have workout specialists (loss mitigators) who strive to find a viable approach to keep you in the house and the loan on the books. In fact, Fannie Mae, Freddie Mac, Ginnie Mae, and the FHA require mortgage companies to do whatever is feasible to keep borrowers out of foreclosure.

While loss mitigation may sound like a new-age buzz word in the mortgage industry, it's been around for decades. In fact, over time, the options available to delinquent borrowers from lenders have expanded to include:

- *Reinstating the mortgage.* If there's money you can borrow from relatives or friends, you can catch up the missed payments along with any interest, penalties, and fees.
- *Accepting partial payments for a predetermined time.* If the amount of the mortgage payment has been the problem but an economic remedy is in sight, the lender might accept partial payments for a predetermined period of time, usually several months. This is often a stop-gap solution when the borrower decides that selling the property is the best solution. It provides the lender with some return on the investment so that it remains a "performing asset" and gives the borrower time to liquidate the property and pay off the loan.
- *Accepting interest-only payments.* This is another stop-gap measure to help make the monthly mortgage payment more manageable short-term for the borrower while allowing the lender to receive timely interest payments on the loan.
- *Catching up the arrearages by adding small additional amounts to payments until paid in full.* This approach would only work if the borrower had new-found cash to catch up the loan since the arrearage would be in addition to the current principal and interest monthly payments due on the mortgage.
- *Adding the delinquent amounts on to the back of the loan.* If the delinquencies were caused by a short-term event that is unlikely to reoccur, this is often the best solution for the borrower. While the borrower will be charged interest on the amounts, there will be no additional out-of-pocket cash.
- *Recasting the loan into a more realistic payment plan (i.e. from an unpredictable adjustable-rate mortgage to a more stable fixed-rate program).* This is afforded borrowers who may appear to be in a rate-rising loan that keeps stretching their ability to pay, often due to interest increases. For example, borrowers in adjustable rate mortgages whose wage increases haven't kept pace with inflation and rising interest rates might find this a viable solution. It can be a win/win situation with the lender charging new loan origination fees while the borrower wraps his past-due mortgage payments into a new, more affordable, payment plan.

Keeping the loan out of foreclosure is a win-win for the borrower and the lender alike. You may be pleasantly surprised at the outcome.

Q. What's a short sale?

A *short sale* is a term that means that the lender has decided to take less than the balance owing on the current mortgage(s) in order to sell the property. It often occurs when mortgage payments are behind and/or the loan has some type of payment insurance coverage such as private mortgage insurance (PMI) or other guarantee for repayment like the FHA or VA. The lender's rationale is that since the property is no longer a "performing asset" on the books (no payments received on a regular basis), it might as well cut its losses and attempt to avoid other carrying costs on the property such as taxes, repairs, maintenance, etc. A short sale can be a good buy for a potential buyer, especially if the lender is willing to waive other costs of purchasing—loan origination fees and other customary closing costs, for instance.

FHA and VA Workout Programs

Foreclosure can be expensive, not only in terms of payments lost, but also in preforeclosure property maintenance fees until foreclosure, and other costs of property repair. Understanding this, the FHA and VA have initiated preforeclosure workout programs for their loans. You can find these explained in Chapters 8 and 9.

Deed in Lieu of Foreclosure

Q. What is the worst that could happen if a borrower gives the property back to the lender?

I don't know about worst, but something adverse could certainly happen.

In this situation, called *a deed in lieu of foreclosure* or a *friendly foreclosure*, the lender agrees to take the property back and the borrower forgoes any equity in the property. But that may not be all that happens.

While the borrower could negotiate with the lender to waive posting negative information on the borrower's credit report (and may even put this agreement in writing), other parties to the default, such as the PMI company, might make a negative posting to the borrower's credit.

Because a deed in lieu of foreclosure can carry major impact for the borrower, giving the property back to the lender or agreeing to a workout program should only be undertaken after consulting with a real estate attorney.

Q. Are there any tax consequences if a borrower gives the property back to the lender?

Pursuant to the "Mortgage Forgiveness Debt Relief Act" of 2007, a three-year temporary change to the IRS tax laws will be in effect for any mortgage debt relief occurring between January 1, 2007, and January 1, 2010. During that time, no federal taxes will be charged on the forgiven debt, including deed in lieu of foreclosure situations. Before passage of this act, forgiven mortgage debt was considered taxable as ordinary income in the year in which it was forgiven.

TOUGH TO WIN WITH
"CASH FOR YOUR HOUSE" COMPANIES

Q. Our financial situation requires that we sell our house immediately. We've seen ads for companies that pay "quick and easy" cash overnight for houses, and claim to charge no commission to do so. How do these companies work and what can we expect if we work with one?

The companies you're referring to are usually real estate investment companies that make money purchasing homes at a discount from distressed sellers and then reselling them to buyers often via creative methods like seller financing or rent-to-own. Most are not real estate brokerages so they don't charge commissions. But that doesn't mean that there won't be costs involved, perhaps substantial ones. You need to make sure that "quick and easy" doesn't equate with parting with a big chunk of your hard-earned equity.

The primary focus of the investment company is to pay as little as possible for the property and receive the largest return possible. That's why if you decide to give this type of company a shot, you'll need to ask upfront questions like the following:

1. How is the sales price determined? Don't expect to receive anything close to market value for the property. It's not uncommon for an investment company to initially discount 10 to 20 percent off potential market value off the top since the seller is receiving cash without the time and money to expose the property to the market place and wait for a potential buyer that may or may not appear.

2. How will my net proceeds be calculated? After the initial discount, the following will be subtracted:

    a. Your outstanding mortgage balance(s) on the property
    b. The cost of any repairs needed to get the property in shape for resale
    c. Property taxes prorated to the closing date
    d. Any other liens or judgments against the property
    e. Closing costs for the sale including title insurance fees, transfer taxes, document prep fees, and recording charges
    f. Much like some mortgage lenders who charge "junk" fees, some investors tack on preparation/administration fees supposedly to cover the overhead costs of facilitating the purchase. These can cost the seller hundreds of additional dollars.

If your urgency to sell is due to delinquent mortgage payments and/or property taxes, you should first seek solutions through your lender. Investors willing to give you quick cash for your house will make sure they, not you, have the greatest financial win.

PROTECTION AGAINST CREDITOR HARASSMENT

Q. Do homeowners have any protection against mortgage lenders who harass them for late payments?

Yes. Though lenders have the right to contact consumers to request payments, consumers are protected under the Fair Debt Collection Act against calls that exceed the type and/or frequency specified by law.

Two free booklets are available to inform the consumer:

1. *Fair Debt Collection,* published by the Federal Trade Commission, Pennsylvania Avenue and 6th Street, NW, Washington, DC 20580, outlines what a debt collector can and can't do, or obtain information online at www.ftc.gov.
2. *Fair Debt Collection Practices Act,* published by the Federal Reserve Bank, P.O. Box 66, Philadelphia, PA 19105-0066, outlines violations under the law and describes how and where to report violations. You can find a copy online at www.ftc.gov.bcp.

Because reporting violations must be backed by proof, the consumer should keep an annotated log of all contacts with the lender and the respective outcomes.

Q. Does a delinquent borrower have any other recourse if the lender is not willing to work with him or her?

If the loan has PMI, or is an FHA or VA loan, other options may be available.

Private mortgage insurance companies insure the conventional lenders' loans against loss. So when the borrower can no longer make the mortgage payments, the PMI company stands to lose as well.

Many PMI companies are focusing their efforts on preforeclosure workout programs, designed to intercept the defaulting loan and work it out before formal foreclosure occurs. Their rationale is that if they can find a way to help a new, stronger buyer get the property by merely paying the lender some of the defaulting owner's back payments, they stand to lose less than if they paid an entire claim for loss. (For a breakdown of these costs, see Chapter 6.) A workout program might create a more equitable solution than foreclosure for all parties.

Q. If it's a conventional loan, how does the borrower find out which PMI company insures the loan?

Lenders are usually willing to contact the PMI company to see if a workout program is possible (especially if the property owner requests this). If not, however, the borrower might check his or her loan settlement papers from the purchase to see which company the initial PMI premiums were paid to. (All of the PMI companies are listed in Chapter 6 and have toll-free numbers.)

BEST WISHES FOR GROWING YOUR EQUITY

I hope that *All About Mortgages*, 4th edition, has helped you secure an affordable loan and provided you with tips for sound equity management, and will continue to be your bible for home affordability issues. Visit my Web site at www.juliegarton-good.com and let me know what information helped you most.

Then sit back and watch that equity grow!

AMORTIZATION FACTORS

To determine the monthly P and I (principal and interest) payment:

1. Locate the factor for the desired interest rate and term.
2. Multiply this rate/term factor by the loan amount.

To determine the principal amount of the loan:

1. Locate the factor for the desired interest rate and term.
2. Divide the monthly P and I payment by this rate/term factor.

Term in Years	INTEREST RATE					
	4 %	4½ %	4½%	4¾ %	4 %	5¼ %
5	.0184165	.0185296	.0186430	.0187569	.0188712	.0189860
8	.0121893	.0123059	.0124232	.0125412	.0126599	.0127793
10	.0101245	.0102438	.0103638	.0104848	.0106066	.0107292
12	.0087553	.0088772	.0090001	.0091240	.0092489	.0093748
15	.0073969	.0075228	.0076499	.0077783	.0079079	.0080388
18	.0065020	.0066319	.0067632	.0068961	.0070303	.0071660
20	.0060598	.0061923	.0063265	.0064622	.0065996	.0067384
25	.0052784	.0054174	.0055583	.0057012	.0058459	.0059925
30	.0047742	.0049194	.0050669	.0052165	.0053682	.0055220
35	.0044277	.0045789	.0047326	.0048886	.0050469	.0052074
40	.0041794	.0043362	.0044956	.0046576	.0048220	.0049887

Term in Years	INTEREST RATE					
	5½ %	5¾ %	6 %	6¼ %	6½ %	6¾ %
5	.0191012	.0192168	.0193328	.0194490	.0195661	.0196835
8	.0128993	.0130200	.0131414	.0132640	.0133862	.0135096
10	.0108526	.0109769	.0111021	.0112280	.0113548	.0114824
12	.0095017	.0096296	.0097585	.0098880	.0100192	.0101510
15	.0081708	.0083041	.0084386	.0085740	.0087111	.0088491
18	.0073032	.0074417	.0075816	.0077230	.0078656	.0080096
20	.0068789	.0070208	.0071643	.0073093	.0074557	.0076036
25	.0061409	.0062911	.0064430	.0065970	.0067521	.0069091
30	.0056779	.0058357	.0059955	.0061570	.0063207	.0064860
35	.0053702	.0055350	.0057019	.0058710	.0060415	.0062142
40	.0051577	.0053289	.0055021	.0056770	.0058546	.0060336

Term in Years	INTEREST RATE					
	7 %	7¼ %	7½ %	7¾ %	8 %	8¼ %
5	.0198012	.0199193	.0200379	.0201570	.0202764	.0203963
8	.0136337	.0137585	.0138838	.0140099	.0141367	.0142640
10	.0116108	.0117401	.0118702	.0120010	.0121328	.0122653
12	.0102838	.0104176	.0105523	.0106879	.0108245	.0109620
15	.0089883	.0091286	.0092701	.0094128	.0095565	.0097014
18	.0081550	.0083017	.0084497	.0085990	.0087496	.0089015
20	.0077530	.0079038	.0080593	.0082095	.0083644	.0085207
25	.0070680	.0072281	.0073899	.0075533	.0077182	.0078845
30	.0066530	.0068218	.0069921	.0071641	.0073376	.0075127
35	.0063886	.0065647	.0067424	.0069218	.0071026	.0072849
40	.0062143	.0063967	.0065807	.0067662	.0069531	.0071414
50	.0060169	.0062089	.0064023	.0065970	.0067927	.0069896

Term in Years	INTEREST RATE					
	8½ %	8¾ %	9 %	9¼ %	9½ %	9¾ %
5	.0205165	.0206372	.0207584	.0208799	.0210019	.0211243
8	.0143921	.0145208	.0146502	.0147802	.0149109	.0150423
10	.0123986	.0125327	.0126676	.0128033	.0129398	.0130771
12	.0111006	.0112400	.0113803	.0115216	.0116637	.0118069
15	.0098479	.0099949	.0101427	.0102919	.0104422	.0105937
18	.0090546	.0092089	.0093644	.0095212	.0096791	.0098382
20	.0086782	.0088371	.0089972	.0091587	.0093213	.0094852
25	.0080523	.0082214	.0083920	.0085638	.0087370	.0089114
30	.0076891	.0078670	.0080462	.0082268	.0084085	.0085916
35	.0074686	.0076536	.0078399	.0080274	.0082161	.0084059
40	.0073309	.0075217	.0077136	.0079066	.0081006	.0082956
50	.0071874	.0073861	.0075857	.0077860	.0079871	.0081888

Term in Years	INTEREST RATE					
	10 %	10¼ %	10½ %	10¾ %	11 %	11¼ %
5	.0212471	.0213703	.0214940	.0216180	.0217425	.0218674
8	.0151742	.0153068	.01544.01	.0155740	.0157085	.0158436
10	.0132151	.0133540	.0134935	.0136339	.0137751	.0139169
12	.0119508	.0120957	.0122415	.0123881	.0125356	.0126840
15	.0107461	.0108996	.0110540	.0112095	.0113660	.0115235
18	0099984	.0101598	.0103223	.0104859	.0106505	.0108162
20	.0096503	.0098165	.0099838	.0101523	.0103219	.0104926
25	.0090871	.0092639	.0094419	.0096210	.0098012	.0099824
30	.0087758	.0089611	.0091474	.0093349	.0095233	.0097127
35	.0085967	.0087886	.0089813	.0091750	.0093696	.0095649
40	.0084916	.0086882	.0088857	.0090840	.0092829	.0094826
50	.0083911	.0085939	.0087972	.0090010	.0092052	.0094098

Term in Years	INTEREST RATE					
	11½ %	11¾ %	12 %	12¼ %	12½ %	12¾ %
5	.0219927	.0221184	.0222445	.0223710	.0224980	.0226254
8	.0159794	.0161158	.0162529	.0163906	.0165289	.0166678
10	.0140596	.0142030	.0143471	.0144920	.0146377	.0147840
12	.0128332	.0129833	.0131342	.0132860	.0134386	.0135921
15	.0116819	.0118414	.0120017	.0121630	.0123253	.0124884
18	.0109830	.0111507	.0113195	.0114892	.0116600	.0118317
20	.0106643	.0108371	.0110109	.0111857	.0113615	.0115382
25	.0101647	.0103480	.0105323	.0107175	.0109036	.0110906
30	0099030	.0100941	.0102862	.0104790	.0106726	.0108670
35	0097611	0099579	.0101555	.0103537	.0105525	.0107519
40	0096828	0098836	.0100850	.0102869	.0104892	.0106919
50	0096148	0098200	.0100256	.0102314	.0104375	.0106438

Term in Years	INTEREST RATE					
	13 %	13¼ %	13½ %	13¾ %	14 %	14¼ %
5	.0227531	.0228813	.0230099	.0231389	.0232683	.0233981
8	.0168073	.0169475	.0170882	.0172296	.0173716	.0175141
10	.0149311	.0150789	.0152275	.0153767	.0155267	.0156774
12	.0137463	.0139014	.0140572	.0142139	.0143713	.0145295
15	.0126525	.0128174	.0129832	.0131499	.0133175	.0134858
18	.0120043	.0121779	.0123523	.0125276	.0127038	.0128809
20	.0117158	.0118944	.0120738	.0122541	.0124353	.0126172
25	.0112784	.0114671	.0116565	.0118467	.0120377	.0122293
30	.0110620	.0112578	.0114542	.0116512	.0118486	.0120469
35	.0109520	.0111524	.0113534	.0115548	.0117567	.0119590
40	.0108951	.0110987	.0113026	.0115069	.0117114	.0119162
50	.0108502	.0110569	.0112637	.0114707	.0116778	.0118850

Term in Years	INTEREST RATE					
	14½ %	14¾ %	15 %	15¼ %	15½ %	15¾ %
5	.0235283	.0236590	.0237900	.0239241	.0240532	.0241855
8	.0176573	.0178011	.0179455	.0180904	.0182360	.0183821
10	.0158287	.0159808	.0161335	.0162870	.0164411	.0165959
12	.0146885	.0148483	.0150088	.0151701	.0153321	.0154948
15	.0136551	.0138251	.0139959	.0141675	.0143400	.0145131
18	.0130587	.0132374	.0134169	.0135972	.0137782	.0139600
20	.0128000	.0129836	.0131679	.0133530	.0135389	.0137254
25	.0124217	.0126147	.0128084	.0130026	.0131975	.0133929
30	.0122456	.0124448	.0126445	.0128446	.0130452	.0132462
35	.0121617	.0123647	.0125681	.0127718	.0129758	.01318.01
40	.0121213	.0123267	.0125322	.0127380	.0129440	.0131502
50	.0120930	.0122973	.0125072	.0127148	.0129225	.0131303

Term in Years	INTEREST RATE					
	16 %	16¼ %	16½ %	16¾ %	17 %	17¼ %
5	.0243181	.0244511	.0245846	.0247184	.0248526	.0249872
8	.0185288	.0186761	.0188240	.0189725	.0191215	.0192710
10	.0167514	.0169075	.0170643	.0172217	.0173798	.0175385
12	.0156583	.0158225	.0159874	.0161530	.0163193	.0164862
15	.0146871	.0148617	.0150371	.0152133	.01539.01	.0155676
18	.0141425	.0143257	.0145096	.0146942	.0148795	.0150654
20	.0139126	.0141005	.0142891	.0144782	.0146681	.0148584
25	.0135889	.0137855	.0139825	.0141800	.0143780	.0145764
30	.0134476	.0136494	.0138515	.0140540	.0142568	.0144599
35	.0133847	.0135895	.0137945	.0139998	.0142053	.0144109
40	.0133565	.0135630	.0137696	.0139764	.0141832	.0143902
50	.0133381	.0135459	.0137538	.0139617	.0141697	.0143777

Term in Years	INTEREST RATE					
	17½ %	17¾ %	18 %	18¼ %	18½ %	18¾ %
5	.0251222	.0252576	.0253935	.0255296	.0256662	.0258032
8	.0194212	.0195719	.0197233	.0198751	.0200274	.0201804
10	.0176979	.0178579	.0180186	.0181798	.0183417	.0185041
12	.0166539	.0168222	.0169912	.0171608	.0173311	.0175021
15	.0157458	.0159247	.0161043	.0162844	.0164652	.0166467
18	.0152519	.0154391	.0156269	.0158153	.0160042	.0161938
20	.0150494	.0152410	.0154332	.0156258	.0158190	.0160127
25	.0147753	.0149746	.0151743	.0153744	.0155748	.0157757
30	.0146633	.0148669	.0150709	.0152750	.0154794	.0156841
35	.0146168	.0148228	.0150289	.0152352	.0154417	.0156483
40	.0145973	.0148045	.0150118	.0152192	.0154266	.0156342
50	.0145858	.0147939	.0150020	.0152101	.0154183	.0156264

acquisition cost Cost of acquiring a property, in addition to the purchase price, such as title insurance and lender's fees (e.g., with FHA, acquisition is a set amount based on the appraised value of the property).

addendum rider An addition to the standard contract (e.g., the lender attaches the due-on-sale clause to the loan via an addendum rider).

adjustable-rate mortgage (ARM) A mortgage tied to an index that adjusts based on changes in the economy.

adjustment period The period during which an ARM adjusts (e.g., six months, one year, or three years).

alienation clause (due-on-sale clause) A type of acceleration clause in a loan, calling for payment of the entire principal balance, triggered by the transfer or sale of a property.

amendatory language Language usually added to FHA and VA sales contracts when the contract is written prior to the completion of the appraisal. (This specifies what the options are if the appraisal amount varies from the offering price.)

amortization Retiring a debt through predetermined periodic payments, including principal and interest.

annual percentage rate (APR) The mortgage interest rate that includes both interest and any additional costs or prepaid finance charges including prepaid interest, private mortgage insurance, points, and closing costs. The APR represents the total cost of credit on a yearly basis after all charges are calculated.

appraisal An estimate of value.

ARM *See* adjustable-rate mortgage.

assignment The transfer of rights to pay an obligation from one party to another, with the original party remaining secondarily liable for the debt, should the second party default.

assumption To take over one's obligation under an existing agreement.

(Note: This can be achieved with varying degrees of release—*see* assignment, novation, and subject to).

automatic approval The processing of a VA loan, solely by the lender, without prior submission of the documents to the regional office.

automatic underwriting system (AUS) The process of using technology to underwrite a mortgage loan.

balloon payment A principal sum coming due at a predetermined time (may also contain payment of accrued interest).

biweekly mortgage A mortgage under which one-half of the regular amortized monthly payment is payable every two weeks, giving the benefit of 13 full payments per year; depending on the interest rate, this allows a 30-year loan to be retired in approximately 18 years.

blended rate The melding together of two rates to create a lower overall rate of interest. For example, blending the rate of an 8 percent first mortgage and a 10 percent second mortgage allows the buyer to more readily qualify.

buydown *Permanent:* prepaid interest that brings the note rate on the loan down to a lower, permanent rate.

Temporary: prepaid interest that lowers the note rate temporarily on the loan, allowing the buyer to more readily qualify and to increase payments as income grows. (A common example of a temporary buydown is the 3-2-1 plan—3 percent lower interest the first year, 2 percent the second, and 1 percent the third.)

cap A ceiling, usually found on ARM loans; can be expressed as per period (e.g., annual or lifetime, meaning for the entire loan term).

cash reserves The amount of buyer's liquid cash remaining after making the down payment and paying all closing costs.

certificate of commitment The lender's approval of a VA loan, which is usually good for up to six months.

certificate of eligibility VA certification, showing the amount of entitlement used and the remaining guaranty available.

certificate of reasonable value (CRV) The formal name for a VA appraisal.

chattel Personal property.

collateral/collateral agreement Means *additional*, but is generally termed to mean security for a debt.

commitment period The period during which a loan approval is valid.

conforming loans Mortgage loans that meet the FNMA/FHLMC underwriting guidelines in regard to loan type, amount, and other secondary market criteria.

contract for deed (aka, installment sales and land sales contract) A document used to secure real property when it is seller-financed; contains the full agreement between the parties, including purchase price, terms of payment, and any additional agreements.

convertibility option The clause that allows the ARM loan to be converted to a fixed-rate loan during a certain period.

convertible ARM An adjustable-rate mortgage containing a clause allowing for the rate to become fixed during a certain period (e.g., between months 13 and 60 of the loan term).

credit scoring Electronically giving a numerical weighting to various financial factors in the borrower's credit to determine the risk of lending to that borrower.

CRV *See* Certificate of Reasonable Value.

debt assumption letter/assignment of debt The formal transfer of debt from one person to another, backed by a formal contract of assumption, signed by the parties. This is undertaken to reduce the amount of a person's long-term debt.

debt ratios The comparison of a buyer's housing costs to his or her gross or net effective income (based on the loan program); and the comparison of a buyer's total long-term debt to his or her gross or net effective income (based on the loan program used). The first ratio is termed *housing ratio* or *"front end"*; the second ratio is *total debt ratio* or *"back end."* (*See* particular programs for applicable ratios.)

deed of trust (trust deed) A document used to secure the collateral in financing the property; title is transferred to the trustee, with payments made to the beneficiary by the trustor (grantor in some states).

Desktop Underwriter® (DU) The proprietary technology product of the Federal National Mortgage Association used to underwrite mortgage loans.

direct endorsement lender Lenders approved by the FHA to make loans without having loans first approved by the regional FHA office.

direct loan, VA A loan made to the veteran borrower by the VA without using a lender (undertaken infrequently, and then only in remote outlying areas).

discounting, seller Reducing the sales price in lieu of paying points or other fees from the seller's gross price.

discount points (points) A point is equal to 1 percent of the amount financed. Points are used to increase the lender's yield on the loan to bridge the gap between what the lender could get with conventional monies and the lower rates of the VA and the FHA.

distributive share MIP The FHA mortgage insurance plan in effect prior to 1983.

dual contracts Double contracts on the same property by the same buyer. Usually refers to an illegal second contract requesting a higher loan amount from a lender, even though the first contract bears the agreed-upon price between the seller and buyer.

due-on-sale clause (alienation clause) *See* alienation clause.

Equal Credit Opportunity Act (ECOA) A federal law requiring creditors to make credit equally available without discrimination based on race, color, religion, national origin, age, sex, marital status, or receipt of income from public assistance programs.

entitlement Also known as VA guaranty; the amount of the veteran's eligibility in qualifying for a VA loan.

equity The difference between what is owed and what the property could be sold for.

equity loans Tapping into an owner's equity, with the property used as the collateral.

escrow A financial account set up by the lender, funded by the borrower, to collect monthly installments for annual property tax payments and homeowner's insurance policy renewals. Also known as an *impound account*; on the West Coast of the United States, escrow can also mean placing the purchase and sale documents with a third-party escrow agent to oversee the closing of the transaction.

escrow holder An impartial third party who holds the documents pertinent to the transfer and sale of real estate.

Fannie Mae Foundation A nonprofit foundation affiliated with the FNMA, designed to educate consumers on home affordability and homebuying options.

Federal Home Loan Mortgage Corporation (FHLMC) Called Freddie Mac; a part of the secondary market, particularly used to purchase loans from savings-and-loan lenders within the Federal Home Loan Bank Board.

Federal Housing Administration (FHA) The FHA is part of the federal government's Department of Housing and Urban Development. It exists to underwrite insured loans made by lenders to provide economical housing for moderate-income persons.

Federal National Mortgage Association (FNMA) Also called Fannie Mae, a privately owned part of the secondary mortgage market used to recycle mortgages made in the primary market; purchases conventional, FHA, and VA loans.

fixed-rate mortgage (FRM) A fixed-rate mortgage is a conventional loan with a single interest rate for the life of the loan.

FICO The Fair, Isaac & Company credit-scoring system used by many leaders to determine a borrower's ability to repay a mortgage; uses a scoring range of 300 to 850—the lower the score, the higher the risk.

FHLMC *See* Federal Home Loan Mortgage Corporation.

FNMA *See* Federal National Mortgage Association.

foreclosure A proceeding, in or out of court, to extinguish one's rights in a property and to pay off all outstanding debts via a sale of the property.

fully indexed rate The maximum interest rate on an ARM that can be reached at the first adjustment.

funding fee An origination fee on VA loans, usually equal to 1 percent of the amount financed.

GEM *See* growing equity mortgage.

gift letter A letter from a relative (or party with whom a strong relationship has been established—for some loans) stating that an amount will be gifted to the buyer and that said amount is not to be repaid.

GNMA *See* Government National Mortgage Association.

Government National Mortgage Association (GNMA) Ginnie Mae is a governmental part of the secondary market that deals primarily in recycling VA and FHA mortgages, particularly those that are highly leveraged (e.g., no or low down payment).

graduated payment mortgage (GPM) A type of conventional loan containing a fixed rate for the life of the loan, but graduates, or increases, the payment during a certain period of the loan. (Example: 7.5 percent payment increase for the first seven years of the loan, then the payment remains fixed at that level.)

growing equity mortgage (GEM) This mortgage has a fixed interest rate for the life of the loan; but payments increase 3 percent, 5 percent, or 7.5 percent (depending on the program) for a period during the loan (usually not to exceed ten years), with all payment increases applied directly to reduce the principal. Thirty-year amortized GEM loans typically pay off between 13 and 15 years.

guaranty, VA The amount that the Department of Veterans Affairs will indemnify the lender against loss on a VA loan.

home equity line of credit (HELOC) A credit line secured by the property that works much like a credit card. The borrower writes a check against the equity available, making repayments only on the outstanding amount.

housing expense ratio The amount of either gross income or net effective income (depending on the loan program) that can be allocated for the borrower's housing expense. This percentage will also vary based on the loan-to-value ratio of the loan.

hybrid ARM An adjustable rate mortgage that allows the borrower to receive a fixed rate in the early years of the loan (selecting from three, five, seven, or ten-year periods, term 3/1, etc.) followed by the balance of the loan term as an ARM adjusting annually.

income qualifications The amount of either gross income or net effective income (depending on the loan program) required by the lender for loan qualifying.

index An indicator used to measure inflation, which is a basis for the ARM loan. There are various sources of indexes, including treasury securities, Treasury bills, 11th district cost of funds, and the index of the Federal Home Loan Bank Board. The index, plus the margin, becomes the interest rate in the ARM.

inflation An increase in value; most often used as an indicator of the economy. When inflation is high, real estate performs well, because it appreciates in times of inflation.

initial interest rate The introductory interest rate on a loan; signals that there may be rate adjustments later in the loan.

in-service eligibility Qualifying a veteran buyer for a VA loan while still on active duty.

installment sales contract *See* contract for deed.

interest only Payments received are only applied to accrued interest on the loan; therefore, there is no principal reduction.

interest rate The note rate charged on the loan.

interest-rate cap The maximum amount of interest that can be charged on an ARM loan. Can be expressed in terms of annual or lifetime figures.

jumbo loans Mortgage loans that exceed the loan amounts acceptable for sale in the secondary market; these jumbos must be packaged and sold differently to investors and therefore have separate underwriting guidelines.

kickback The illegal payment of a fee or other compensation for the privilege of securing business referrals from a source. (Example: A lender illegally receives $50 per referral sent to the title company.)

lease option A lease with an option to buy; said option can be either exercised to culminate in a purchase or forfeited by the optionee.

lease purchase A type of delayed closing. A lease purchase is drafted on a purchase and sales contract, stating the terms of the purchase, as well as a date for closing the sale. Should the buyer default, the seller has all the remedies available under the sales contract.

leverage Using a small asset to purchase a larger asset. Leverage allows a buyer's down payment to go further. (Example: Instead of using $50,000 down on a $100,000 property, the buyer could use $10,000 down on five properties of $100,000.)

liability, release of The type of liability release for the original borrower, found under a novation.

LID (local improvement district) A legal entity (district) established under state law to benefit a certain geographic area. Districts issue bonds to finance real property improvements such as water-distribution systems, sidewalks, and sewer systems. To repay funds, districts then levy assessments on real estate located in the geographic area affected.

lifetime cap The maximum amount of interest an ARM loan can reach during the life of the loan.

Loan Prospector® (LP) The proprietary technology product of the Federal Home Loan Mortgage Association used to underwrite mortgage loans.

loan qualifying Meeting the criteria for a loan as required by a mortgage lender; varies greatly from program to program.

loan-to-value ratio (LTV) The amount of the loan as compared to the appraised value of the property.

lock in Fixing an interest rate or points at a certain level, usually during the loan-application process. It is usually established for a certain period of time, such as 60 days.

long-term debt For qualifying purposes, debt that cannot be paid off within a certain period of time (i.e. 10 months) and/or debt with a term less than 10 months that require payments so large as to cause a severe impact on the family's resources for any period of time.

margin An amount added by the lender to an ARM index to compute the interest rate. The margin is set by the lender at the time of the loan inception and remains constant for the life of the loan. The margin is considered the lender's cost of doing business plus profit.

maximum entitlement The maximum amount of VA guaranty available to a veteran.

mortgage insurance premium (MIP) The mortgage insurance required on FHA loans for the life of said loans; MIP can either be paid in cash at the closing or financed in its entirety in the loan. The premium varies depending on the method of payment.

mortgage meltdown A series of events which began to topple both the primary and secondary markets in 2006, due, in large part to increased defaults in subprime mortgages, resetting ARMS, rising foreclosures, and less-than-stellar returns to secondary market investors who purchased mortgage-backed securities.

negative amortization An interest payment shortfall that is added back onto the principal balance.

no-cost mortgage A mortgage transaction where the lender pays the borrower's closing costs (except for per diem interest and escrows/prepaids) with the offset being that the borrower is charged a slightly higher interest rate.

nonconforming loan A mortgage that does not meet the purchase requirements of the secondary market due to loan size, poor credit, or inadequate documentation.

nonsupervised lender An FHA lender that operates outside of strict governmental control (such as mortgage companies) and is able to be an automatic approval lender on application to the FHA regional office.

note rate The rate of interest shown on the face of the promissory note or in the contract of sale language; the rate of interest charged on an obligation.

notice of separation The VA form received when the veteran is discharged from the service.

novation From the root word *nova,* meaning new. A novation is a total release of liability to the first borrower under a loan, and the substitution of a subsequent borrower; usually not automatic, requiring a lender's approval (*see* assignment, assumption, and subject to).

online lending Accessing mortgage programs and lenders via the Internet.

on-the-job benefits Noncash compensation to an employee, such as a car or day care provided, or extra guaranteed per diem. Lenders may consider this for loan qualification if a trackable history can be shown.

owner occupancy Occupied by the buyer of the property; a requirement in VA loans; many times a requirement in conventional and FHA programs as well.

package mortgage A mortgage loan that includes the financing of personal property.

PAM *See* pledged account mortgage.

payment cap The maximum amount the payment can adjust at any one time (e.g., 7.5 percent per period).

payment option feature A feature in a mortgage that allows the borrower one of several payment options each month. These are typically a fully amortized payment of principal and interest, an interest-only payment, and a minimum or limited payment that is less than the amount of interest due for that month. The latter option will result in the interest shortfall being added back onto the principal balance, termed negative amortization.

payment shock The shock of the payment change affecting the buyer's ability to repay the loan.

PITI Principal, interest, taxes (property), and insurance.

pledged account mortgage (PAM) Instead of using all the down payment at the closing, part of the funds are placed in an interest-bearing account and drawn from over time to help pay the mortgage payment. These impounded funds are said to be pledged to the lender.

PMI *See* private mortgage insurance.

POC (paid outside of closing) Funds disbursed on behalf of the borrower outside the formal closing with that borrower.

portfolio lending Instead of selling the mortgage into the secondary market, the lender keeps it *in portfolio* (in the in-house file) for the life of the loan.

power of attorney Also termed *attorney in fact*. A legal power given to a person to act on behalf of another. This right can be either specific (for special circumstances) or general (in all activities).

premium yield adjustment, aka yield spread premiums (YSP). Denotes that a lender is receiving compensation from the party funding the real estate mortgage.

prepaids Property expenses that are paid in advance and are usually prorated at the time of the closing (e.g., insurance).

prepayment privilege The right of the borrower to prepay the entire principal sum remaining on the loan without penalty.

private mortgage insurance (PMI) Insurance that indemnifies the lender from the borrower's default, usually on the top 20 percent of the loan. Premiums are paid as an initial fee at the time of the closing, and as a recurring annual fee based on the principal balance, but paid monthly with the PITI payment. Both the initial and recurring fees are customarily paid by the buyer.

prohibited costs Certain costs that cannot be paid by a particular party to the transaction, as determined by a certain type of loan. (Example: Buyers cannot pay discount fees under VA loan guidelines.)

planned unit development (PUD) A type of housing development based on high density (cluster buildings) and maximum use of open space generally resulting in lower-cost housing requiring less maintenance.

The common areas of ground are owned by a nonprofit community association not by individuals. Developers will often mix residential with light commercial zoning to maximize land use. PUDs can also be used for resort housing and shopping center projects.

qualifying ratio Percentages used by lenders to compare the amount of housing expense and total debt to that of the buyer's gross income or net effective income (depending on the loan program).

RAM *See* reverse annuity mortgage.

rate cap The maximum amount of interest that can be charged on an ARM loan; expressed as either per period or lifetime, or both.

rate ceiling The maximum to which the rate can go in an ARM loan, specified in an interest amount (e.g., 14 percent).

rate gap The difference between where the rate is now and where it could adjust to on an ARM. Also used to compare the difference between a current conventional rate and that of an ARM.

ratio A percentage; used as a qualifying guideline in mortgage lending.

Regulation Z A federal regulation requiring disclosure of the overall cost of borrowing (truth in lending); states that if you disclose one piece of financial information, you must disclose it in its entirety (including the total of all payments and the number of payments). The only exception to this rule is the use of the annual percentage rate. If this is used, no other piece of financial information is necessary.

release clause A clause allowing a portion of the real estate to be released as security from the loan; usually occurs upon a payment of a substantial portion of the principal.

renegotiable rate mortgage (RRM) The forerunner of today's ARM; RRMs got a black eye in the late 1970s when lenders required the borrowers to renegotiate and requalify at specified intervals during the loans.

Reservist A person who has served in a reserve branch of the armed forces.

residual income Monthly leftover income after deducting housing costs and fixed obligations from the net effective income in qualifying for a VA loan.

RESPA The Real Estate Settlement Procedures Act is the up-front view of the costs of borrowing in a mortgage loan, including the APR (annual percentage rate), which is the note rate plus the up-front costs of borrowing.

restoration of eligibility/entitlement When a VA loan is paid in full or otherwise satisfied, or when a veteran assumes another veteran's VA loan, reinstating the first veteran's eligibility.

reverse annuity mortgage (RAM) A loan developed for senior citizens to unlock a portion of their equity in their home without selling the properties.

sales concession A cost paid by the seller or other third party, even though the cost is customarily paid by the buyer. Some loan programs have limits on the amount of sales concessions that can occur before the overage would decrease the amount of loan available.

secondary market Comprised of FNMA, GNMA, and FHLMC, which recycle lent funds from the primary market.

Section 203 FHA programs, divided as follows:

203(b): the standard single-family FHA program
203(h): disaster-victim financing
203(i): loans to outlying areas
203(k): rehabilitation loan program
203(n): co-op financing
203(v): (FHA/VA) for veteran borrowers

Section 220 Urban renewal

220(h): urban renewal repair

Section 221 Low-cost housing

Section 222 In-service military FHA plan

Section 245 Graduated payment mortgage

Section 251 Adjustable-rate mortgage

security document A legal document that creates a lien against a property as security for repayment of a debt (such as mortgages or deeds of trust).

seller financing The seller allows the borrower to finance the property, using a portion of the seller's equity in the property.

shared appreciation mortgage (SAM) A mortgage under which a coborrower investor contributes; facetiously called the CYD (call your dad) loan.

shared equity mortgage (SEM) A coborrower mortgage by which the equity of the property is shared when the property is sold.

simple assumption A type of loan assumption that is actually a no-qualifying assignment with the lender. The original obligor remains secondarily liable should the assumptor default.

subject to The transfer of rights to pay an obligation from one party to another, with the first party remaining secondarily liable should the second party default. In addition, the first obligor could be responsible for any deficiency judgment caused by the second borrower. (*See* assignment, assumption, and novation.)

subprime loan (aka nonprime loan) Subprime loans are made to people with less than "prime" credit. Blemishes can range from late mortgage payments to seriously damaged credit like judgments or bankruptcy. Borrowers can expect to pay a higher interest rate and more fees to obtain a subprime loan.

sweat equity Materials or labor used by a buyer in addition to, or in lieu of, cash.

teaser rate An unusually low introductory rate, used to entice borrowers into a loan and allow them to more readily qualify.

transfer charge The cost of transferring or assuming an existing mortgage.

Veterans Affairs, Department of (VA) A branch of the federal government that guarantees lenders against borrowers' default in order to assist veterans in the purchase of single-family dwellings.

WDAGO A veteran's notice of separation.

wraparound An original loan obligation remains stationary, while a new amortizing obligation wraps around the other loan. One payment is made (many times to an escrow holder), out of which the underlying payment is made, with the remainder going to the seller.

yield Return on investment.

zero net When the seller is receiving little or no net proceeds from selling the property.

Print Resources
for Buyers and Sellers

The following booklets are available free of charge from:

The Mortgage Bankers' Association
1125 15th Street, NW
Washington, DC 20005
www.mbaa.org

A Consumer's Glossary of Mortgage Terms
Great for the first-time buyer who needs to know the language, the
players, and the plays.

Self Test
Ideal to use prior to qualifying with a lender. Will help you determine
how much house you can afford and what documentation the lender
may require.

What Happens after You Apply for a Mortgage
Walks you through the process and explains the mysteries of underwriting
the mortgage loan.

The following booklets are available from:

Federal National Mortgage Association
Drawer MM
3900 Wisconsin Avenue, NW
Washington, DC 20006
www.fanniemae.com

Unraveling the Mortgage Loan Mystery
Great for information on who makes loans, the types of loans available, and how to choose the best loan.

When Your Home Is on the Line
A comprehensive booklet describing how to evaluate an equity line of credit.

A Homebuyer's Guide to Environmental Hazards
Alerts you to the various environmental red flags that could impact the property and its value.

When writing, ask the FNMA for a list of other publications available, or request information on a certain topic.

Available from the:
Federal Trade Commission Bureau of Consumer Protection
Pennsylvania Avenue and 6th Street, NW
Washington, DC 20580
www.ftc.gov

The Mortgage Money Guide
Gives detailed comparisons of costs borrowers can expect to pay for various types of loans. Good for loan comparison shopping.

Miscellaneous Real Estate Booklets

Home Accessibility and Safety

Home Modifications for the Elderly, available from the National Association of Home Builders (NAHB). A preplanning home safety audit. For a free copy write to NAHB Research Center, 400 Prince George's Boulevard, Upper Marlboro, MD 20772, Attn: L. Rickman. www.nahb.org

Home safety booklet for the elderly, *The Doable, Renewable Home,* is available free of charge from AARP. Write for booklet D12470, AARP Fulfillment, EE094, 1909 K Street, NW, Washington, DC 20049. www.aarp.org

Regarding home accessibility, free of charge from the National Easter Seal Society, a booklet entitled *Easy Access Housing*. Write to the society at 70 East Lake Street, Chicago, IL 60601. www.easter-seals.org

Home Ownership Issues

A selection of booklets on homebuying, insurance, radon, and home hazards. While most of the government's booklets are free of charge, others may cost up to $1.50 to order. Write for a free catalog from:

United States Federal Government
Consumer Information Center
P.O. Box 100
Pueblo, CO 81002
www.pueblo.gsa.gov

Discriminatory Housing Practices

Call the HUD hotline at 800-669-9777 to speak to a HUD representative or to order a free booklet, *Fair Housing: It's Your Right* (publication #HUD-1260-FHEO/July 1990). www.hud.gov

Turning Equity into Cash

Free homemade money booklet describing the reverse annuity mortgage loan. Contact:

American Association of Retired Persons (AARP)
Home Equity Information Center
601 E Street, NW
Washington, DC 20049
800-424-3410
www.aarp.org

Real Estate Consultants

National Association of Real Estate Consultants® (NAREC®). Sponsors of the Consumer-Certified Real Estate Consultant® (C-CREC®) designation.

NAREC®
404 4th Avenue
Lewiston, ID 83501
800-445-8543
www.narec.com

Online Resources

Affordable housing

efanniemae.com
fanniemae.com
fanniemaefoundation.org
freddiemac.com
ginniemae.gov
habitat.org
www.nehemiahprogram.org

Attorneys

abanet.org

Auctions

auctioneers.org
internetauctionlist.com
sothebysrealty.com

Buyer's agents

naeba.org
rebac.org

Calculators (real estate) online

interest.com
mtgprofessor.com
quicken.com
ziprealty.com

City comparisons

cityguide.com
homefair.com

Credit agencies/information

annualcreditreport.com
experian.com
equifax.com
myfico.com
truecredit.com

Crime information

homefair.com

Environmental information

ashi.com
epa.gov
independentinspectors.org
inspectorusa.com
nahi.org

FHA (Federal Housing Administration)

www.hud.gov
www.huduser.org

Flood insurance

fema.gov

Foreclosure

fanniemae.com
freddiemac.com
foreclosure.com
foreclosures.com
ginniemae.gov
www.hud.gov
realtytrac.com
va.gov

For sale by owners

4salebyowner.com
buyowner.com
fiftystatesfsbo.com
forsalebyowner.com
fsbo.com
fsbonetwork.com
homesbyowner.com
ired.com
isoldmyhouse.com
nationalforsalebyowner.com
oldhouses.com
open-house-online.com
ziprealty.com

Governmental sites

epa.gov
ftc.gov
www.hud.gov
irs.gov

Home building

buildingahome.net
buildscape.com
homedepot.com
nahb.org

Homebuyer information (general)

fanniemaefoundation.org
houseandhome.msn.com
inman.com
ired.com
juliegarton-good.com
ourbroker.com
realtor.com
realtytimes.com

Home inspections

ashi.com
nahi.org

Home repair

askbuild.com
misterfixit.com

Home seller information (general)

inman.com
ired.com
juliegarton-good.com
ourbroker.com
realtytimes.com

Improve versus move

buildscape.com
bobvila.com
homedepot.com
nahb.org
thisoldhouse.com

Inflation statistics

hsh.com
wsj.com

Insurance

geico.com
homeownerinsurancequote
  group.com
insWeb.com
netquote.com
prudential.com
safeco.com

Interest rates

bankrate.com
hsh.com
interest.com
realtytimes.com

International real estate

ired.com
sothebysrealty.com

Listings online

cyberhomes.com
erealty.com
homes.com
homeseekers.com
houseandhome.com
ired.com
realtor.com

Manufactured housing

mfdhousing.com

Mortgage comparison shopping

eloan.com
gomez.com
interest.com
juliegarton-good.com

Mortgages

bankofamerica.com
championmortgage.com
citimortgage.com
e-loan.com
getsmart.com
lendingtree.com
loanworks.com
loanvibe.com
mortgage.com
mycountrywide.com
myhomebank.com
myhomeloan.com
quickenmortgage.com
usbank.com
wellsfargo.com

New homes

buildingahome.net
move.com
nahb.org

Payment calculators

interest.com
mtgprofesssor.com
quickenmortgage.com
ziprealty.com

Predatory lending

ftc.gov
ncrc.org

Pricing property

experian.com
zillow.com
ziprealty.com

Private mortgage insurance

mgic.com
mica.org
pmirescue.com
privatemi.com
rmic.com

Real estate consultants (unbundled fee for services)

ccrec.com
coloradohomefront.com
davidkpowell.com
flatfeeMLSlisting.com
flatfeerealty.CA (located in
   Canada)
narec.com
new-all.com
onepercentrealty.info
realestateunplugged.com

Real estate education

dearbornRE.com
homeloanlearningcenter.com
narec.com
reea.org

Refinancing

championmortgage.com
eloan.com
mycountrywide.com
quickenmortgage.com

Relocation

homefair.com
nationalrelocation.com

Rent versus buy

interest.com
mtgprofessor.com

School information

homefair.com
schoolreport.com

Signage (homesellers)

ired.com
ziprealty.com

Tax rates

irs.gov

Title and escrow companies

ctic.com (Chicago Title)
escrow.com
firstam.com (First American
   Title)
landam.com (Land America)
stewart.com (Stewart Title)

Unbundled real estate services—à la carte

ccrec.com
fsbo.com
helpusell.com
juliegarton-good.com
narec.com
owners.com

VA (Department of Veterans Affairs)

va.gov

A

B

qualifying form, 201
recently discharged veterans,
    202
refinancing, 216
residual incomes by region, 200
second mortgage, 245-46
30-year term, 77
types, 210-11
underwriting guidelines, 211-12
workout programs, 294
Verification of deposit, 27
Veterans Affairs, Department of, 24
Veterans' Benefits of 2004, 195

W-Y

Wall Street Journal, The, 139, 140,
    153
Web sites, 7-8
When Your Loan Is Transferred to
    Another Lender, 260
Wraparound financing, 234-35, 247
Yield spread premium (YSP), 18

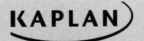